AF612431

In defense of degrowth

Opinions and Minifestos

Giorgos Kallis
Edited by Aaron Vansintjan

First published March, 2017
Uneven Earth Press

Paperback ISBN : 9789090306612

To cite this book:
Kallis, Giorgos. (2017) *In defense of degrowth: Opinions and minifestos*. Ed. by Aaron Vansintjan. Brussels: Uneven Earth Press.

Uneven Earth Press
Nevelestraat 5
Hansbeke, Nevele
9850
Belgium

Praise for *In defense of degrowth*

"Whatever your level of familiarity with the subject, the book's mix of engaging commentary, bold analysis, and creative policy tools is certain to deepen your thinking."

—Naomi Klein, author of *This changes everything* and *The shock doctrine*

"In defense of degrowth … shows why its author, and the Barcelona group to which he belongs, have become the indisputable world leaders in the vital project of crafting novel economic imaginaries and feasible frameworks for an age where, literally, everything has to change."

—Arturo Escobar, author of *Encountering development: The making and unmaking of the Third World* and *Feel-thinking with the Earth.*

"An easy-to-read answer to many interesting questions around degrowth."

—Joan Martinez Alier, author of *The Environmentalism of the Poor: A study of ecological conflicts and valuation.*

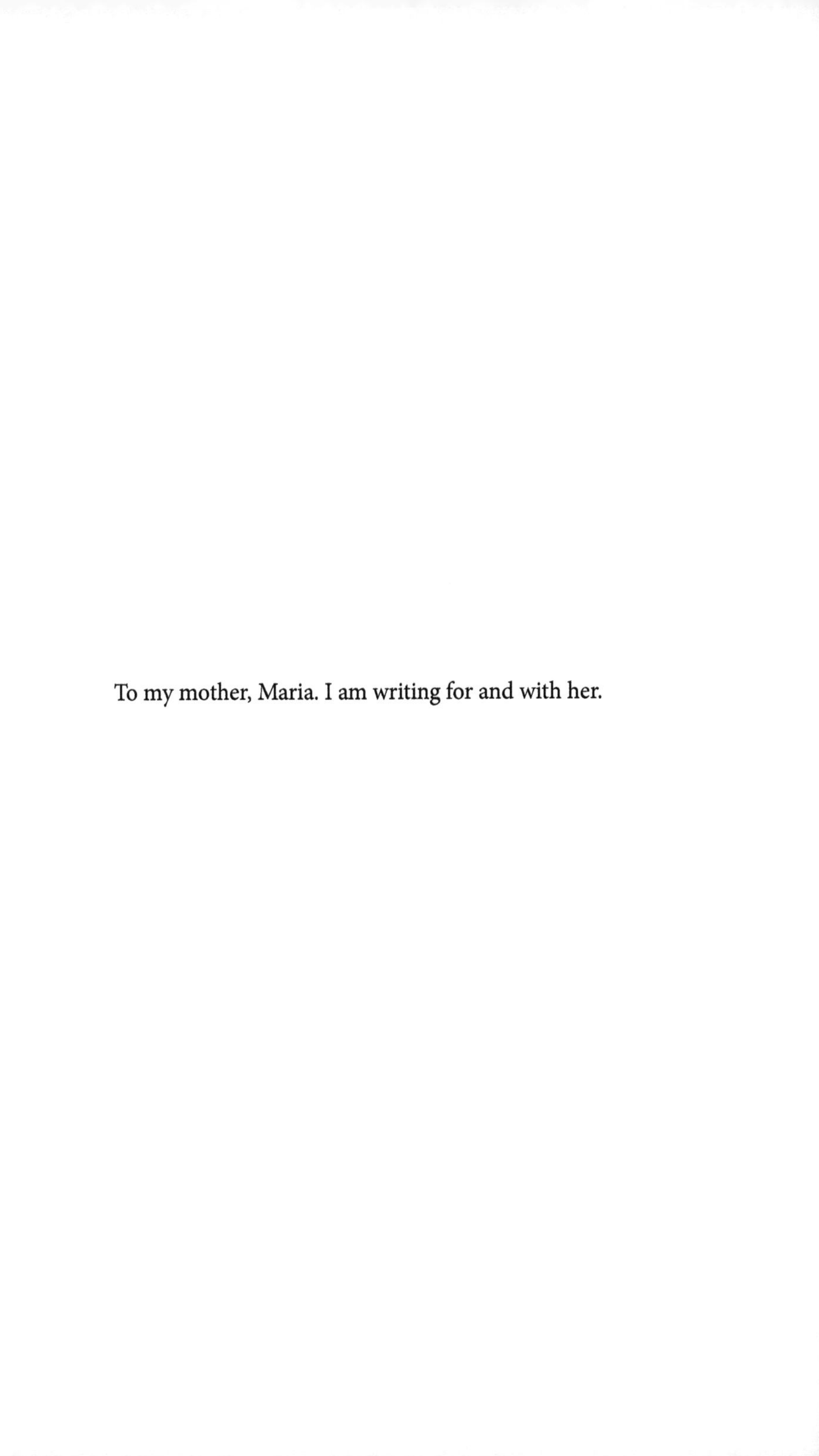

To my mother, Maria. I am writing for and with her.

Contents

Part VII: A view from the South (of Europe)

Preface

This book is a collection of opinion essays, newspaper articles, and blog posts I wrote the last four years to communicate my thoughts and research to a non-academic audience. I wrote them for three reasons. First, because I wanted to talk to—and with—people outside the university. I wanted to make sure that the ideas we were developing with my friends in Research & Degrowth Barcelona did not stay locked within the pay walls of scientific journals. Second, because I felt a need to intervene in public debates; that I am doing something that may make some, even if tiny, difference in the face of the turmoil, chaos, but also hope, that was engulfing us in the South of Europe. Third, because I wanted to throw and test some half-baked ideas, without waiting for the long academic process of researching the literature, examining what others have said before, confronting my hypotheses with evidence and all the rest. There is a place and moment for reason and rigour, and there are also moments where intuition and passion are called for. Some of my essays are communicating well-founded and empirically supported claims. Others are just pitching concepts and ideas that someone else might want to follow up on, or are simply making emotional pleas for a different course of action.

Writing these essays was not an easy experience. I have mastered the art of writing an academic paper and getting it published, but I was never taught how to write something that a friend can read. My academic writing is clunky at times, but this is fine since it is other clunky writers that evaluate my work. A clunky blogpost, though, will simply not be read. It is a hard moment of truth when you try to simplify your ideas, only to find that you can't. You can no longer hide your own confusion behind complex concepts, impenetrable language, or elaborate math. What you say either makes sense, or doesn't. And if it doesn't, or if you can't express it in a way that it does even if you feel that it does, then frustration, if not depression reigns. What a great satisfaction though, when it does make sense, when language and emotion sync, as I feel they do in "The battle for Harvard" (chapter 8), or "The Wolf of Wall Street" (chapter 10)!

The essays included here were written at different times, for different audiences and with different purposes in mind. Some are more academic, others, more direct. Some of the same ideas may appear and re-appear in different articles, in different forms with different words. I want to think that this is not repetition, the same refrain played over and over, but rather different variations on the same musical motive, played one way here, and in another there.

We organized this collection in seven parts. The first part consists of four articles I wrote to present the idea of degrowth in simple terms. These four essays were written at different stages of development of my thoughts on degrowth, and for different audiences. I call them minifestos. They are passionate declarations in support of degrowth, but without the claim to grand theory or certainty that would characterize a manifesto. They are the entry point to this book for the reader not familiar with the core claims behind the missile slogan "degrowth".

Part II includes three essays establishing an antagonistic dialogue between degrowth and its arch-nemesis, eco-modernism—that is, the idea that all environmental and social problems can ultimately be solved with the application of technology, and that the only solution to the problems of modern technology is more modern technology. I argue that eco-modernism is factually and conceptually wrong, though funny at times.

Part III is about economics, but its three essays are very different in content and scope. First, I tell a little known story of how dissident voices were purged from the field of economics and university campuses in the early 70s. Then I propose five principles for a new economics, drawing from concepts and ideas developed in our recent book *Degrowth: A vocabulary for a new era* (vocabulary.degrowth.org). Then I turn film critic to describe the enigma and magic of capital in Martin Scorsese's *The Wolf of Wall Street*.

Part IV has some half-baked thoughts on capitalism, socialism, and degrowth, and Part V turns into the politics of and the policies for degrowth, starting with ten policy commandments and moving on to a series of mini-interventions ranging from work-sharing and Keynesian policies by Spain's Podemos, to AirBnb, the Pope's *Laudato Si*, and the hopes fueled from Barcelona's new city government.

In Part VI I engage with critiques. It is through these engagements that the nuances and uncertainties in my own claims come to the fore. Common criticisms concern both whether degrowth is necessary, and whether the term is appealing and mobilizing. Sometimes the two critiques, or my own responses, mix the two issues. I am sure that what is expressed by degrowth is valid, and the transformations we espouse are necessary. I am less certain of the term, though I defend its use. But no doubt, the debate on both questions is open and ongoing.

In Part VII I come back home. I close with three essays originally written in Greek, which concern the country where I was born and raised, Greece. A few years ago, a focus on Greece might have seemed an idiosyncratic and too personal of a choice, but today it no longer is. Greece with its Great Depression has come to signify the economic crisis at its worst and to embody all that is going wrong with Europe and the West. I am sharing here three fragments of a thought, the two cents of a Greek of the diaspora.

The ideas in the essays were developed over the years through discussions and debates within the Institute for Environmental Sciences and Technology (ICTA) at the Autonomous University of Barcelona (icta.uab.es), and the Research & Degrowth collective in Barcelona (degrowth.org). I am grateful to all my companer@s in R&D, and my colleagues and students at ICTA, especially to my good friends and co-authors Giacomo D'Alisa and Federico Demaria with whom I have co-developed most of my thoughts on degrowth. I thank the editors of the outlets for which I wrote these essays and my co-authors for those articles that were co-written.

The book was edited, formatted, and published by Aaron Vansintjan. Aaron did not just put the essays together: he read them carefully, refined them, contextualized them and made the whole better than the sum of its parts. Without him, this book would not have been available.

All the articles in this book were originally published on various news outlets, online magazines, and blogs and several were co-written with friends and colleagues:

"For a radical environmentalism" was published by *Nous Horitzons* in 2011.

"The degrowth alternative" was published on the website of The Great Transition Initiative in 2015.

"The left should embrace degrowth" was published on the website of *The New Internationalist* in 2015.

"Let's be less productive" was published in the book *Degrowth: A vocabulary for a new era*, and co-authored with Giacomo D'Alisa and Federico Demaria.

"Political Ecology gone wrong" was published on the *ENTITLE Blog* in 2015.

"Why eco-modernism is wrong" was published on the *ENTITLE Blog* in 2015.

"Tweeting with the enemy" was published on the Degrowth.de blog in 2015.

"The battle for Harvard, or, how economics became economics" was published in *Adbusters* in 2014.

"For a Political Ecological Economics" was presented as the plenary lecutre at the 11th conference of the European Society for Ecological Economics in Leeds, 2015.

"The Wolf of Wall Street and the spirit of capitalism" was published by *The Press Project* in 2014.

"Is there a growth imperative in capitalism?" was published on the *ENTITLE Blog* in 2015.

"Socialist growth is an oxymoron" was published on the *ENTITLE Blog* in 2015.

"Yes, we can prosper without growth" was published in *El Diario* in 2014 , after which it was translated and published by The Press Project in 2015, and was co-authored by the Research & Degrowth network.

"The right to leisure" was published on *Greeklish* in 2013.

"Fridays-off" was published in the *European Financial Review* in 2013 and co-authored by Nicholas Ashford.

"Barcelona's new commons" was published by *The Huffington Post* (Spain) in 2015.

"The "sharing" economy is not a commons" was published by *The Press Project* in 2014.

"A Pope for degrowth" was published by *La Vanguardia* in 2015.

"Spanish Keynesianism without growth?" was published by *The Guardian* in 2015.

"A society without growth: The planet of *The Dispossessed*" was published by the Center for Humans and Nature in 2012.

"The degrowth debate" was published on the website of The Great Transition Initiative in 2015. This chapter includes abridged responses by Nicholas Ashford, Maurie Cohen, Herman Daly, Al Hammond, Michael Karlberg, Rajesh Makwana, Mary Mellor, Robert Paehlke, Richard Rosen, Tilman Santarius, and Anders Wijkman.

"Will trees grow in a degrowth society?" was published on the website of the STEPS Centre in 2016. This chapter includes an abridged essay by Andy Stirling and my own response.

"Is degrowth a compelling word?" consists of three essays. The first was originally published on the blog *News Frames*, written by Brian Dean, in 2015. The second, written by Kate Raworth, and third, written by Giorgos Kallis, were originally published on the Oxfam blog, *From Poverty to Power*, also in 2015.

"Will degrowth be voluntary or involuntary?" features two essays by Brian Davey and Giorgos Kallis, both published by Feasta in 2014.

"How the tigers became PIIGS" was published by *The Press Project* in 2014.
"Extractivism, the Greek way" was published by *The Press Project* in 2015.
"Islandizing the city" was published by *Greeklish* in 2013.

"I am not proposing a return to the Stone Age. My intent is not reactionary, nor even conservative, but simply subversive. It seems that the utopian imagination is trapped, like capitalism and industrialism and the human population, in a one-way future consisting only of growth. All I'm trying to do is figure out how to put a pig on the tracks."

- Ursula K. Le Guin

Image: Still from the film *Black Cat White Cat* by Emir Kusturica

Part I: The degrowth alternative

1. For a radical environmentalism

Author's note: This article was written for the Catalan publication Nous Horitzons *(New Horizons), a magazine of a foundation supported by the Catalan political party Iniciativa per Catalunya Verds (Initiative for Catalonia-Greens). The article was written back in 2011, and it was one of my first attempts to capture and articulate in a relatively simpler language what I was trying to say about degrowth in my more academic articles. The main thesis is that degrowth is first and foremost a re-radicalization of environmentalism, a return to the radical roots of the green movement of the 1970s, and as such a response to the de-politicizing discourse of "sustainable development".*

The vision

Sustainable degrowth is defined as an equitable downscaling of production and consumption that increases human well-being and enhances ecological conditions.[1] Those of us who write about degrowth envision a future wherein societies live within their ecological means, with localized economies, which distribute resources more equally through new forms of democratic institutions. Such societies will no longer have to "grow or die". Material accumulation will no longer hold a central position in the cultural imaginary. The primacy given to efficiency will be substituted by a focus on sufficiency. The organizing principles will be simplicity, conviviality, and sharing. Innovation will no longer be directed to new technology for technology's sake but to new social and technical arrangements that will enable a convivial and frugal living.

Why should we degrow?

1. To avoid climatic catastrophe, ecosystem destruction and resource depletion. This cannot be done with technological improvements and simple behavioral changes: the scale of the economy has to decline too.[2] During 300 years of industrialization, there has been a strong correlation between econom-

1 Schneider, F., Kallis, G., & Martinez-Alier, J. (2010). "Crisis or opportunity? Economic degrowth for social equity and ecological sustainability. Introduction to this special issue." *Journal of Cleaner Production, 18*(6), 511-518.

2 Jackson, T. (2009). *Prosperity without growth: Economics for a finite planet.* Routledge.

ic growth and many forms of resource use and environmental damage, most notably energy use and CO_2 emissions. The few countries, mostly in Europe, that have lately stabilized their CO_2 emissions or their material flows have done so either because of economic shocks, such as the ex-Communist countries, or by exporting the production of their consumer goods elsewhere, such as countries like the U.K. After years of intergovernmental deliberations following the Stockholm and Rio environmental conferences, and tons of ink spilled in the name of "sustainable development", the only concrete declines in CO_2 emissions came since 2008 as a result of the recent economic crisis.

2. Growth is no longer economic; increasing GDP does not necessarily increase human welfare.[1] Studies by psychologists and economists show that both happiness and essential welfare (such as public health or education) correlate with economic growth only up to a level. After that, growth yields diminishing returns; more and more economic growth does not improve them. We run faster to stay in the same place. In most Western societies we've reached this plateau decades ago. Yet we are investing more and more natural and labor resources for new gadgets and consumer products that yield marginal, if any, welfare improvements for those that use them, and have terrible impacts on those that produce them or those that are forced to deal with the waste, our disposed boats, computers, or cellphones. Communities at the frontiers of oil and metal extraction or waste disposal live in hell today,[2] they don't have to wait for climate change. And all this for nothing: most people in the West, which is driving this consumerist craze, are not happier today than they were 20 or 30 years ago; public and social security, health standards, living quality are all at the same level and are quickly worsening as a result of the current crisis. Then why does economic output, meaning production and consumption, have to grow continuously?

Because capitalist economies are designed to grow, merely in order not

1 Daly, H. (1996). *Beyond growth: the economics of sustainable development.* Beacon Press.

2 Martinez-Alier, J., Kallis, G., Veuthey, S., Walter, M., & Temper, L. (2010). "Social metabolism, ecological distribution conflicts, and valuation languages." *Ecological Economics*, 70(2), 153-158.

to collapse.[1] Debts, pensions, employment—all rest on constant economic growth. But is this reasonable? No other entity in the physical world is programmed to grow indefinitely. Our economic systems are an anomaly that needs to be corrected.

How to degrow?

Sustainable degrowth is not equivalent to economic recession or depression, i.e. unplanned and involuntary economic degrowth within a growth-driven system; this has devastating social implications to which we are not oblivious. Sustainable degrowth denotes an intentional process of a smooth and "prosperous way down",[2] through a range of social, environmental, and economic policies and institutions, orchestrated to guarantee that while production and consumption decline, human welfare improves and is more equally distributed.

Various concrete and practical proposals are being debated for enabling such a degrowth transition.[3] These include both policy-institutional changes *within* the current system—such as drastic changes to financial institutions, resource and pollution caps and sanctuaries, infrastructure moratoria, eco-taxes, work-sharing and reduced working hours, basic income and social security guaranteed for all—as well as ideas for creating new spaces *outside* of the system, such as eco-villages and co-housing, cooperative production and consumption, various systems of sharing, or community issued and regulated currencies, barter and non-money market exchanges. "Exiting the economy", to create new spaces of simplicity, sharing and conviviality, is the driving motto of degrowth.[4]

Such non-capitalist alternatives have always co-existed at the margins of the capitalist economy. We may even speculate that older economic crises were felt more lightly by populations precisely because there were several non-capitalist social networks of support that were not affected by the fall of the core money economy. Those non-monetary networks of mutual support and solidarity have traditionally sustained livelihoods in times of crisis. It is their erosion during the last years and their swallow-

1 Jackson, T. (2009). *Prosperity without growth: Economics for a finite planet.* Routledge.

2 Odum, H. T., & Odum, E. C. (2008). *A prosperous way down: principles and policies.* University Press of Colorado.

3 See www.degrowth.eu; Jackson, T. (2009). *Prosperity without growth: Economics for a finite planet.* Routledge.

4 Latouche, S. (2009). *Farewell to growth*: Polity.

ing up by the ever-expanding capitalist economy in its quest to commodify everything that doesn't have a money value, which is responsible for the reduction of social resilience and the quick conversion of a financial crisis into a social crisis.

Non-capitalist alternatives are reinvigorated when a crisis hits. In Catalunya, from where I write, there is a wealth of innovative emerging experiences, ranging from the proliferating urban food gardens at various barrios of Barcelona and other cities, to the growing network of production-consumption food cooperatives, co-housing cooperatives such as SostraCivic and local currencies such as the EcoSeny in Monseny.[1] The vibrant Barcelona squatting movement should also be mentioned, with the occupation of abandoned houses and their conversion into exemplars of alternative communal, community-oriented, ecological living.[2] All these initiatives, which are not only confined to Catalunya, are what Chris Carlsson has called "nowtopias":[3] utopias materialized in the present. This "other life" is not only possible; it is already forming[4] within "the belly of the beast". The question is: can it be sustained and expanded to form a true society of degrowth?

Escaping the capitalist economy and forming nowtopias is not an idyllistic ecologist call for a return to a bucolic past that has never existed. It is of course a romantic project, and this is fine, since a dose of romanticism is precisely what we need in this era of cold-blooded and self-destructive individualistic utilitarianism. Nowtopias are not just "life style choices": they represent conscious "life projects" for their participants, and are political actions, consciously and explicitly for some and unconsciously and implicitly for others. But "escaping the economy" is unlikely to become a massive movement on its own without an interlocked change at the political-institutional level that will make its flourishing

---

1 These and other initiatives are depicted in the wonderful documentary *Homenatge a Catalunya II*, a product of sociological research by Joana Conill and Manuel Castells at Universitat Obierta de Catalunya.

2 See Cattaneo and Gavalda, 2010 for an ecological-economic assessment of the squats at Colserolla Hill; and Cattaneo and Tuleda, 2014 for a history of Barcelona's squatting movement.

Cattaneo, C., & Gavaldà, M. (2010). "The experience of rurban squats in Collserola, Barcelona: what kind of degrowth?" *Journal of Cleaner Production, 18*(6), 581-589.

Cattaneo, C., & Tudela, E. (2014). "¡El carrer es nostre! The autonomous movement in Barcelona, 1980-2012." In B. Van der Steen (Ed.), *The city is ours: squatting and autonomous movements in Europe from the 1970s to the present.* PM Press.

3 Carlsson, C. (2008). *Nowtopia: how pirate programmers, outlaw bicyclists, and vacant-lot gardeners are inventing the future today.* AK Press.

4 Castells, M. 2011. "Otra vida es possible." *La Vanguardia*, 2 April 2011, p.19.

possible. Institutions to limit the expansion of the economy and to open spaces for alternative life projects are a prerequisite for nowtopias.

Of course the core capitalist system and the political and economic elites that govern it are not going to sit back quietly and watch the internal dismembering of the system without putting up a fight. The system will undermine, oppose, and if necessary oppress those who want to "exit the economy", as soon as "nowtopias" start expanding from the marginal population of the few dedicated activists that are currently involved to reach the population at large. The movement of nowtopias and of a new economy will either evolve into a strong social and political movement or it will perish. Escaping alone is not enough; the danger of becoming irrelevant is acute. There is nothing particularly new in escaping a failing capitalist system. The very first wage laborers in 15th century Northern Italy fled the cities *en masse* hit by, probably the first ever, crisis of capitalism, returning to the countryside and devoting themselves to food gardening, as Marx noted on the chapter on Primitive Accumulation of Capital Vol 1. Their survivalist escape of course changed little in the historical trajectory of capitalism, and the role of wage labor in it. Rather than—only—escapist "eco-villages" and food gardens, degrowth is about the construction and, importantly, political defense of new "urban villages",[1] i.e. nowtopias in the city that aim to change the city itself. Institutional and grassroots action are part and parcel of each other.

Environmentalists' illusion with green growth

Instead of engaging with the creative construction of political alternatives beyond the capitalist growth economy, many environmentalists in positions of influence, in green parties, NGOs, or the academia, insist on "techno-fixing" our way out of our current ecological-economic conundrum. Their vision is one of a dematerializing, "green growth" future based on efficiency and new, environmental-friendly technologies. The illusion here is that capitalist economies can grow as always, just by switching to renewable energies, organic farming and pollution abatement, substituting "dirty" industrial development fed by fossil fuel and material extraction.[2] Much hope is put on efficiency, be it in the form of better technologies (e.g. energy-efficient or hybrid cars) or conservation by individuals (change

1 Latouche, S. (2009). *Farewell to growth*. Polity.

2 UNEP. (2011). *Towards a green economy: Pathways to sustainable development and poverty eradication*. United Nations Environment Programme.

your lamps, retrofit your house, use less water, etc).

These strategies of technological innovation and social moralizing have been on the table for a long time and they are not working. There is a good reason for this. Any efficiency gains that have been realized are generally reinvested back to further growth. This is what some analysts have named the "rebound effect", i.e. less consumption rebounding to more consumption eventually. Leaner cars travel faster and farther way. The money we save with energy-efficiency lamps in our houses, we use to fly farther away for our holidays. Economist Stanley Jevons writing in the 19th century, the era of steam-fired coal engines, noted how technological efficiency improvements were leading to using more coal, not less. As efficiency makes resources cheaper, demand increases and new technologies emerge to make use of the affordable resources. If we remain within a growth economy, efficiency and conservation simply mean capital accumulation plowed back to further growth.

Physicist-economist Nicholas Georgescu-Roegen[1] noted that the first source of wealth on Earth is the sun's energy. While solar flow will last for a very long time, the undeground stocks upon which industrial society has been based will end sooner or later. As fossil fuels are burnt, they cannot be recycled and fresh supplies are needed all the time. Entropy increases. While entropy degradation cannot be averted, its pace can be arrested by shifting timely and smoothly from stock to flow sources. Renewable technologies capture flows but do not escape the laws of physics; they also use energy, resources (such as rare metals); and they occupy space. Renewable sources have much lower EROI (energy return on energy investment) than the oil and gas sources whose surpluses provided the "invisible labor" of the industrial revolution. Environmentalists who calculate how much energy we will need in 50 years and then proclaim that we can meet it all with renewable energy commit a vital factual error: they forget to calculate the energy that will be consumed for producing and maintaining the renewable sources themselves.

All this is not to discard the usefulness of renewable energies and the need to shift from oil and carbon stocks to solar and wind flows. It is only a reminder that whereas a solar and wind future is possible, it will by necessity be a simpler one: a degrowth future, indeed.

1 Georgescu-Roegen, N. (1971). *The Entropy Law and the Economic Process*. Cambridge.

From pragmatic environmentalism to a radical, degrowth environmentalism

In an even more sinister twist, a growing number of self-proclaimed "pragmatic" environmentalists have recently come out in favor of nuclear energy, calling it the best solution in the face of climate change and peak oil. James Lovelock, inventor of the concept of Gaia advocates nuclear as the "only green solution". More controversially given the timing, The Guardian's world-renowned environmental journalist George Monbiot wrote on the 23rd of March "how Fukushima made him stop worrying and love nuclear power". Ted Nordhaus and Michael Schellenberger, 2008's "heroes of the environment" according to Times magazine, have gone as far as proclaiming the "death" of environmentalism and calling for a new post-environmentalism grounded on a pragmatic engagement with—among other enemies of "old" environmentalism—nuclear power! (see more on ecomodernism in Part II)

It would be easy to join other anti-nuclear environmentalists and discard Nordhaus and Schellenberger as "sell-outs", Lovelock as an old man who is losing his reason, and Monbiot as a provocative journalist. But there is something bigger going on here. Their pro-nuclear stance, or in Monbiot's case his flirtation with nuclear, is not an aberration but the logical conclusion in the evolution of an environmental movement which—at least since the early 1980s and the victory of "pragmatists" over "fundamentalists", not least in the German Green Party—has lost its radical roots for the sake of a political expediency that has led it nowhere. Rather than a political stance in defense of an alternative way of organizing society, environmentalists have been trapped into a technical, depoliticized debate about how to best manage the environment without harming the economy or changing the current political order.

But this path is a dead-end. Indeed in technical terms, and within the coordinates of the present capitalist economy, Nordhaus and Schellenberger may be correct, and I don't feel competent to judge. Between coal and nuclear, nuclear may just as well be less bad. Perhaps the costs of nuclear accidents like Fukushima are lower than the human and environmental cost of coal mining and climate disasters (of course they are not taking into account here the energy consumption and contribution to climate change of nuclear energy production and waste disposal itself; and one wonders how we can we ever estimate and compare lost lives from nuclear versus lost lives from coal). More importantly, they are definitely right that renewables alone cannot power our current industrial economy at its present scale. If we were to install decentralized, local energy sources everywhere to produce the same economic output, then the environmental impacts would be horrible too (imagine a landscape full of windmills and rivers full of hydro-power dams).

But is this what environmentalism has come down to? Making pragmatic choices between the lesser of two terrible evils? Should we die from coal tomorrow or from nuclear waste the day after? Unfortunately, that is what it has been reduced to, from questions of local development in the "first" and "third" world's peripheries to every single resource issue, food, water, energy, climate change, everything. The framing is strikingly similar: should we have mining or tourism? Mass tourism or high-end eco-tourism? Landfills or incinerators? One is tempted to wonder what the point is of being an environmentalist nowadays, and not let scientists do their job quietly, deciding whether nuclear or coal costs more.

The absurdity of being a "pro-nuclear environmentalist" makes us see that the problem is not in the answer but in the framing of the question, i.e. the assumption of a given and growing economy, no matter what its cost, no matter what its real usefulness. What is missing from the narrative of "pragmatic" (sic) environmentalists is the "missile option" in Paul Aries'[1] terms: a simpler, downscaled, communal economy, that can indeed be powered by renewables and provide meaningful livelihood; a frugal and convivial one though with much less material goods and comforts than today, but much more welfare. "Pragmatists" are quick to dismiss this as an unrealistic, bucolic vision. Never mind that we used 50% less resources just a few decades back and our lives were anything but bucolic. In their view, our present levels of consumption are god-given and to consider that we can backtrack is unthinkable. Well, then time to think the unthinkable.

Epilogue

I hope that in this essay I convinced the reader that degrowth is not a naïve or unfounded call for a return to a bucolic past. It is an informed maturing of a radical environmentalism, at the roots of which has always been the creation of an alternative socio-ecological and political-economic order. Freed from deep ecologists' a-political misconceptions about a passive submission to an inherently balanced "mother earth", degrowth presents a radical political project of constructing an alterna-

1 Ariés, P. (2005), *Décroissance ou Barbarie*. Golias: Lyon.

tive socio-ecological future, one that is simpler by enlightened choice, not by passive conformity to nature's laws. Degrowth is a radical political project in Slavoj Žižek's terms of what a radical project is: one that challenges and aims to change the very ideological coordinates of our society. It attacks the semi-religious totem of modern societies, capitalist and communist alike: economic growth.[1] Unlike failed radical projects of the past, degrowth does not offer only a new way of realizing humanity's dreams; it changes the dreams themselves.[2]

If someone is pragmatic today then it is the radical degrowth nowtopians. Let the self-proclaimed "pragmatists" simply debate the optimal path for civilization's demise: should it be nuclear or should it be coal? Let them wonder.

---

1 Castoriadis, C., & Murphy, J. (1985). "Reflections on 'rationality' and 'development'". *Thesis Eleven, 10*(1), 18-36.

2 Žižek, S. (2011). *Living in the end times*. Verso.

2. The degrowth alternative

Author's note: this is a more recent essay, written in 2015 for the Great Transitions Initiative in Boston. I met the GTI team at the Tellus Institute back in 2013, while visiting my good friend and colleague Nicholas Ashford, a professor at MIT. As part of their amazing work in constructing scenarios for a Great Transition, they also invite debates on important topics. And so we debated whether degrowth is a necessary ingredient of sustainable scenarios (my position), or whether we should be agnostic to the question of growth and frame future scenarios in different terms (the position of some of my interlocutors). In this essay I try to argue the case for degrowth a bit better, and frame a long-term vision of societies without growth and the transition to them. In Chapter 21 you can read some critiques to my article and my rebuttal.

Both the name and the theory of degrowth aim explicitly to repoliticize environmentalism. Sustainable development and its more recent reincarnation "green growth" depoliticize genuine political antagonisms between alternative visions for the future. They render environmental problems technical, promising win-win solutions and the impossible goal of perpetuating economic growth without harming the environment. Ecologizing society, degrowthers argue, is not about implementing an alternative, better, or greener development. It is about imagining and enacting alternative visions to modern growth-based development. This essay explores such alternatives and identifies grassroots practices and political changes for facilitating a transition to a prosperous and equitable world without growth.

Ecology vs. Modernity

The conflict between environment and growth is ever-present. For "developers," the value of growth is not to be questioned: more mining, drilling, building, and manufacturing is necessary to expand the economy. Against developers stand radical environmentalists and local communities, who are often alone in questioning the inevitability of "a one-way future consisting only of growth."[1] In this opposition to development projects, philosopher Bruno Latour sees a fundamental rejection of modernity's separation of means and ends.[2] Radical environmentalists recognize that ecology, with its focus on connecting humans with one another and with the non-human world, is inherently at odds with growth that separates and conquers.

The rise of mainstream discourse on sustainable development effectively erased the radical promise of ecology. The notion of sustainability that emerged from the 1992 Earth Summit neutralized and depoliticized the conflict between environment and growth. Since then, negotiations between government, businesses, and "pragmatic" environmentalists have assumed that new markets and technologies can simultaneously boost economic growth and protect natural systems. Environmental problems have been largely consigned to the realm of technical improvement, the province of experts and policy elites.

Ten years ago, the provocative formulation of "degrowth"—a so-called "missile concept"—was put forward to challenge this de-politicization of environmentalism and attack the "oxymoron of sustainable development."[3] The use of a negative word for a positive project was intentional: by subverting the desirability of growth, degrowth aimed to identify and question the ideology that must be confronted in order to transition to a truly sustainable world: the ideology of growth. Degrowth theorists call for an "exit from the economy," an invitation to abandon economistic thinking and construct viable alternatives to capitalism. However, proposing alternative economic models is not enough. We must also question the existence of

---

1 The phrase is from Ursula Le Guin (1982), whose social science fiction novel *The Dispossessed* (1975) provides a vivid exposition of a degrowth world. See the article "The planet of *The Dispossessed*", in this book (chapter 20).
Le Guin, U. (1982). A Non-Euclidean View of California as a Cold Place to Be. *Dancing at the Edge of the World: Thoughts on Words, Women, Places* (pp. 80-100). Grove Press.
Le Guin, U. (1974). *The Dispossessed*. New York: Harper & Row.

2 Latour, B. (1998). "To Modernize or to Ecologize? That's the Question". *Remaking Reality: Nature at the Millennium*. Noel Castree and Bruce Willems-Braun (Eds). New York: Routledge, 221-242.

3 Latouche, S. (2009). *Farewell to growth*. Polity.
For a review of the unpublished francophone literature, see Fournier, 2008. The choice of the term "degrowth" (décroissance in French) was inspired by the title of Nicholas Georgescu-Roegen, Jacques Grinevald, and Ivo Rens (Georgescu-Roegen et al., 1979). On degrowth as a "hypothesis," see Kallis et al., 2012.
Georgescu-Roegen, N., Rens, I., & Grinevald, J. (1979). Demain la décroissance: Entropie-écologie-économie. P.-M. Favre.
Fournier, V. (2008). "Escaping from the economy: the politics of degrowth." International Journal of Sociology and Social Policy, 28(11/12), 528-545.
Kallis, G., Kerschner, C., & Martinez-Alier, J. (2012). "The economics of degrowth." Ecological Economics, 84, 172-180.

an autonomous sphere called "the economy." The "free market" is not a natural process; it has been constructed through deliberate governmental intervention. Repoliticization of the economy will require hard-fought institutional change to return it to democratic control.

Envisioning Degrowth

Advocates of degrowth refrain from offering any one blueprint to replace today's growth-centric "free" market. Their objective is to open up conceptual space for imagining and enacting diverse alternative futures that share the aims of downscaling affluent economies and their material flows in a just and equitable manner. Reducing such material flows would likely lead to a decrease in GDP as currently measured. However, degrowth is not synonymous with recession or depression, the terms we use for negative growth in a growth economy. Degrowth, instead, involves a rethinking of the organization of society signaled by terms such as limits, care, and dépense.[1]

Degrowth proposals generally incorporate collective limits, such as caps on carbon emissions or 100% reserve requirements for banks. These are understood as "self-limitations," collective decisions to refrain from pursuing all that could be pursued. Moreover, only social systems of limited size and complexity can be governed directly rather than by technocratic elites acting on behalf of the populace. Fossil fuels and nuclear power are dangerous not only because they pollute, but also because an energy-intensive society based on increasingly sophisticated technological systems managed by bureaucrats and technocrats will grow less democratic and egalitarian over time. Many degrowth advocates, therefore, oppose even "green" megastructures like high-speed trains or industrial-scale wind farms.

Care can become the hallmark of an economy based on reproduction, rather than expansion. Reproduction refers to the activities that sustain the life cycle, typically within the family. But more generally, it encompasses all processes of sustenance and restoration. In the present economy, care work remains gendered, undervalued, and pushed into the shadow of the formal economy. Degrowth calls for the equal distribution of care work and the re-centering of society around it. A caring economy is labor-intensive precisely because human labor is what gives care its

1 D'Alisa, G., Demaria, F., & Kallis, G. (2014). *Degrowth: a vocabulary for a new era.* Routledge.

value. It thus has the potential to offset rising unemployment today while fostering a more humane society.

Dépense refers to the unproductive expenditure of the social surplus. How civilizations allocate their surplus—the expenditures they make above and beyond what is necessary to meet basic human needs—gives them their essential character. The Egyptians devoted their surplus to pyramids, the Tibetans to an idle class of monks, and the Europeans of the Middle Ages to churches (and this is an analytical observation, I am not suggesting that we should repeat such expenditures today!). In today's capitalist civilization, as the surplus is accumulated and invested to produce more growth, dépense is displaced to privatized acts of exuberant consumption. Since limiting excessive consumption alone would fuel even more saving and investment, degrowth envisions radically reducing the surplus and deploying it for a festive society in which citizens devise new, non-harmful ways to dispense it, ways that help build community and collective meaning.

The degrowth imperative

There is a substantial body of evidence that demonstrates how growth threatens both environmental and social well-being.[1] Continued economic growth makes us more likely to exceed the safe operating space defined by planetary boundaries, making life harder for everyone, especially the most vulnerable. Although "green growth" has become a buzzword in recent years, it remains an oxymoron. Its emphasis on enhanced efficiency creates a paradox: decreased resource requirements lead to lower costs and—by the simple workings of supply and demand—a rebound in the consumption of resources.[2] This is part of the fundamental dynamic of capitalism: increasing productivity frees up resources that are invested to provide yet more growth.

Continued economic growth in wealthy nations is also proving inimical to well-being. As Herman Daly observed, "illth" (congestion, crime, and other undesirable side effects) increases as fast as, or faster than, wealth as measured by GDP.[3] Redistribution, not growth, is what

1 Daly, H. (1996). *Beyond growth: the economics of sustainable development.* Beacon Press.
Jackson, T. (2009). *Prosperity without growth: Economics for a finite planet.* Routledge.

2 Alcott, B. (2005). "Jevons' paradox." *Ecological Economics*, 54(1), 9-21.

3 Daly, H. (1996). *Beyond growth: the economics of sustainable development.* Beacon Press.

improves well-being in affluent nations. Growth can never quench the desire for positional goods; only redistribution and new values can.

What about those in poor nations who have yet to see the benefits of growth? Degrowth in the Global North can provide ecological space for the Global South. For example, strong carbon caps for the North and better terms of trade for the South can help compensate for past carbon and resource debts, redistributing wealth between North and South. Economic growth in the South, moreover, threatens alternative, non-monetized means of livelihood, generating the poverty that, in turn, makes more growth "necessary." Degrowth in the North, then, can provide space for the flourishing of alternative cosmovisions and practices in the South, such as buen vivir in Latin America or ubuntu in Africa. These are alternatives to development, not alternative forms of development.

Seeds of a degrowth transition

Degrowth alternatives have begun to flourish as the formal economy has fallen into crisis. These include food production in urban gardens; co-housing and ecocommunes; alternative food networks, producer-consumer cooperatives, and communal kitchens; health care, elder care, and child care cooperatives; open software; and decentralized forms of renewable energy production and distribution. These alternatives are often accompanied, or even supported, by new forms of exchange such as community currencies, barter markets, time banks, financial cooperatives, and ethical banks.[1]

Such projects display various facets of degrowth. They promote a shift to a more locally based economy with short production and consumption cycles. They emphasize reproduction and caring, to satisfy use values, not profits. They replace wage labor with voluntary activity. They do not have a built-in tendency to accumulate and expand, and they are less resource-intensive than their counterparts in the formal economy. Such practices of "commoning" cultivate solidarity and humane interpersonal relations, and generate shared, non-monetary wealth.

As these alternative forms of provisioning suggest, a degrowth transi-

1 Conill, J., Cárdenas, A., Castells, M., Hlebik, S., & Servon, L. (2012). *Otra vida es posible. Practicas económicas alternativas durante la crisis (incluye DVD)* (Vol. 9). Editorial UOC.
Gibson-Graham, J. K. (2006). *A postcapitalist politics.* University of Minnesota Press.
Dittmer, K. (2013). "Local currencies for purposive degrowth? A quality check of some proposals for changing money-as-usual." *Journal of Cleaner Production, 54,* 3-13.

tion will be heavily bottom-up. However, broad institutional changes will be needed to foster adoption of such practices. For example, a guaranteed basic income would provide universal access to national wealth, securing basic sustenance for all and liberating time for non-paid activity. With the complementary policy of a job guarantee, the state could provide employment for all who wish to work in activities that support the common good. A shorter workweek and job sharing without a reduction of monthly wages could also combat unemployment and create more time for leisure and commoning. Adoption of these policies would reduce economic insecurity without the need for further economic growth.

A transition beyond growth will entail a transition beyond capitalism, since the essence of capitalism is accumulation and expansion.[1] A degrowth transition would likely follow a pattern similar to those of past systemic economic shifts. Capitalism arose from feudalism as connections were forged between new economic practices and entities (firms, corporations, trade contracts, banks, investments) and political and institutional developments supportive of these practices (abolition of monarchies and feudal privileges, enclosure of the commons, liberal democracy, laws protecting private property).

Analogously, contemporary grassroots practices and institutional changes can seed a transformation of the current system, as economic growth approaches its limits. Degrowthers see deepening democracy as essential to a degrowth transition. They welcome experimentation with direct forms of popular democracy, such as those practiced by the Occupy movement. They envision a regime that combines elements of direct and delegative democracy, such as the "radical ecological democracy" advocated by Ashish Kothari.[2]

A degrowth transition would differ sharply from the revolutions of the twentieth century, not only because it would be resolutely non-violent and democratic in character, but also because the target would not just be capitalism, but also productivism. An exit from growth requires an exit from capitalism, but an exit from capitalism does not necessarily bring an exit from growth. Twentieth century socialist regimes replaced the capitalist relations of production without changing the basic objective

---

1 Capitalism can experience involuntary negative growth, but not for long, as this would lead to intensifying inequalities and socio-political instability, and the threat of the imposition of some form of autocracy.

2 Kothari, A. (2014). "Radical Ecological Democracy: A Path Forward for India and Beyond". *The Great Transition*. Retrieved from http://www.greattransition.org/publication/radical-ecological-democracy-a-path-forward-for-india-and-beyond

of resource exploitation and surplus accumulation for the sake of mass production and consumption.

Governing degrowth

Despite the richness of degrowth theory, proponents are still grappling with questions of scale and governance. Advocates of degrowth privilege relocalization, anticipating that it will emerge and flourish, leading to a national political movement that can change the state from within. However, there is a tension between a desire for local autonomy and the need for action at a broader scale. A certain degree of hierarchy is unavoidable because the redistribution of burdens and resources among more and less privileged localities will require intermediation and decision-making at broad geographic levels. Some of the degrowth reforms discussed above are, in fact, quite interventionist and would require strong state action.

Likewise, engagement with governance at a global scale is largely absent from the discussions within the degrowth movement. This is curious given the centrality of issues like climate change, free trade, and relentless global competition. Many degrowth advocates appear to assume that limitations on trade and capital at the national level will extricate a country from global economic forces, or that generalized global change will ensue as the aggregate effect of local grassroots initiatives. However, such developments remain unlikely. Climate change, for instance, cannot be tackled solely by summing up various local low-carbon initiatives in the absence of international agreements that cap total greenhouse gas emissions.

Under the prevailing neoliberal regime, global interdependence makes it impossible for a country to undertake a degrowth transition on its own. Doing so would entail substantial penalties from capital flight, bank and currency collapses, asset devaluations, collapse of public and security institutions, and political isolation. This would undermine the ability of a nation to pursue a quiet contraction on its own. Likewise, if a single country or block of countries were to successfully downscale their economies, a global reduction of resource prices would likely follow, producing a rebound in consumption elsewhere. In a sense, then, escaping growth is a global collective action problem. To be successful, the transition to degrowth must be global.

Epilogue

Degrowth requires a commitment not just to protect nature or to manage and mitigate the impacts of capitalism, but also to create an alternative social-ecology and a fundamentally different basis for action. From this new perspective, environmentalists opposing a mega-project need not perform cost-benefit calculations or devise alternatives that accommodate growth. They can simply assert that such projects do not fit the world in which they want to live. They can say that there is alternative, and it is called "degrowth".

3. The Left should embrace degrowth

Author's note: this article was written in 2015 for the online edition of The New Internationalist *magazine, and it has a more political outlook. The audience I had in mind while writing were the ecologically-minded participants of leftist social and political movements. My argument is that a new left can no longer afford to be productivist and developmentalist. I then reflected on some hopeful, and other less hopeful, developments in Europe's New Left.*

Origins

Intellectually, the origins of degrowth are found in the Continental *écologie politique* of the 1970s. André Gorz spoke of *décroissance* in 1972, questioning the compatibility of capitalism with earth's balance "for which … degrowth of material production is a necessary condition".[1] Unless we consider "equality without growth", Gorz argued, we reduce socialism to nothing but "the continuation of capitalism by other means—an extension of middle-class values, lifestyles and social patterns".[2]

"Demain la décroissance" (tomorrow, degrowth) was the title of a 1979 translated collection of essays of Nicholas Georgescu-Roegen,[3] a Romanian émigré teaching in the US and a proto ecological economist who argued that economic growth accelerates entropy. These were the times of the oil crisis and the Club of Rome. For continental "red-green" thinkers, however, the question of limits to growth was first and foremost a political one. Unlike Malthusian concerns with resource depletion, overpopulation and collapse of the system, theirs was a desire for pulling the emergency brake on the train of capitalism, or, to quote Ursula Le Guin, "put a pig on the tracks of a one-way future consisting only of growth".[4]

The slogan *décroissance* was revived in the early 2000s by activists in the city of Lyon in direct actions against mega-infrastructures and ad-

1 Bosquet M. (1972). "Proceedings from a public debate organized in Paris by the Club du Nouvel Observateur." *Nouvel Observateur*, Paris, 397, p. IV.

2 Gorz, A., Vigderman P., and Cloud J.. (1980) *Ecology as politics*. Black Rose Books, p. 13.

3 Georgescu-Roegen, N., Rens, I., & Grinevald, J. (1979). *Demain la décroissance: Entropie-écologie-économie*. P.-M. Favre.

4 Le Guin, U. K. (1982). "A Non-Euclidean View of California as a Cold Place to Be." *Dancing at the Edge of the World: Thoughts on Words, Women, Places*. Grove Press.

vertising. Serge Latouche, a professor of economic anthropology and vocal critic of development programmes in Africa, popularized it with his books, calling for an "end to sustainable development".[1] For French intellectual Paul Ariès, degrowth was a "missile word", a subversive term that questioned the taken-for-granted desirability of growth-based development.[2] A small but dedicated network of degrowthers sprang around the monthly *La Decroissance* magazine.[3] The word registered in French political debates,[4] with even a failed attempt for a degrowth political party.[5]

Degrowth today

From France, the new meme spread to Italy, Spain and Greece. In 2008, just before the Spanish crisis, Catalan degrowth activist Enric Duran "expropriated" 492,000 euros via loans from 39 banks. He gave the money to social movements, denouncing Spain's speculative credit system and the fictitious growth it propelled.

Starting in Paris in 2008, a series of international gatherings—a mix of scientific conference with social forum—introduced degrowth to the English-speaking world. In September 2014, 3,500 researchers, students and activists met in Leipzig for the 4th International Conference on Degrowth. Activities spanned from panels on growth and climate change, Gramscian critiques of capitalism, or the 20-hour workweek, to civil disobedience outside a coal power plant and courses on how to make your own bread.

Proliferating academic literature[6] in peer-reviewed journals has buttressed key degrowth claims: the impossibility to avoid disastrous climate change with growth as usual; fundamental limits in decoupling resource use from growth; the disconnection between growth and improved well-being in advanced economies; the rising social and psychological costs of growth. Recent works highlight the imperative of compound growth

---

1 Latouche, S. (2009). *Farewell to growth.* Polity.

2 Ariès, P. (2005). *Décroissance ou barbarie.* Golias.

3 http://www.ladecroissance.net

4 Baykan, B. G. (2007). "From limits to growth to degrowth within French green politics." *Environmental Politics, 16*(3), 513-517.

5 See http://www.partipourladecroissance.net

6 For a list, see http://www.degrowth.org/publications and the database run by Degrowth.de: http://www.degrowth.de/en/media-library/

for capitalism[1] (what David Harvey called the most lethal of its contradictions[2]), and explore how employment or equality could be sustained in post-capitalist economies without growth.

Policy proposals range from carbon caps and extraction moratoria to a basic citizens' income, a reduced working week, a reclaim of resource commons and a debt jubilee, as well as a radical restructuring of the tax system with carbon instead of income taxes, salary caps, and capital taxes. By demanding the impossible, such "non-reformist reforms", as Andre Gorz called them, call for systemic transformation (as Slavoj Žižek noted, social-democratic reforms are revolutionary in an era that capitalism can no longer accommodate them).

Politically, there is a clear understanding that system change is necessary, and that this requires a movement of movements, or an alliance of the dispossessed, including a coalition of the global social and environmental justice movements. Whereas degrowth is incompatible with capitalism, degrowth rejects also the illusion of a so-called "socialist growth", whereby a rationally, centrally planned economy somehow magically will bring technological developments that will allow a reasonable growth without impinging upon the ecological conditions. In the spirit of Gorz, degrowthers take issue with fellow socialists who find it easier to imagine the end of the world or the end of capitalism, but for some inexplicable reason, not the end of growth.

Another way

For others "degrowth" signifies mostly an everyday (politicized) living practices. Our three-day degrowth forum in Athens in 2015 was attended by hundreds of participants: not only academics, environmental and human rights activists or members of Syriza, the Greens, and the "anti-authoritarian" Left, but also back-to-landers and organic farmers from rural Greece, and many of the "ground troopers" of the solidarity economy of peoples' clinics and urban agriculture. In Barcelona, degrowth is symbolized in projects such as Can Masdeu, an occupied squat with a network of food gardens in the working-class neighbourhood of Nou Barris and a history of "right to housing" activism; or the Cooperativa Integral Catalana, a co-operative consisting of 600 members and 2,000

1 Binswanger, M. (2015). "The growth imperative revisited: a rejoinder to Gilányi and Johnson." *Journal of Post Keynesian Economics, 37*(4), 648-660.

2 Harvey, D. (2014). *Seventeen contradictions and the end of capitalism.* Oxford University Press (UK).

participants, which also functions as an umbrella for independent producers and consumers of organic food and artisanal products, houses eco-commune residents, and runs co-operative enterprises and regional networks of exchange that issue their own currencies.

Francois Schneider, instigator of the international conferences and founder of the Research & Degrowth think-tank in Paris (now in Barcelona), embodies degrowth's hybridity: a PhD graduate in industrial ecology, he walked for a year with a donkey around France explaining degrowth to passers-by who stopped him bewildered. He lives now in Can Decreix, a bare-basics house on the French-Catalan border, a center of experimentation and education in frugal living.

Some speak of a grassroots degrowth "movement", but the attendants of the conferences are not a cohesive group of people with a shared agenda or unified purpose,[1] nor do we still reach the numbers of a movement. Unlike the "anti-globalization" movement, there is no WTO building to be stormed or free-trade treaty to be stopped. Degrowth offers a slogan that mobilizes, brings together, and gives meaning to a diverse range of people and movements without being their only, or even principal, horizon. It is a network of ideas, a vocabulary as we called it in our recent book, that more and more people feel speaks to their concerns.

Redistribution, not growth

A new Left has to be an ecological Left, or it won't be left at all. Environmental change "changes everything" for the Left too, as Naomi Klein argued.[2] Capitalism requires constant expansion, an expansion predicated on exploitation of humans and non-humans, that irreversibly damages the climate. A non-capitalist economy will have to sustain itself while contracting. But how can we redistribute or secure meaningful work without growth? There is not yet a concrete "economics of degrowth". Lamentably, Keynesianism is the most powerful tool the Left, even the Marxist Left, has for dealing with issues of policy. But this is an economics of the 1930s when unlimited expansion was still possible and desirable.

Without a tide to raise all boats, it is the time to rethink which boat

---

1 Eversberg, D., & Schmelzer, M. (2016). "Über die Selbstproblematisierung zur Kapitalismuskritik." *Forschungsjournal Soziale Bewegungen, 29*(1), 9-17.

2 Klein, N. (2015). *This changes everything: Capitalism vs. the climate.* Simon and Schuster.

gets what. The Left's response to Piketty's $r>g$ conundrum[1] should not be "we will increase g". After all, we always wanted to degrow r, i.e. reduce capital accumulation! Piketty himself, hardly an ecologist, does not believe in the possibility of higher growth. Redistribution is the central question for a 21st century without growth.

The Left has to liberate itself from the imaginary of growth. The growth of anything at a compound rate quickly turns towards infinity, an absurd and dangerous idea. Growth is an idea that is part and parcel of capitalism. It is the name the system gave to the dream it was producing, the dream of material plenty.[2] GDP was invented to count war production,[3] and evolved into an indicator "objectively" measuring and confirming the "success" of the US in the Cold war.[4] Growth is what capitalism needs, knows, and does. As Gareth Dale notes,[5] socialist politics were never about quantitative increases in abstract exchange value. They were about specifics, about concrete use values: employment, a decent wage, dignified conditions of living, a healthy environment, education, public health or clean water for all. All these need resources; but there is no reason why they would need a perpetual expansion of resources, 3% each year.

And here is a stronger claim: the things we in the Left would like to see "grow" would not bring aggregate growth (unless we totally redefined what we measure as economic activity, but this is then a play of words). Spreading wealth evenly, using more hands and minds than otherwise necessary, leaving environments and people idle, spending time to care for one another: all these are "taxes" on productivity and growth. We may as well be better off being less productive.[6] But industrialization took off by concentrating surpluses in the hands of a few (capitalists or states), reinvesting profits for more growth; not by spreading the wealth to everyone or leaving the pastures and the fossils idle.

---

1 Piketty, T. (2013). *Capital in the twenty-first century.* Belknap Press.

2 Yarrow, A. L. (2010). *Measuring America: How economic growth came to define American greatness in the late twentieth century.* University of Massachusetts Press.

3 Mitchell, T. (2011). *Carbon democracy: Political power in the age of oil.* New York: Verso.
Mitchell, T. (2014). "Economentality: how the future entered government." *Critical Inquiry, 40*(4), 479-507.

4 Yarrow, A. L. (2010). *Measuring America: How economic growth came to define American greatness in the late twentieth century.* University of Massachusetts Press.

5 Dale, G. (2012). "The growth paradigm: a critique." *International Socialism, 134.*

6 Jackson, T. (2012). "Let's be less productive." *The New York Times.* Retrieved from http://www.nytimes.com/2012/05/27/opinion/sunday/lets-be-less-productive.html?_r=0

Changing the dreams

This may be too hard to swallow. After all, many of us often advocate for equality, democracy, full employment, a minimum wage, education, or renewables (you name it) in the name of growth. The belief is that an alternative to the capitalist system that has eyes only for profits will be more "rational" and do better what capitalism does, and even more. This is wrong politically: as Slavoj Žižek claims, the Left cannot exhaust itself to new ways of realizing the same dreams; it has to change the dreams themselves. It is also wrong factually. The "glorious" (sic) post-War era of reconstruction and catch-up is over. There are few indications that debt-fuelled Keynsianism, brown or green, capitalist or socialist, can revive it. This is independent of the fact that neoliberal austerity is disastrous. Redistribution, democracy and equality, yes; but not in the name of growth.

Degrowth revives the spirit of Enrico Berlinguer's "revolutionary austerity", an austerity born out of solidarity. The petrol that fuels our cars, heats our homes or even powers our hospitals and schools is the same that destroys livelihoods and forests in the Peruvian Amazon or Nigeria. We do not need the Pope to remind us that.[1] The reason for a 'sober' life, as Berlinguer before or the Pope now calls it, is because our actions 'here' affect people and ecosystems 'there'. Not because the capitalist machine is running out of things (Malthusians' worry), or because, as the neoliberals want it, 'we live beyond our means' (by which they mean 'we the 99%' who use the services of the welfare state, not they the 1% who live by their capital).

From a degrowth perspective, the issue is not that the Global North consumes more than it produces (or produces more than it consumes, à la Keynesians). The issue is that it produces and consumes more than what is necessary, at the expense of the Global and inner 'South', other beings, and future generations. Producing and consuming less will reduce the damage done to others. This is a question of social and environmental justice: a 'shrink and redistribute' from the global 1% (and to a lesser extent the 10%, which includes the middle classes of the EuroAmericas) to the rest. Such invocations of sober simplicity may resonate with dormant common senses about the 'good life' present in many cultures, East and West. It can recover the commonsensical critique of

1 Krüger, O. (2015). "*Laudato Si" as signalling towards Degrowth*. Retrieved from http://www.degrowth.de/en/2015/06/laudato-si-as-signalling-towards-degrowth/

'excess' from the grip of austerians, who hypocritically use it to justify their regressive policies.

Political possibilities

Degrowth is a keyword circulating mostly among activists. In Greece and Spain, it resonates with anarcho-cooperativists and eco-communalists, including many in the youth bases of parties like Syriza or Podemos. It was a word present, though not dominant, in the occupied squares and the solidarity economies that spun off from them. Among Greens it has woken up old, pre-'sustainable development' divisions between radical 'fundis' and pragmatist 'realos'. A sign of the re-radicalization of Europe's Greens, Spain's Equo, represented in the European Parliament, has endorsed explicitly a 'post-growth' agenda (its MEP writing in favor of degrowth[1]). The national campaign of the UK Greens was also 'post' or 'de'-growth in spirit, though not in name.

Calling for degrowth explicitly is electoral suicide in an environment dominated by corporate media. More groundwork is necessary to make degrowth a widespread common sense. For now, the closer a radical party gets to power, the more likely it is to disassociate itself from degrowth. Pablo Iglesias signed the degrowthist 'last call' manifesto.[2] But as *The Economist* noted approvingly[3], as Podemos matured it left behind more 'nutty' ideas like 'degrowth' and 'anti-capitalism'. The parallels with the New Left in Latin America are obvious. Correa or Morales were elected with the support of indigenous and ecological movements with philosophies similar to degrowth. Once in power, real-politik and growth-based redistributive politics dictated that capital be accomodated and the economy be fuelled by extractivism.

One would hope that at least New Left parties in Europe refrain from making growth their central objective. No doubt, crises reassert the imaginary of growth, this time as a progressive goal. A Podemos activist in Catalonia commented to me that "in the current crisis, we can only talk about growth". And yet this is not totally true. It takes courage and

1 See a collection of Florent Marcellesi's writings on the topic: http://florentmarcellesi.eu/category/decrecimiento/

2 (2016). "The Manifesto." Retrieved from https://ultimallamadamanifiesto.wordpress.com/el-manifiesto/last-call-the-manifesto-english/

3 (2015). "Restless and resentful: A year of electoral turbulence lies ahead." *The Economist.* Retrieved from http://www.economist.com/news/europe/21637423-year-electoral-turbulence-lies-ahead-restless-and-resentful

imagination, but is not impossible. *Barcelona en Comú* won the elections of the city without mentioning growth once in its programme. This might have to do with the organic rooting of degrowth and associated ideas in Barcelona's civil society and the flourishing, alternative solidarity economy of the city. Many of my friends and colleagues worked for the party's programme, which commits to a citizens' income, green taxes, reclaiming of green spaces, a municipal energy co-operative, less resource use and waste, or social housing. Among the first decisions of the new mayor, Ada Colau, were a moratorium on new hotels and an end to the bid for the 2026 Winter Olympics. Santi Villa, Catalonia's minister for the environment until 2015 and an aspiring young conservative, accused her for leading "a party of degrowth"[1] (omitting though that a few months back, and trying to stay on top of the latest international ideas in debates around climate change, he too had talked favorably of degrowth in Parliament).

Keynesianism without growth?

Podemos' economic programme was drafted by two socialist-Keynesian economists (Vicenc Navarro and Juan Torres), who had frequently written opinion pieces against degrowth. Fortunately, it avoids clear references to growth. Might this signal room for a "Keynesianism without growth"? I have argued that it does.[2] One can imagine fiscal and tax policies that shift resources in favor of the working classes and toward green, caring or alternative activities stimulating a low-intensity consumption by those in need, within an overall pattern of economic contraction. Hardly Keynes' vision, but perhaps one apt for secularly stagnant economies.

Unlike a municipality, of course, whose fiscal responsibilities are limited, a nation without growth may have problems to finance its welfare services. At least in principle, however, I see no good reason why health or education costs have to grow at 2 or 3% per year (the rate of the supposed necessary growth). There is immense scope for saving by reversing outsourcing and expensive procurements, banning mega-projects, or de-

1 Pellicer, L. (2014, 16 July). "Barcelona's crackdown on Airbnb renters." *El País*. Retrieved from http://elpais.com/elpais/2014/07/16/inenglish/1405501012_966041.html

2 Kallis, G. (2015). "Podemos party's plan to "stimulate consumption" needs more ambition." *The Guardian*. Retrieved from http://www.theguardian.com/sustainable-business/2015/jan/15/spain-podemos-should-further

centralizing services, like preventative health or child care, sharing them with solidarity networks. Poorer countries such as Cuba and Costa Rica have world-class public health and education. Higher capital taxes can also offset revenue lost from degrowth. Welfare without growth is theoretically possible, but no Left party has dared to think what it would take to put it into practice.

A major sticking point is debt. Without growth, debt as a percentage of GDP increases. Borrowing rates sky-rocket, as the likelihood of repayment declines. This is what makes a degrowth Keynesianism less plausible. Without growth, public debt has, sooner or later, to be restructured or eliminated either by decree or by inflation. There are historical precedents for this. But once done, it cannot be repeated. Without new debt, the room for fiscal expansion is limited.

The urgency of the public-debt question may explain differences between Spain and Greece. The rise of Syriza initially fuelled hopes for 'another world' becoming possible: the base, especially the youth, of the party consisted of greener 'co-operativists' who, akin to a degrowth spirit, bet on—an arguably not fully defined—'solidarity economy'. All high cadres of the party, however, talked unreservedly in favor of growth, framing it as the alternative to austerity. In the negotiations with the Eurogroup there was a short-lived attempt to advance Joseph Stiglitz's proposal for a 'growth clause': Greece would link debt repayments to growth. Such demands were deemed as 'ultra-radical'; speaking of a solidarity economy without growth would be nuttier than nutty.

A solidarity economy

Some foreign commentators dreamed that a 'No' to the Troika and an exit from the euro would open the road for a degrowth transition and a solidarity economy.[1] There was no political force, however, in Greece advocating this. The pro-drachma Left of Syriza, now a separate party called "Popular Unity" is ardently productivist, its leader having a dismal environmental record as Minister of Energy, including plans for new domestic coal production and fuel subsidies to industries. Despite the phenomenal expansion and the important achievements of the solidarity economy in Greece, this is still a marginal social movement (much smaller than in Spain), and its networks are insufficient for satisfying the

1 Hinton, J. (2015). "This endless quest for growth will see Greece self-destruct." *The Guardian*. Retrieved from https://www.theguardian.com/sustainable-business/2015/jul/07/this-endless-quest-for-growth-will-see-greece-self-destruct

population's needs in case of a transitional period. A smooth economic contraction out of the euro is unlikely: it was precisely the fear of imported food or drug shortages and economic chaos in the interim period that scared Alexis Tsipras into signing a new memorandum. Countries like Japan, with fiscal and monetary independence, and an ability to issue and finance debt in their own currency, are better positioned to sustain employment and welfare without growth (Japan has not seen growth for more than 10 years, a decade "lost" only in the eyes of economists). But, of course, a capitalism without growth is inconceivable, and Japan tries as hard as possible to relaunch growth (with little success to date).

The impossibility of imaging political forces rising to power with a degrowth agenda makes some degrowthers argue that change can only come from the grassroots and not the state, through an "involuntary" path, whereby citizens will self-organize as the economy stagnates and lack of growth brings crisis. I agree that a degrowth transition is unlikely to be voluntary and take place in the name of "degrowth"; it will be a process of adaptation to the actual stagnation of the economy. I can't see, however, how this can happen without also occupying the state, with a mutual reinforcement of civil and political society, grassroots practices, and new institutions.

No political party of the Left might dare to openly question growth, but I find it hard to see how in the long-term, willingly or not, the European Left (which, unlike its Latin American counterpart, cannot bank on a commodities bubble) can avoid thinking about how to manage without growth. Growth is not only ecologically unsustainable but, as economists openly admit (from Piketty to Lawrence Summers and the "secular stagnationists"), increasingly unlikely for advanced economies.[1]

Capitalism without growth is savage. Degrowth is not a clear theory, plan, or political movement. Yet it is a hypothesis whose time has come; and one that the Left can no longer afford to avoid.

---

1 Summers, L. (2013). "Transcript of Larry Summers speech at the IMF Economic Forum." Retrieved from https://www.facebook.com/notes/randy-fellmy/transcript-of-larry-summers-speech-at-the-imf-economic-forum-nov-8-2013/585630634864563

4. Let's be less productive

Author's note: this minifesto was the epilogue to our book Degrowth: A vocabulary for a new era *(Routledge, 2015) and was separately published in the magazine* Adbusters. *Most of the ideas are from my good friend and colleague Giacomo D'Alisa. Within our Research & Degrowth group in Barcelona, Giacomo has been insisting that we should avoid the utilitarian trap to which environmentalists often fall, justifying the protection of the environment on the grounds of a self-interested survival. The idea though of unproductive expenditure, of wasting rather than saving, is one that is hard for Western environmentalists to stomach. It shouldn't be, because it is not as paradoxical as it first seems, we argue in this essay. We claim that the core challenge of each and every society is what to do with its surplus, i.e. how to handle its excess, not how to confront scarcity. Our intention here is to turn upside down the traditional concern of environmentalism with "things running out", a concern that is at the heart of capitalism and modern economics, more than environmentalists often realize. This is a very different road to degrowth than the one of the three previous essays.*

> – [A] big duel, Uncle … Great things are in the offing, and I don't want to stay at home ….
>
> – You're mad, my boy, to go with those people! They're all in the mafia, all troublemakers. A Falconeri should be with us, for the King.
>
> – For the King, Uncle, yes, of course. But which King? … If we want things to stay as they are, things will have to change.
>
> -Giuseppe Tomasi di Lampedusa, *The Leopard*

> [A]ll that city … You just couldn't see an end to it … It wasn't what I saw that stopped me, Max. It was what I didn't see.… In all that sprawling city, there was everything except an end … Take a piano. The keys begin, the keys end. You know there are 88 of them … They are not infinite, you are infinite. On those 88 keys the music that you can make is infinite.… But you get me up on that gangway and roll out a keyboard with millions of keys, and … there's no end to them, that keyboard is infinite. But if that keyboard is infinite there's no music you can play.
>
> -From the movie *The Legend of 1900*

Back in November of 2013 David Cameron, then the Prime Minister of the UK, gave a memorable speech in the Lord Mayor's banquet calling for austerity and a "fundamental culture change, while sitting in a golden throne, a contradiction that many commentators found hard to stomach."[1]

Cameron condemned idleness and invoked the traditional British value of hard work. "Put simply," he said, "no country can succeed in the long term if capable people are paid to stay idle and out of work." People are trapped into unemployment by high benefits, Cameron noted: "For generations, people who could work have been failed by the system and stuck on benefits." Benefits will be lowered, he promised, and no one will see any reward in staying idle or working less: "we are ensuring that for every extra hour you work and every extra job you do, you should always be better off." In Cameron's talk, the State is the problem, not the solution; it has to be shrunk, become leaner and limit itself to setting and enforcing rules, letting markets and the private sector produce wealth. His talk was a celebration of private enterprise: "The UK economy should be based on enterprise ... we need to support, reward, and celebrate enterprise ... make sure it is boosted everywhere, promoted in schools, taught in colleges, celebrated in communities."[2]

At around the same time, famous economist Paul Krugman commented on Lawrence Summers' talk at the IMF where the latter raised the specter of a "secular stagnation" for the U.S. economy, that is, a long-term zero growth state.[3] For Krugman this is the result of a liquidity trap, which makes state spending vital. Ideally such spending should be productive; but even unproductive spending is better than nothing, Krugman argues. The important thing is to get circulation going. Hide money or gold in caves and have enterprises dig it up, as Keynes proposed. Fake a threat from non-existent space aliens and spend for military protection (Krugman's "own favorite"). Or get U.S. enterprises "to fit out all their employees as cyborgs, with Google Glass and smart wristwatch-

---

1 Hardy, R. (2012, 13 November). "It was hard to stomach David Cameron preaching austerity from a golden throne." *The Guardian*. Retrieved from https://www.theguardian.com/commentisfree/2013/nov/13/david-cameron-austerity-public-sector-cuts

2 Cameron, D. (2013). "David Cameron's Lord Mayor's Banquest speech: in full." *The Guardian*. Retrieved from http://www.telegraph.co.uk/finance/economics/10442263/David-Camerons-Lord-Mayors-Banquest-speech-in-full.html

3 Summers, L. (2013). "Transcript of Larry Summers speech at the IMF Economic Forum." Retrieved from https://www.facebook.com/notes/randy-fellmy/transcript-of-larry-summers-speech-at-the-imf-economic-forum-nov-8-2013/585630634864563

es everywhere." Even if this does not pay off, "the resulting investment boom would have given us several years of much higher employment, with no real waste, since the resources employed would have otherwise been idle."[1]

These two discourses, that still dominate the public debate of our times, the discourses of austerity and stimulus spending appear on the surface to be worlds apart. Cameron calls for an unprecedented cultural change, when in fact he re-invokes Locke's instructions to the emerging bourgeoisie, what Max Weber later called "the protestant ethic": work hard, and deny self-indulgence and pleasure. This way capital will accumulate and enterprises produce wealth, Cameron suggests.

In the current conjuncture there is no doubt that a project like Cameron's is classist, redistributing upward. The working classes are asked to tighten their belt and accept the loss of services provided to them, free or subsidized, by the common wealth, so that the rich do not have to shoulder higher taxes to sustain the common wealth in the absence of growth. The Keynesian project instead seems to put the employment of the working classes first; its advocacy of public spending seems, at least in principle, not to be regressive (even if it is not destined to what one would normally call public services).

But, we maintain, what is common between the two discourses is more instructive than what separates them. Both Cameron and Krugman are concerned with "investment." The former thinks that investment will be unleashed by raising the confidence of the markets that State expenditures are under control. The latter wants the state to kick-start investment by pouring money in the economy. They differ on the "how," but what both want is to see capital circulating and expanding again. The second feature they share is their abhorrence of "idleness." For Cameron, the problem is the idleness of workers and the resources wasted by the State to support it. For Krugman the problem is the idleness of capital and the waste of productive resources that could otherwise be invested. For Cameron the problem is the worker who doesn't work, for Krugman the capital that doesn't flow.

On the contrary, we who advocate for degrowth are not afraid of idleness. Paul Lafargue's provocative "right to be lazy" is our inspiration.[2] A society that has developed so many resources surely can extend the

1 Krugman, P. (2013). "Secular stagnation, coalmines, bubbles, and Larry Summers." *New York Times*. Retrieved from http://krugman.blogs.nytimes.com/2013/11/16/secular-stagnation-coalmines-bubbles-and-larry-summers/?_r=0

2 Lafargue, P. (1969). *The right to be lazy*. Solidarity Publications.

right to idleness from the few rich to everyone, Lafargue argued in 1883, and André Gorz elaborated 100 years after.[1] We degrowthers also are not afraid of the idleness of capital; we desire it. Degrowth involves slowing capital down. The essence of capitalism is the continuous reinvestment of surplus into new production. Wealth in industrialist societies is what can be invested again.

The spending proposed by Krugman and Summers appears wasteful and unproductive in the short-term, but is productive in the long-term: it is a utilitarian spending whose goal is to value capital, so that it does not stand idle, re-launching its circulation and growth. Worse, implicit in their proposal is the assumption that public policies must not engage with the meaning of life and the creation of a political collective. On the contrary, for us, the current socio-ecological crisis urges to overcome capitalism's senseless growth through the means of a social dépense. Dépense refers to a genuinely collective expenditure — the spending in a collective feast, the decision to subsidise a class of spirituals to talk about philosophy, or to leave a forest idle — an expenditure that in strictly economic sense is unproductive. Practices of dépense "burn" capital out and take it out of the sphere of circulation, slowing it down. Such collective "waste" is not for personal utility or for the utility of capital. It aspires to be political. It offers a process through which a collective could make sense of and define the "good life," rescuing individuals from their illusionary and meaningless privatized lives.

Dépense generates horror, not only among the supporters of austerity, but also among Keynesians, Marxists, and radicals of all sorts, including many ecologists. Witness the reaction to the set-up for Cameron's talk. Progressives panicked because the PM was calling for austerity while standing in a sumptuous hall surrounded by furniture crafted in gold. Instead, we are not particularly concerned with such lavish expenditure, by a public institution such as the City of London Corporation that was founded in the Middle Age. The gold of the Mayor's Hall is an unproductive expenditure with the anti-utilitarian essence of a by-gone era that preceded capitalism. For Keynesians, what was appalling in this picture is the display of idle wealth; not for us. The contradiction is not between Cameron's call for austerity in the midst of golden furniture; the real contradiction is between his call for an austere state, in the midst of a place that symbolizes an era during which sovereigns were not shy of dépense.

1 Gorz, A. (1994). *Capitalism, socialism, ecology*. Verso.

The Mayor's Hall is a form of public dépense, in a form that we do not want to reproduce, but that we do not reproach as such. We are aware that the gold in London's Guildhall is the outcome of the exploitation of workers, colonies, and ecosystems by the British Empire. We are against such dispossessions and depletions. Social surplus might be, and has often been, the outcome of exploitation, but it doesn't have to: commonwealth can be generated without exploitation. The progressives who took issue with Cameron's talk condemned the contradiction between the display of wealth and his call for austerity. Indeed, there is nothing contradictory to call upon between this wealth being a product of exploitation, and Cameron's call for austerity, i.e. more exploitation of workers.

Many ecologists will find it hard to accept a non-utilitarian waste of resources, because their imaginary is so strongly wedded to the idea of natural scarcity. But scarcity is social. Since the stone-age we have had more than what we need for a basic standard of living. The original affluent societies of Sahlins[1] did not experience scarcity—not because they had a lot, but because they did not know what scarcity means and thought they always had enough. They consumed what they gathered, and they never accumulated. Scarcity calls for economizing and accumulating; this is why the common sense in industrial society is that scarcity is the major problem of humanity. This is why scarcity is the sine qua non of capitalism. Our message to frugal ecologists is that it is better to waste resources in gold decorations in a public building or drink them in a big feast than put them to good use accelerating even more the extraction of new resources and the degradation of the environment. It is the only way to escape Jevon's paradox: the fact that the more efficient we become, and the more resources we save, the more we end up consuming as their cost goes down. Accumulation drives growth, not waste. Even in a society of frugal subjects with a downscaled metabolism, there will still be a surplus that would have to be dispensed, if growth is not to be reactivated.

For those who are concerned that there are not enough resources to secure basic needs, let alone waste them uselessly, let us note the incredible amount of resources currently dispensed in bubbles and zero-sum positional games, whose aim is nothing else than the circulation of capital (in fact what Krugman calls for). Economists realize now that bubbles are not an aberration; they are vital for capitalism and growth. Think of the immense amount of resources spent on professional sports, cinema

1 Sahlins, M. (1995). "The original affluent society." *Sociological Worlds: Comparative and Historical Readings on Society*, 2.

and commercial modern art, financial services, or all sorts of positional consumption (the latest cars, houses, or gadgets whose only fleeting value is that they are the latest). A football game is as pleasant as 50 years ago, when sports were practiced by amateurs, and a movie or a painting no better today than then, despite the huge amounts of capital that circulate to finance and market sports and arts. "Ferraris for all" is the elusive dream of growth, but when everyone has a Ferrari, Ferrari will be the Fiat of its generation. Economists have called for limits on such zero-sum competition for positional consumption, limits that would liberate resources for real growth. We instead want to liberate these resources to secure basic needs and to collectively feast with the rest to avow the political of a new era.

At the same time that capitalist discourses blame the idleness of the "factors of production" at the societal level, they foster the privatization of wasteful consumption: the individual can get drunk, spend all their savings at the casino, organize private parties with champagne and caviar for his or her entourage, deplete accumulated resources in luxurious hobbies or conspicuous shopping, or lease beautiful bodies of women and men for orgiastic VIP parties. All this personalized dépense is allowed in the name of the liberty of each individual to elusively search in his or her personal sphere for the meaning of life. The unquestionable premise of a modern society is the right of each person to accumulate resources beyond basic needs and use them for realizing what he or she thinks is a "good life." As a consequence the system has to constantly grow to allow each and every one the opportunity to pursue this right, as it pretends to do in the abstract.

This central feature of modernity has affected many strains of Marxism too, which pushed the dream of collective emancipation to the extreme by means of a life of material abundance for everyone. Actually existing socialist regimes found that basic needs could well be satisfied for everyone. But in doing so, they repressed private dépense and disavowed socialized dépense (counting out military parades and ceremonies in honor of Stakhanovite bureaucrats). The hypothesis put forward here is that it was the nullification of both private and social dépense that led to the social failure and eventually the collapse of these regimes.

In the degrowth society we imagine, dépense will be brought back to the public sphere, but sobriety will characterize the individual. We are inspired here by the use of the notion of sobriety by Italian Communist Party's historical Secretary, Enrico Berlinguer, for what he called a "revolutionary austerity," an austerity which stands at the antipode of today's conservative and imposed one. This call for personal sobriety is not in the name of financial deficits, ecological limits or moral grounds; ours is not the Protestant call of conservatives. Our claim for sobriety is based on the premise that finding the meaning of life individually is an anthropological illusion. Consider for example those rich individuals who after having it all get depressed and don't know what to do with their lives. Finding meaning alone is an illusion that leads to ecologically harmful and socially unjust outcomes since it cannot be sustained for everyone. The sober subject of degrowth that we envision does not aspire to the private accumulation of things; because he or she wants to be free from the necessity to find the meaning of life individually. People should take themselves less seriously, so to say, and enjoy living free from the unbearable weight of limitless choice. The pianist in the movie *The Legend of 1900* was born in an Atlantic cruiser and chose not to step out of it because he was content with his world there, and the mastery of the piano. Like the pianist, in the opening quote of this essay, the sober subject knows well not to desire a piano with limitless keys. Like the pianist, he or she will always prefer a limited vessel over the limitless city. The sober subject finds meaning in relations, not in itself. Liberated from the project of individually finding the meaning of life, they can be devoted to a daily life centered around care, reproduction, and leisure, and participate in democratically determined societal dépense. Anthropologically, this subject of degrowth already exists. The open question is how it can spread and replicate; but this is a political question, not an individual question.

The pair individual sobriety-social dépense is to substitute the pair social austerity-individual excess. Our dialectical imaginary is political in the deep sense of the term. Compare it to the supposedly "political" economy of Krugman, who like the character in Lampedusa's *The Leopard*, wants to change everything (even invent aliens!), just for things to stay the same.[1] It is indeed the paradox of the contemporary political economy that it must not be political, i.e. it must not participate to build the meaning of life, the latter being an affair left to individuals and their private networks. Instead, we maintain that once basic needs have been secured, it is in deciding collectively "what to dépense" that a sense of the "good life" can be constructed and the political of a new era be liberated. The realm of meaning starts where the realm of necessity ends. A degrowth society would have to build new institutions to choose collectively how to dedicate its resources to basic needs on the one hand, and different forms of dépense on the

1 Di Lampedusa, G. T., & Colquhoun, A. (2007). *The leopard.* Pantheon Books.

other. The political does not end with the satisfaction of basic necessities; it starts there. The choice between collective feasts, Olympic games, idle ecosystems, military expenditures, or voyages to space will still be there. The weight on democracy and on deliberative institutions will be more intense now that the dogma of growth and continuous reinvestment has evaded the difficult questions of what we want to do once we have enough. The political economy will be interested in the sacred again. And the economy of austerity for the most and private enjoyment for the few will become the economy of the common feast for all sober people.

"The ecologist movement was always against nuclear power, not only because of its indisputable and terrible environmental risks and effects, but because it didn't fit with its vision of the good and just life.... the hypothesis for radical ecologists is, as Ivan Illich put it, that 'socialism will come on a bicycle.'"

Image: Scarecrows ward off migrating birds from massive toxic tailings ponds, byproduct of the Albertan Tar Sands. Pembina Institute / Flickr

Part II: Against eco-modernism

5. Political Ecology gone wrong

Author's note: I wrote this essay in response to the eco-modernist manifesto published in 2015. As I explained in Chapters 1 and 2, if something is at the core of degrowth this is its opposition to the techno-managerial imaginary of eco-modernism. The Breakthrough Institute, with its Eco-modernist Manifesto, brought the obsession with techno-managerial fixes to their logical conclusion, or rather perversion. The argument is that environmentalists should promote precisely what those who deny any environmental problem promote too (nuclear power, GMOs, intensified agriculture and urbanization), because science actually tells us that what appears on the surface "anti-environmental" is in reality environmental. When I read the manifesto I was blown away by this discursive play and the surrealism of this post-modern, post-environmentalism. But I was perplexed when I found that radical political ecologists whose work I admire were fellows of the Breakthrough Institute (one of them, Bruno Latour, fortunately later ridiculed the Manifesto). This essay, written for the ENTITLE blog, *a blog on political ecology launched by the fellows of the European Network of Political Ecology, a PhD training project I had the honor to coordinate from 2011 to 2015, tried to make sense of what it is in political ecology that might lead to a support of the ideas expressed by the eco-modernists.*

The ecomodernist manifesto by the "post-environmentalist" think-tank the Breakthrough Institute[1] starts with premises familiar to political ecologists.[2] Earth has become a human planet. There is no wild nature out there. We are part of nature and we constantly transform it. What landscapes we produce, what we conserve and what we do not, is a matter of choice. Yet most political ecologists, even the most "modernist" among them, would feel uneasy (or so I hope) with the resulting eco-modernist agenda: nuclear power, genetically modified agriculture and climate geo-engineering—and all this in the name of, well, preserving "wilderness" …

---

1 Asafu-Adjaye, J., Blomquist, L., Brand, S., Brook, B., DeFries, R., Ellis, E., … Lynas, M. (2015). "An ecomodernist manifesto." Retrieved from: http://www.ecomodernism.org/manifesto-english/

2 Political ecology is a wide-ranging and interdisciplinary academic field whose practitioners study the interactions between political, economic, and social institutions and environmental issues. In particular, political ecologists seek to understand environmental issues as issues of power: who wins, who loses? Part of this involves acknowledging that there is no "nature" outside of human involvement: society is not separate from the environment, nature is always political and shaped by powerful interests.

How did we come to this point: a pro-nuclear political ecology?

The philosophical premises of the manifesto can be partly traced to the work of Bruno Latour, a supporter of "post-environmentalism".[1] For Latour, there is not—and there should not be—any separation between humans and nature. We have never been truly modern, Latour argues, in so far as existing modernity has sought to liberate humans from nature, and ignore its effects to it. To become truly modern, we have to take final responsibility of our products and their effects: we should control our technological "Frankensteins", rather than shy away from producing them.

Slavoj Žižek, in arguing that "nature does not exist", strikes a similar tone: "we are within technology… and we should remain strongly within it".[2] For Žižek, like Latour, there is no going back to an un-alienated relationship with nature; we should double up our efforts and be in control of our alienation. Žižek's communist politics are worlds apart from the green, somewhat statist, capitalism of post-environmentalists. But I am afraid that, as far as our metabolic relationship to the non-human world is concerned, the result is the same, independent of whether the control of the means of producing this metabolism is to be private, state, or communal.

Claiming that "there is nothing unnatural about nuclear power plants" (paraphrasing David Harvey's dictum that there is nothing unnatural about New York City) we risk reproducing the logic of the Soviet regime, where environmental problems did not exist, in so far as what was being produced was by the people and for the people. A stance on "ecology" is necessary.

Including by the eco-modernizers, whose manifesto without an "eco" becomes a pure call for modernization, advocating nuclear power for the sake of nuclear power. To justify the "eco" in the title, the manifesto performs theoretical acrobatics, arguing that somehow a more intense use of technology will liberate space and resources for preserving wilderness. This is not only factually wrong. It is also inconsistent with the overall premise of the manifesto that there is no wild nature out there independent of us.

Contra Latour, the manifesto continues to treat nature as a means to an end (using this nature more intensively to save that other, wild nature). And it assumes that somehow magically the resource extraction

1 Latour, B. (201is 1). "Love your monsters." *Breakthrough Journal, 2*, 21-28.

2 Žižek, S. (2011). "Nature does not exist." [Video] Retrieved from https://www.youtube.com/watch?v=DIGeDAZ6-q4

and transformations we conduct "here" will not affect nature "out there". In effect, the manifesto is what Latour criticizes as modernism 1.0; that is, a modernism still premised on the idea of separating ourselves from the non-human world.

Paradoxically, Latour's own work can come to our rescue from the eco-modernizers. After all, he is the one who wrote: "to modernize or to ecologize—that's the question".[1] Indeed, unlike the eco-modernists, Latour argues that the "challenge demands more of us than simply embracing technology and innovation. It requires exchanging the modernist notion of modernity for what I have called a 'compositionist' [note: what when younger he called 'ecologist'], one that sees the process of human development as neither liberation from Nature nor as a fall from it, but rather as a process of becoming ever-more attached to, and intimate with, a panoply of nonhuman natures."[2]

And here is the mistake (dare I say in the knowledge that they will never read me) of Latour or Žižek. Recognizing our alienation from nature, and the power to contribute to the production of new socio-natures, does not logically lead to the conclusion that more "control" or more and bigger technology is what we should do.

There are multiple ways in which we can become "ever-more attached to ... nonhuman natures".[3] And there are many ways we can produce technologies and associated socionatures. We can choose a world of bicycles or spacecrafts and we can choose a world powered by DIY-windmills or nuclear plants. Each suggests a different type of connection and relation with the non-human world. There is nothing to suggest that we connect more to a river by damming it and using it to produce electricity, than by walking along its shores or talking to it.

The ecologist movement has always been about a different type of connection, both among humans, and between humans and nonhumans. It has advocated smaller scale, and more direct connections, what Ivan Illich called "convivial" relations: technologies that can be controlled by their users, and not by others on their behalf. The ecologist movement was always against nuclear power, not only because of its indisputable and terrible environmental risks and effects, but because it didn't fit with its vision of the good and just life.

---

1 Latour, B. (2007). "To modernize or to ecologise? That is the question." *The Politics of Interventions, 249.*

2 Latour, B. (2011). "Love your monsters." *Breakthrough Journal, 2*, 21-28.

3 *Ibid.*

Contra Žižek, the hypothesis for radical ecologists is, as Ivan Illich put it, that "socialism will come on a bicycle": large-scale technological systems create a society divided into experts and users. It is only a short pass for the former to become the bureaucrats or the bosses who control and appropriate the surplus of the system. A society powered by nuclear energy cannot be a society of equals or of mutual aid.

The ecologists' call for limits to growth has mistakenly been thought of as a call for a harmonious co-existence with nature, one of leaving "nature" alone (I am not denying that many ecologists argue for limits on these grounds, but I believe they are wrong). On the contrary, as we have argued elsewhere,[1] the basis for limits should be different: fully aware of our capacity to keep pursuing what can be pursued, the choice is "not to".

We ecologists do not want to produce radioactive or genetically modified Frankensteins. This "not to" is an affirmative choice for the world we want to produce, a world where we live a simpler life, in common, a world of connection rather than disconnection, approaching rather than distancing, coupling rather than decoupling. A world where we control the controllers. This is an ecological vision.

The choice has always been, and still is, the same. To modernize or to ecologize? That is the question.

1 D'Alisa, G., Demaria, F., & Kallis, G. (2014). *Degrowth: a vocabulary for a new era.* Routledge.

6. Why eco-modernism is wrong

Author's note: Here I took off my political ecologist hat, and wore my ecological economic one. The objective is the same: expose the fallacies of eco-modernism. The basic argument in this chapter is that the science of eco-modernism is wrong. The eco-modernists confuse efficiency/intensity with scale. Using existing resources more intensively leads to more, not less, resource use, because the relative cost of resources decreases, and because the savings from the increased productivity of intensive use are re-invested back to more resource use. This is the historical pattern of capitalism, the one that eco-modernists want to see accelerated.

The ecomodernist manifesto is the latest and most visionary document under the auspices of the "post-environmentalist" think-tank the Breakthrough Institute. I first heard the Institute's founders Ted Nordhaus and Michael Shellenberger speak at Berkeley some eight years ago, presenting their case for the "death of environmentalism" (hence the "post" prefix). For half of the presentation I was thinking how much I agree. They claimed that environmentalists have to let go the idea of a pristine nature with which we have to live in harmony. We constantly rework nature, they argued; what worlds we create is a matter of choice. They also took issue with the professionalization of the "big green" NGOs and their transformation into a vested interest fighting for this or that legislative gain—while losing the overall picture of systemic change which had inspired the early green movement. I couldn't add more. Next I expected to hear about growth and capitalism, the type of worlds environmentalists may want to produce, the political choices at stake and the alliances they have to forge with labor, feminist or social justice movements to bring about systemic change.

Nope. In an amazing mishmash of critical theory, political liberalism and technological cornocupianism they came up with a government-funded "Apollo plan" instead. Not one that would fly us to the moon again, but to an earth powered by nuclear plants and fed with GMOs. Post-environmentalists' preferred allies were Monsanto and the nuclear industry, it turned out. This mishmash full of contradictions continues in the new manifesto.

A manifesto for what will happen anyway

The document starts with a celebration of technological progress, centralized production, and urbanization. It assures us that population is peaking (true) and so is resource consumption (untrue). "Land-use change, overexploitation and pollution can peak and decline this century", they argue, if the forces that brought us here continued. Well, then why write a manifesto in the first place? To "accelerate" things, is the answer. This must be the first manifesto whose goal is to save a few years down the line. And why accelerate things? Ah, because problems are hitting the fan, it is implied. So we aren't doing that well, are we? Could it be that, rather than accelerating the train of history, we might have to "pull the emergency brake", as Walter Benjamin memorably put it?

Confusing efficiency with scale

"Cities", we are told, "perform far better than rural economies in providing efficiently for material needs while reducing environmental impacts." Here, efficiency is confused with scale. Cities may use less resources per unit of product, but they produce and use more resources overall. This is precisely why footprints have increased, not declined with urbanization. Actually, the very indicator of "ecological footprint", invoked in the manifesto, was invented to calculate the extent to which the consumption of cities extends beyond their borders. "Cities occupy just one to three percent of the Earth's surface", the manifesto says. Yes, but they are largely responsible for the transformation of the remaining 97%.

"The technologies that humankind's ancestors used to meet their needs [had] much higher per-capita impacts on the environment", we read. The "proof" for this is that, in the Pleistocene, native Americans had cleared forests and hunted mammals to extinction. If older technologies had more impact per capita indeed, industrialization in China would have come with a decline, not an increase in per capita emissions, energy, or resource use. Everywhere, and without exception, the transition from rural to urban/industrial economies has come with a total increase, not decrease, of resource and energy use, both in absolute and per capita terms (this should not be confused with the fact that the environmental impact per unit of product declines as an economy grows). The only resource whose use has declined are forests, but this has to do with the shift to fossil fuels, not with efficiency improvements in the use of forests. (The effects of so-called forest transitions on biodiversity are also questionable, to say the least).

Of course, if the 8 millions of New Yorkers were to be dispersed in the countryside and to live exactly as they did in New York, the total environmental impact would be much higher. It would even be worse if New Yorkers were to pursue their current standard of living by hunting mammals and clearing forests. But the point is precisely that "our ancestors" or the people who live in the countryside (other than the suburbanized countryside of the U.S.) could never achieve the same standard of material consumption achieved in cities. They consumed less, precisely because life in the countryside was less productive than in the city. If you have to fetch your own water or raise and milk your own cows, you won't shower and you will drink less milk. Being less productive per unit of product, you can only produce less. Hunter and gatherer societies consume fewer resources, in total and per capita, than agrarian societies, who in turn consume less than industrial ones. The efficiency of new technologies and the economies of scale the authors celebrate are causally related to the increasing scale of resource use they want to see inversed.

This is a fundamental aspect of the economic process: productivity and efficiency fuel growth. This is why economists love them. The so-called "Jevons' paradox"[1], whereby improved efficiency in the use of resources drives down their prices and leads to more resource use, is a paradox only for the mindset of environmentalists. Centralized production and new technologies liberate labor and resources for more production and more resource use. This is after all the magic of capitalism. This is the source of the growth take-off. And this is why footprints have been growing and the authors had to write their manifesto. If urbanization and technological progress did the trick we wouldn't be here talking about climate change.

The manifesto suggests that the linkage between growth and resource use may be breaking in modern economies, as they become materially lighter "knowledge economies". However, Facebook and Google might seem materially light on screen, but their servers have become among the highest consumers of energy and emitters of carbon. Huge resources, natural and human, are necessary for training the next Brins and Zuckerbergs or powering the military and University labs where the next internets will be invented. All these costs are hidden. Energy use in the US is not increasing, not because a peak is being reached due to technological efficiency and dematerialization, but because the US economy imports its garments from China and has its servers in Norway.

The authors argue that "humans are as likely to spare nature because it is not needed to meet their needs as they are to spare it for explicit

1 Alcott, B. (2005). "Jevons' paradox." *Ecological Economics, 54*(1), 9-21.

aesthetic and spiritual reasons". The issue is that nature is never spared under capitalism. If temporarily spared it becomes cheaper, and then new needs are created by innovations on the consumption side and by advertising—to make sure that surplus nature is put to profitable use, including tourism for "aesthetic reasons". Only a political act of setting limits, of keeping this land out of circulation, of enclosing this resource for the public good, leaving that oil under the soil or getting these emissions capped, can spare "nature". But this, as all regulation and institutional change, requires social struggles. It is not something that will happen automatically because of technological progress and "modernization". It is a battle against such modernization.

Philosophical mishmashes

The philosophical and epistemological posture of the text is self-contradictory, perhaps betraying differing views among its authors. The manifesto starts with the recognition that the planet has become a human planet, aka "the anthropocene". There is no wild nature out there, sure. And yet somehow the goal of the manifesto is to "make more room for nature" and "re-wild" and "re-green" the earth.

Section 5 argues that the way we come to know "nature", i.e. through science, is shaped by our own constructions and therefore dependent on our own choices. Correct. Yet the whole manifesto is permeated by a blind belief in the power of science to solve whatever problems may be, while constantly invoking science for proving that this or that technology is better than the other.

The authors suggest that they write "out of deep love and emotional connection to the natural world" (again, presuming that there is such a natural world "out there", which they said there isn't). "To preserve wilderness, biodiversity, and a mosaic of beautiful landscapes [beautiful for whom?] will require a deeper emotional connection to them". The manifesto itself undermines the case for preservation in a spirit of connection, since "it is the continued dependence of humans on natural environments that is the problem". It seems that the manifesto calls for less material connection and more "emotional" connection to nature. Yet it is unclear how the latter will come without the former in the urban, genetically modified paradises envisaged. Playing Tarzan video games?

I was reminded by one of the authors that French philosopher Bruno Latour has written in favor of the "breakthrough" of "post-environmentalism".[1] Following Latour could provide more epistemological consistency to the manifesto, but would, however, expose the authors to the risk of alienating the wilderness environmentalists they obviously want to convince.

True, Latour himself suggests that new technologies, such as the ones advocated by the manifesto, are part of connecting to nonhuman natures, and that putting limits to growth is a form of detachment. But he is misunderstanding the call for limits here. Limits do not have to mean detachment. They are a means for allowing different, possibly stronger and qualitatively different forms of connection. There is nothing to suggest that we connect more to a river by damming it and using it to produce electricity, than by limiting its damming, allowing us to walk along its shores or talk to it.

Anyway, these philosophical complications are too much for the manifesto to handle. The authors finally conclude that no matter what ones' views on nature are (and they are all fine according to them), "decoupling" our economic activity from it will be for the better and full stop.

"Anthropogenic choices"

The authors repeatedly refer to "anthropogenic choices" about how to transform landscapes or what to conserve and what not. But what is their choice then, their politics? These are never articulated explicitly. Modernization for modernization's sake I would say. Pursuing what can be pursued, without limits, as philosopher of technology Jacques Ellul used to put it.[2]

And they do like their modern technologies big. Dams, but not windmills. Nuclear, but not solar. Why so is never clear. We hear that "most forms of renewable energy are, unfortunately" not up to the task, because of their "scale of land use". Yet somehow, hydroelectric dams are nice "even though their land … footprint is very large". Their "anthropogenic choices" here are disguised as objective science. And a bad science, that is. The decisions of Germany, Japan or California to shutter nuclear power plants are "counterproductive". Why? Because somehow nuclear is "clean". And what about all the carbon and energy necessary for extracting and transporting uranium, constructing, operating and dismantling

---

1 Latour, B. (2011). "Love your monsters." *Breakthrough Journal, 2*, 21-28.

2 Ellul, J. (1967). *The technological society*. Vintage books.

nuclear plants or handling their waste?[1] Calculated over the lifetime of a plant, this makes nuclear far from "clean" and far from clear whether it produces any energy surplus to begin with. But these are too specific details for a manifesto.[2]

I am comfortable with the fact that the preference for nuclear energy, dams or GMOs is the "anthropogenic choice" of the authors, although I would prefer them not to hide it with semi-scientific reasoning or allusions to preserving "wilderness". Even so, they owe an answer "why". Why do they desire a planet populated by nuclear plants and bunkers with radioactive waste? Why do they desire becoming ever more attached to nonhuman radioactivity? What is it that excites them with a nuclear future, so as to make them blindly confident to the eternal capacity of our civilization to have the resources to handle nuclear plants and nuclear wastes? Are earthquakes or civilization downturns ruled out in the eco-modernist future?

The other face of modernization

The benefits of modernization the manifesto celebrates (higher material living standards, higher life expectancy and the rest) are confined in time and space much more than the authors admit. The atrocities of colonialization and the two World Wars are not something modernizers should be proud of, nor the near nuclear holocaust, which wouldn't have let us be here discussing manifestos today. The improvements in birth, living, and working conditions the authors rightly celebrate are concentrated in a small part of the world (the Euro Americas) and in a small period of time after the outmost modern disaster that was the second world war (the "30 golden years" as the French like to call them, which for the authors of the manifesto are curiously "the planning fallacy of the 1950s").

No word that it was the working classes who won public health or free education, and that these did not naturally trickle down from growth and technological progress. Also no word of the evidence that since the 1970s growth has become "un-economic" in the already "modernized"

1 Lenzen, M. "Life cycle energy and greenhouse gas emissions of nuclear energy: A review." *Energy conversion and management* 49, no. 8 (2008): 2178-2199.

2 Diaz-Maurin, F., & Giampietro, M. (2013). "A "Grammar" for assessing the performance of power-supply systems: Comparing nuclear energy to fossil energy." *Energy, 49*, 162-177.

parts of the world, such as the U.S. for which this manifesto is written. No word that it has more social and environmental costs than benefits and doesn't increase self-reported or objectively measured wellbeing.

Why keep pursuing growth then? Presumably because it can be pursued. This is what it is about to be modern after all. And please spare me the paternalistic argument that the Global North needs to grow out of concern and solidarity for "the poor" of this world, who without "our" growth will not grow up too. "We" seemed to have grown pretty well without them growing in the past. In fact we did grow by exploiting their cheap labor, plundering their resources, and shifting our costs to them. From the comfort of my University armchair I do not feel entitled to speak about what the "back-breaking agrarian poor of this world" (sic) want, and neither should the eco-modernizers.

For degrowth and the commons

Which brings me to my own "anthropogenic choice". If we want to reduce the footprint of the economy, then let's downscale the economy as a whole, and find ways to make the transition socially sustainable: to prosper without growth, as Tim Jackson put it.[1] If we are to leave land aside, then let's organize for making land a commons, leaving some of it aside for non-productive purposes.

This call for degrowth is neither a call for a harmonious co-existence with nature, nor one of leaving "nature" in peace. It is not about succumbing to external limits to growth. It is about limiting growth because we dislike the detached world produced by growth; a world controlled by others for our sake.

The conscious and collective decision of a society to limit itself, without recourse to spirits and totems, gods and kings, charts or graphs, is the essence of what Cornelius Castoriadis called "democracy". This, and not eco-modernism's more of the same, faster and faster, is the necessary next civilizational step.

1 Jackson, T. (2009). *Prosperity without growth: Economics for a finite planet.* Routledge.

7. Tweeting with the enemy

Author's note: This was a lighter text, following a series of twitter exchanges with supporters of the Breakthrough Institute, after the publication of my two previous essays. I mostly poke friendly fun on eco-modernists, but there is also a serious insight here. I realized that the core of the Manifesto, the premise upon which it rests or falls, is the assumption of an abundant, unlimited, angelic source of energy that can fuel a modernizing planet for ever and ever. The Alchemists would have liked this.

Well, that was an interesting week! After publishing two rebuttals of the eco-modernist manifesto, I got swirled into twitterlandia, and exchanges with an amazing cadre of characters.

First came the leaders of the Breakthrough Institute, with whom I had civilized conversations about the GDP of Japan and whether it is growing or not; the energy return on investment (EROI) of solar vs. nuclear energy; or -at the late hours and over a virtual beer among pals—about life in Fukushima and how it compares to the African countryside.

Next came the army of science wonks with "kick-ass" degrees. They flooded me with studies I did not know. Meta-analyses proving that nuclear is safe and clean. Graphs showing increasing numbers of whales, rabbits and rats (proof of decoupling if you were wondering). I would cherry-pick studies against theirs, and they would throw more cherries in response. I decided to stop. Not because of back pain from cherry-picking, but because I realized that my interlocutors were fellows of the Breakthrough Institute doing their job, unlike me wasting my time on twitter.

And then came a circus crowd, straight out of a Fellini movie. People with nicknames like "Thor" (a super-hero of Thorium, whose motto is "nuclear energy? Yes, please!"). They called me "enviro". They informed me that Fukushima has lower levels of radioactivity than the French Riviera. That they would move there if only I paid for their trip and Japanese language classes. At their most artistic, they would post pictures of Fukushima looking like a forested Eden. At their most touching, they would post retro, night-view photos of American nuclear reactors from the 1960s.

Getting to know this parallel universe of "nucleos" can be depressing. After all, no matter how hard I work and no matter what I write, I don't think I can ever convince a guy called "Thor" about the merits of degrowth.

On the positive side though, at long last these meditation classes I took at Berkeley years ago paid off. "Take a deep breath in … now, slowly, out…." "Release the anger in you." This spared me the trouble of tweeting pictures of Fukushima in flames, or inventing fake characters like "Rastafarian Bambi" to start insulting "Thor".

And, yes, I also did learn a lot this week.

It's nuclear, stupid!

Not least I came to better understand the eco-modernizers' thesis. This can be summed up in three words: "nuclear, nuclear, and nuclear". The terminology of "decoupling" and "dematerialization" had me confused. This manifesto is not the standard call for energy efficiency. Neutral terms such as "centralized and clean energy production" are just euphemisms. No, this is a call for substituting fossil fuels with nuclear energy, pure and simple. Producing an abundant and unlimited source of energy in centralized reactors will let the economy grow unstoppably—here and in the rest of the world that most needs it. Carbon will be unnecessary and left aside, and land spared for wildlife. All the rest (urbanization, the critique to conservationism, etc.) are secondary afterthoughts of the manifesto, which stands or falls upon its nuclear thesis.

This thesis is a fantasy of the nth order as I was at pains to argue in 5-word tweets. Of course, if an alchemist's dream came true and we found an unlimited, clean, and safe source of energy, we could spare humanity most of the natural and social ills! The only problem is that this is not how the real world works. Previous "substitutions" (from forest trees to fossil fuels, or the mythical one from whales to kerosene[1] that the eco-modernizers love the most) did not reduce environmental damage; they scaled it up. Forests spared, climate screwed. Georgescu-Roegen's key insight was not that there are entropic limits to growth (even if there are, they are not that relevant for our time frame). It was that increasing rates of energy use unavoidably speed up disorder, aka "entropy". Oil, which seemed comparatively "clean" when first found, disordered the climate. The disorder nuclear radioactivity will bring is not hard to guess.

Even if the wonks were right and nuclear power till now had been proven "safe" (sic), the number of accidents stands only to increase with

1 Kovarik, B. (2008). "The whale oil myth." *Environmental History*. Retrieved from http://www.environmentalhistory.org/brilliant/bioenergy/the-whale-oil-myth/

an exponential growth of reactors. Consider also the implications from an expansion of nuclear reactors beyond the most advanced economies where they are currently located or countries like Ukraine where they currently rot, to non-nuclear countries like Greece, or most of Africa and Latin America (necessary for the manifesto's vision of the rest of the world growing and converging with an abundant source of energy other than oil). I can't even begin to imagine the risks involved in assuming that, from here to eternity, all countries will have the capacity to deal with nuclear reactors, their dismantlement and their wastes. Not to mention the changes in social relations and the new forms of colonialism involved in exporting complex nuclear technologies to the "less developed" parts of the world.

Desiring nuclear

Of course, such reasonable arguments cannot convince retired engineers who dream of living in Fukushima and who find white suits and protective masks beautiful. I didn't know how close to the truth I was when I wrote about a "desire" for nuclear energy in my last post. Perhaps at the risk of psychoanalyzing too much, this is a desire strongly linked to a modern imaginary of control, of the powerful male engineer controlling unruly feminine nature to his whims.

But what about the "eco"—modernizers; those for whom nuclear is not the goal in and of itself? They, I think, reach the logical conclusions of the absurdity of wanting both to protect "nature"; and refuse, in line with the prevalent thinking of modernity, to accept any "limits". This position cannot be sustained without recourse to the fantasy of an infinite and clean source of energy, be it nuclear (for Breakthrough's eco-modernizers) or solar and wind (for green-growthers). It has to be something, and this something has to be true. If not, they would have to think the unthinkable, a world without perpetual growth, a world with limits.

What do we understand when we say we're "ecologists"?

What I also learned this week is that we who call ourselves "political ecologists" need to do much more work in clarifying what we understand by the word "ecologists". My motivation for writing the two pieces was in fact not to convince the Breakthrough crowd, but to make sense of how it is possible that people whose work I admired came to associate themselves with the Breakthrough Institute. Could it be that we have such diverse definitions of what it means to be an ecologist? Ecologists in support of nuclear energy? The very foundation of the ecologist movement was its opposition to nuclear power.

If "ecology" is not about preserving frogs and pine trees in some pristine and stable state free of human influence—a state that we agree does not exist and never has—then what is it? My pieces hinted to ecology as a different quality and structure of connections among humans and between humans and non-humans. And to Cornelius Castoriadis' thesis that "ecology is not 'love of nature', but the need for self-limitation (which is true freedom) of human beings …". But this is not the last word philosophers had to say about ecology and no doubt, I have much, much more homework to do.

If I find time from twitter that is.

"Invented abstractions are not any less real. However imperfect, they may represent things and processes that correspond to actual experiences. Fantasies become real if we act on the basis of such fantasies. Think of wars in the name of gods. The god may be a fantasy; your dead body is as real as it gets. Or the lives of people sacrificed by austerity policies to push GDP a few points up."

Image: "Maison modéle (model home)" by Aaron Vansintjan

Part III: Rethinking the economic

8. The battle for Harvard, or, how economics became economics

Author's note: Back in 2012 and already a professor, I decided to go back to school and study macroeconomics in one of Europe's Meccas of the neo-classical school, the Barcelona Graduate School of Economics at Pompeu Fabra University. I caught myself being not only a student of economics, but also an "ethnographer" of the community of economists, and its initiation rituals. I witnessed how young economists were disciplined into their discipline. I watched the indirect (and occasionally more direct) ways my peers were reprimanded by our professors when they tried to raise political issues or question the foundations or assumptions of the underlying model. I also realized the instrumental usefulness of mathematics in the discipline of economics: I experienced how it cultivated a sense of insecurity, how it made us hesitant to ask a question or levy a criticism in fear that we did not understand or master the model well enough to speak about it. When did economics become like that? When was it cleansed of alternative theories, methods, and ideas? When were dissident voices silenced? What ever happened to critical Keynesian or Marxist theories? Why didn't we hear anything of them in our masters program? I was soon to find a little-known story from Harvard in the early 70s, a story that explains how economics became ... economics.

The economic crisis has supposedly started a soul-searching process in the economics profession. Five years into the crisis and economists still offer more of the same in response. "Create new bubbles" to boost the economy. "Cut red-tape." "Liberalize finance in the rest of the world." Why do economists keep getting it so wrong?

Innovation feeds on diversity, but diversity is scarce in economics.

A little-remembered episode in the history of the discipline, told by Tiago Mata in his dissertation at LSE[1], reveals how diversity was killed in economics. Back in 1968, a group of young radical economists, the product of the campus unrest of the 60s and the anti-war movement,

1 Mata, T. (2009) "Migrations and boundary work: Harvard, radical economists, and the Committee on Political Discrimination." *Science in Context* 22, no. 01: 115-143.

came to rock the discipline. Organized by the Union for Radical Political Economics, they called for a politicization of economics, accusing fellow economists of ignoring the important questions and being "instrumental to the elite's attainment of its unjust ends." They rejected the "marginalist approach," today's mantra in economics, for accepting the basic institutions of capitalism, and catering to improve only its administration … marginally.

The front-guard of the group was at Harvard, where non-tenured faculty Arthur MacEwan, Samuel Bowles, Herbert Gintis and Thomas Weisskopf taught a course tellingly named "The capitalist system: conflict and power." Older Harvard faculty found the course a disgrace. But these were still the 60s and economics was not yet economics. Harvard-based John Kenneth Galbraith, a non-conventional political economist, and a notable ally of the young radicals, was President of the American Economic Association. Galbraith was wary of economics becoming a system of belief and used his presidential address in 1972 to support this "new and notably articulate generation of economists" that was coming to ask politically-important questions. Not everyone agreed.

A campaign ensued the next few years to eradicate the young radicals from top positions. Contract after contract and tenure after tenure were denied, including to the Harvard four.

Among them, the most notable case was that of Sam Bowles, one of the brightest economists of his generation, as confirmed by his later work. His tenure candidacy was rejected by a nineteen to five vote in 1973. He had received the support of the most prominent members of the department, J.K. Galbraith, and Nobel-prize winners Wassily Leontief and (yet to be) Kenneth Arrow. Albert Hirschman was one of the other two who voted in his favor, as recounted by his biographer in a talk in memoriam I recently attended in Boston and which brought the whole Harvard affair to my attention.

Hirschman, a moderate economist, bitterly left Harvard in 1974 for Princeton. So did Leontief for NYU in 1975, after serving Harvard for 30 years, and mentoring such conservative heavyweights like Paul Samuelson and Robert Solow. Galbraith retired in 1975 after half a century at Harvard and Arrow departed for the West Coast. Bowles' denial of tenure and the departure of Leontief, Galbraith, Hirschmann and Arrow brought an end to the notorious Harvard faculty battles between moderates and conservatives, not only over tenures but also University governance and student occupations, battles that had brought the department to a stalemate in the early 70s.

The young radicals did not have the luck of their more established elder supporters. They were relegated to universities of lesser prestige, radical refuges such as the New School in New York and UMass at Amherst. UMass offered Bowles the opportunity to set up an institute and host other ousted young radicals from Harvard, Yale and beyond, such as Marxists Stephen Resnick and Richard Wolff.

The American Economic Association judged that there was no political motivation behind the purge of the radicals, other than in cases where the FBI was found to be involved. The rationale, however, often used in many faculty decisions to deny the quality of the radicals' research was that it was "political" and not scientific enough. Science and objectivity in economics came to be defined through these tenure battles not only as mathematical formalism (in this people like Bowles and Gintis excelled), but as one of a particular kind, based on the so-called "neo-classical" assumptions of a world consisting of selfish individuals maximizing their personal gain. This pre-analytic vision of a world of neo-liberal subjects was considered neutral, but deviations from it ideologically-motivated.

Neutrality was defended by Milton Friedman's dictum, that even if the assumptions were wrong, what mattered was empirical verification of the derived propositions (of course this did not apply for those who made too radical assumptions). But as the higher echelons of the discipline and its prestigious journals were cleansed of radicals, disturbing questions and propositions were left untested. Few radicals were around to verify the thousands of studies that hammered neo-liberal propositions, dressed-up in obfuscated math, impossible to be penetrated by the uninitiated. While economics got dominated by neo-liberal ideas (the farthest to the left coming out in the top journals of the discipline today is to the right of the Democratic Party) dissenters ended up founding heterodox schools of lesser influence, or move to other disciplines, like geography. No doubt, ex-establishment figures like Paul Krugman or Joseph Stiglitz do speak vocally about rising inequalities and the pitfalls of unfettered capitalism.

Yet this is too little too late. They hardly researched such stuff in their active careers and their popular books go unnoticed by the discipline or the teaching curricula. Younger economists are in no position to make similar claims in their home departments … at least not before they get a Nobel prize, too.

Next time young students of economics walk out of their classrooms, they could remind their professors of the Harvard story: what is taught in economics today is not the result of a noble struggle of ideas, but of political power and force. It should be no surprise that the discipline is so monolithic and resistant to change.

Economics has become the secular equivalent of religion. It includes an entangled network of scriptures (textbooks), disciples (students), and preachers (professors), trained to believe without questioning the supremacy of the free market and devotedly working to prove it in each and every context, defending it against non-believers. Like the Church and the priests before them, establishment economists will not change on their own. They can only become obsolete, relics of the past, as the world around them changes. And fortunately this seems to be happening sooner rather than later.

9. For a Political Ecological Economics

Author's note: this text was the basis of my plenary lecture at the 11th International conference of the European society for ecological economics in Leeds, in July 2015. I later presented variants of it at SOAS and Oxford. I wrote this lecture with two objectives in mind. First, I wanted to bring some of the insights of political ecology into (ecological) economics. Second, I wanted to make sense of the understanding of the economy that comes out of the work of those of us who write about degrowth. There is a paradox at play here. Degrowth, as in the work of Serge Latouche, is a critique of the economization of everything, and the idea that there is an independent system out there called "the economy" with its own laws and rules that we can ignore only at our own peril. Latouche's degrowth is a call precisely to escape such "economism" and re-embed the economic in the social, the political and the ecological. On the other hand, much of the degrowth literature unavoidably deals with questions that have typically been defined as "economic": limits to growth, debt, productivity and unemployment, etc. I work through this paradox by proposing an understanding of the economy that combines the constructivism of political ecology with the materialism of ecological economics.

This year we had the pleasure to publish a book on degrowth. The cover features a garden. And indeed the book is a garden of interwoven ideas. It would be false to present degrowth as a cohesive theory and practice. This is why we editors chose the format of a vocabulary. We invited the readers to wander through interconnected keywords and make their own sense of what degrowth is.

Here I want to contribute to the advancement of a more cohesive theory of degrowth. There is no axiomatic, economic theory of degrowth. And there shouldn't be one. My approach will be different. I look retrospectively at our book and the literature on degrowth and I decipher the particular view of the economy that comes out of it.

This is a view of the economy, I argue, more complex than that of the standard model that we use in ecological economics. In the latter, the economy is considered a sphere of allocation and distribution, limited by an external ecosystem that provides it with resources and absorbs its wastes. In the degrowth literature instead, as I will argue, the economy is understood as an invention that is political, diverse, and material; and the key question is not scarcity, but surplus.

This essay might appear too theoretical and is for the patient reader. I hope though that it isn't too abstract or esoteric. To convince you of its practical relevance, I will show how this theory helps us rethink growth and the alternatives to it.

The invention of the economy

So, first principle: the economy is an invention. This might sound too constructivist for those ecologically minded. It is not. It is a historical fact, argues Serge Latouche in his book *The invention of the economy*, which lamentably has not been translated to English yet.[1] But when and how did we come to think of an autonomous system out there called "the economy"? According to Columbia anthropologist Timothy Mitchell, surprisingly recently.[2] Before the 1940s, economy meant to economize (and in my native Greek, the word economy still keeps this double meaning, of a system and of the act of saving). The notion of a national economy was an invention of the 1930s, born amidst planning for war production and the quest to control the monetary supply to avoid crises. This was part and parcel of new tools of representation and measuring, such as national accounts and the GDP. New institutions, the Ministries of National Economy, were founded to govern the new system. Invented in a period of unlimited cheap oil, GDP imagined an economy of pure exchange value. Unlike an economy of physical quantities, the GDP economy is from its conception one that in theory can grow indefinitely, Mitchell argues in *Carbon democracy*.

Invented abstractions are not any less real. However imperfect, they may represent things and processes that correspond to actual experiences. Fantasies become real if we act on the basis of such fantasies. Think of wars in the name of gods. The god may be a fantasy; your dead body is as real as it gets. Or the lives of people sacrificed by austerity policies to push GDP a few points up.

The re-invention of the economy by ecological economists as a system profoundly limited by ecosystems may be a better abstraction. But an imperfect abstraction it also is. The fate of our invention does not depend only on how well it models reality. It depends also on whether it will mold institutions and reality to its own image. In a world with carbon

1 Latouche, S. (2012). *L'invention de l'économie*. Albin Michel.

2 Mitchell, T. (2011). *Carbon democracy: Political power in the age of oil*. New York: Verso.
Mitchell, T. (2014). "Economentality: how the future entered government." *Critical Inquiry*, 40(4), 479-507.

caps, the ecological economics model will be a better representation of the economy.

Let me clarify something here. I am not denying the reality of the processes that we typically understand as economic: production, consumption, exchange, etc. What I am arguing, following the work of economic anthropologists, is that the particular understanding of such practices in these terms (e.g. of eating an apple as consumption, and of cultivating the land as production) and furthermore, their bracketing as part of the same phenomenon ("the economy") is not a universal truth, but a particular conceptualization and abstraction performed by our capitalist civilization. It may, or may not, work well for its purposes, but a historically produced abstraction it is.

The political construction of the "free" market

Second, the economy in the degrowth literature is political. It is not an independent system governed by the laws of supply and demand. The imaginary free market does not exist, Karl Polanyi long ago argued.[1] The free market is constantly constructed through state intervention and enforcement. Think of the complex institutions necessary for counting or trading ecosystem services. Or the liberation of Central Banks from political control. This required political intervention. And it was not a neutral or natural development; it had winners and losers and huge distributive implications.

In ecological economics we do recognize the political nature of the economy when we argue that the so-called efficient allocation and the final price of goods and services depends on the initial distribution of property rights: a distribution that is political. Often though we reproduce the economistic distinction between an economy out there, with its own laws and processes, and a political process which distributes the fruits of this process or sets limits to it. We imagine a benevolent planner who is supposed to listen to our diagnosis and maximize the collective good. We need to move to a Polanyian mode of analysis where the political and its change become part of our research.

1 Polanyi, K. (1957). *The Great Transformation: The Political and Economic Origin of Our Time*. Beacon Press.

Seeing diverse economies

Third, the economy is diverse, as feminist economists Gibson-Graham argue.[1] Its visible part is the capitalist economy of private property, wage labor, market exchange and profit-seeking firms. But below the surface, there is a wealth of alternatives. Alternative work, and unpaid labor. Alternative firms, such as cooperatives, or non-capitalist associations, like social centers. Alternative markets, such as fair trade, or non-market exchanges, such as barters, gifts and donations. Free-help and mutual care between friends or family members. Gibson-Graham visualize this in the form of an iceberg. On the visible top is the money-valued market economy; below the surface of the water is all the invisible work done by women and careworkers, volunteers, members of cooperatives, etc. If we focus our attention to the capitalist economy, on the top of the iceberg, ignoring the diversity of economies that exists, then we reify capitalism and help reproduce it, Gibson-Graham argued, criticizing what they term "capitalocentric" analytical approaches.

Gibson-Graham's analysis however should be complemented with an understanding of capitalism and non-capitalist economies. This is often antagonistic, or indifferent; but very often it can be symbiotic, capitalism constantly renewed by drawing from the free labour of non-capitalist practices, or by assimilating them, valorizing them in money terms, and bringing them into the circuit of capitalist accumulation. Ecosystem services, gifts such as hospitality, or domestic carework are increasingly assigned a price-tag, and incorporated in the GDP economy. The creativity of the sharing economy is giving a boost of life to capitalism, as couchsurfing becomes AirBnb.

Historically, capitalism has subsisted and expanded by bringing new uncommodified relations under its realm. But in moments of crisis, society struggles back against its treatment as a commodity. Communism and fascism, Polanyi argued in the 1940s, were two such, very different, social counter-movements. So are today the occupied squares, the alternative solidarity economies, the anti-austerity political parties, but also the rising xenophobic nationalists.

1 Gibson-Graham, J.-K. (2008). "Diverse economies: performative practices forother worlds". *Progress in Human Geography, 32*(5), 613-632.

The ecology of the economy

Fourth, the economy, as everything human, is material and biophysical. Human hands and heads do not work alone. They use energy and raw materials and they produce wastes. This metabolic view will not be news for ecological economists and I don't have much to add. I do take issue though with our representation of the economy, and by extension of society, as ultimately limited by an external ecosystem.

Ecological economists often invoke Georgescu-Roegen's entropy law.[1] Humans, like other forms of life, take energy and matter from their environments, and metabolize it into useful products and waste. In this process, high-order energy is lost forever as low-order heat, increasing entropy. The law of entropy reminds us that there is a direction in life. At some point high order energy will be over and entropy will prevail. In the long-term we will all be dead. But how long is this long-term? Fortunately, very very long. Earth is an open system and there are 5 billion years of ample energy from the sun. But: there is a big difference, Georgescu-Roegen argues, between solar and fossil fuels. Solar power is a flow. Fossil fuels are a stock. Fossil fuels are like "bottled photosynthesis". We uncork them, and there they go. They cannot be recycled. Releasing them accelerated the economy, but also accelerated entropy. The sun's energy in comparison is vast; but it is limited by its rate of flow. It is more like rain, than a reservoir. Energy and space has to be spent for concentrating such a diffuse form of power.

The entropy law should not be misread as a diagnosis of looming limits. Given solar energy and recycling, it is questionable whether there is an ultimate limit for activity on planet Earth. Even if there is, it is billion years from now and cannot reasonably concern us at the moment. What I keep from Georgescu-Roegen is that the production of order in some places and times shifts disorder or entropy elsewhere. Any techno-fix, such as nuclear power, which increases the throughput of energy, will accelerate entropy somewhere sooner or later.

Rather than a view of the economy as essentially limited by ecological factors, I find Richard Norgaard's metaphor of coevolution more useful.[2] Unlike the view of nature as a reservoir that is close to running out, coevolution suggests that we constantly mold our environments, and we are con-

1 Georgescu-Roegen, N. (1971). *The Entropy Law and the Economic Process.* Cambridge.

2 Norgaard, R. B. (2006). *Development betrayed: The end of progress and a co-evolutionary revisioning of the future.* Routledge.

stantly molded by our molded environments. Human activity constantly transforms ecosystems, and then adapts, for good or for bad, to its transformations. Like beavers building dams, we humans are co-producers of new natures. But we are extremely powerful producers. The question is not whether humanity as a whole will survive a climate or resource disaster, but who will live how and where, with what non-human natures. This is ultimately a question of justice, not of resource technicalities.

I do not discard the idea of limits. But I see limits as the object of political choice; not as something out there imposed upon us. We want to limit our production and consumption so as to pass a better and more egalitarian environment to our kids. Not because we are running out of things. In the face of uncertainty, I side with peak oil, peak phosphorus and the impossible arithmetic of climate change. But this says as much about my desires for limits as about the facts.

Limits, or better self-limitation, should be distinguished from scarcity. Scarcity is a very problematic concept. To move beyond growth, ecological economics should also move beyond scarcity. The concept of scarcity, Nicholas Xenos shows, appeared precisely at a time when capitalism was creating a material abundance never seen before.[1] This is no coincidence. Scarcity and capitalism go hand in hand. Capitalism produces scarcity by enclosing the commons and fueling positional inequalities. And it promises to resolve scarcity by developing the means of production. Economics declared as its mission the study of scarcity. A scarcity that is by definition perpetual as needs are assumed to be unlimited. Permanent scarcity—different from temporal shortages or population overshoots—is an invention of capitalism. Past civilizations did not know of scarcity. They did not have a word for it.

Scarcity is a function of aspirations, not natural conditions. The Sahara dessert was not scarce for the Berbers. Marhsall Sahlins showed that there was no scarcity in the Stone Age.[2] Not because resources were abundant, but because people found ways to live with enough. Self-limitation and sharing dissolve scarcity. The vision of a limited world that chokes our needs is at the heart of modern economics. It is the *raison d'être* of capitalism and growth. And we must do away with it.

---

1 Xenos, N. (1989). *Scarcity and modernity.* Routledge.

2 Sahlins, M. D. (1974). *Stone age economics* (Vol. 130): Transaction Publishers. Sahlins, M. (1995). "The original affluent society." *Sociological Worlds: Comparative and Historical Readings on Society*, 2.

The unproductive expenditure of surplus

The fifth principle of the economy is the one we propose at the epilogue of the degrowth book. This is the idea that the key economic problem is excess, not scarcity. We borrow this from French philosopher Georges Bataille[1], via the contribution of Onofrio Romano in our book.[2]

All societies have a surplus. Even the Berbers in the dessert had their occasional feasts. All societies produce more than what is necessary for their mere reproduction. Such absolute surplus should be distinguished from relative or social surplus. The latter refers to the excess of work and services provided by wage or domestic labor without compensation (or by active or fossilized ecosystems without replenishment, we might add as ecological economists). If wageworkers were compensated for all their work there would be no surplus profit.

The core question of political economy is the distribution of surplus. But in addition to distribution, an equally important question is the expenditure of surplus. Stone-agers just let it be. The Egyptians used it to build pyramids, and the medievals to decorate churches and palaces. The Tibetans instead devoted it to idleness and spirituality. The use of surplus gives each society its essence and its purpose. The key innovation of capitalist civilization was that it invested surplus into further production creating even more surplus. This was the source of the growth take off. Growth is the essence of capitalism.

Surplus though has to be constantly dissipated. When it over-accumulates, its dissipation can be destructive: a war or a devaluation. The key insight of Keynes was this: to become stable, a capitalist economy needs to plan non-destructive outlets for its surplus. The generalization and the privatization of consumption; the creation of new, artificial needs; this is what stabilized capitalism after the wars. Depense, the expenditure or dissipation of surplus, was privatized. Small portions of it were distributed to everyone: binging parties, swimming pools, and summer holidays. All of them non-productive expenditures. Consumerism became the pleasure and meaning offered by capitalism.

One might say that this surplus is not real. Without fossil fuels, we will face lack, not excess, I am often told. But lack to do what? There are currently so many artificial needs, and so many bullshit jobs, as David

1 Bataille, G. (1933). "La notion de dépense." *La Critique Sociale, 1*(7).
Bataille, G. (1988). *The accursed share* (Vol. 1, p. 22). New York: Zone Books.

2 Romano, O. (2014). "Dépense." In G. D'Alisa, F. Demaria, & G. Kallis (Eds.), *Degrowth: A vocabulary for a new era* (pp. 86-89). New York and London: Routledge.

Graeber called them.[1] They are all ways of dissipating the bonanza of the oil surplus. It is not unthinkable that renewables could satisfy the basic reproduction needs of everyone and leave a surplus. The standard ecological economic idea that we can determine an optimal scale and consume exactly that, is a very technocratic one. Even before the advent of fossil fuels, societies wasted exorbitant surpluses. Think of the Chinese Great Wall or the Pyramids; or the golden palaces of Sultans and Maharajas. *(Author's note: I have found it extraordinary how often people confuse the use of these examples for us arguing that these forms of unproductive expenditure were desirable and should be reproduced. I have no sympathy for Egyptian Pharaohs using slave labour to build pyramids. I am not making a normative argument here, but an analytical one: each and every society has an excess that it dispenses of unproductively. This then poses a normative question: what will an egalitarian, degrowth society do with its surplus?)*

Conclusion

Let me now use these five principles to think about economic growth and alternatives to it. Ecological economists have engaged with the materiality of the economy. That is only one of the five components of the economy that I underlined. We have shown how energy and resources influence or limit economic growth. And why a dematerialized economy is much more difficult in practice than in theory. We have documented the impacts of growth, especially in the world's commodity frontiers, as registered in the Environmental (in)Justice Atlas.[2]

But we should also understand growth as a recent invention and trace its origins. Growth is not a trans-historical objective. Economists perpetuate the myth of a Malthusian trap, the two thousand years of stagnation. A trap that all civilizations tried to escape, but only one, ours, managed to do so. Growth is indeed what capitalist civilization produced. To other civilizations it hadn't ever occurred to pursue growth. GDP counted and reified what the capitalist system was already producing. It turned an outcome into an ideology. Escaping growth requires re—inventing, re-counting, and re-representing the economy.

Second, growth and neoclassical economics are not dominant be-

1 Graeber, D. (2013). "On the phenomenon of bullshit jobs." Strike! Magazine, (2013), 10-11.

2 See www.ejatlas.org

cause they won a noble battle of ideas and facts. Political force molded the world in the image of these ideas. These are powerful ideas, but not because they are true. They have to be treated as true because they are powerful. Any alternative will have to change the institutions toward its own image. Implementing carbon caps or reducing working hours is first and foremost a question of political struggle and political transformation. Ecological economics has to go beyond addressing non-existent benevolent planners, and engage with the analysis of real world politics and with transformative action research.

Third, growth is part and parcel of commodification. Growth involves counting what previously was left uncounted or provided for free. Yet this is a self-contradictory process. Commodifying what was a free subsidy, be it women's work or ecosystem services, pushes accounts up, but only for a while. In the long term, it is a tax on growth. As Polanyi noted, the creation of fictitious commodities undermines their very provision.[1] In times of crisis societies strike back and attempt to take back and decommodify the economy. Consider the proliferation of commons, urban gardens, time banks, community currencies and the like, in the countries worst hit by the crisis. A new economy is reinvented from the ground up. Our job as ecological economists is to provide the concepts and models that will help it flourish.

Finally, growth is fundamentally a process of yielding surplus and re-investing it for further growth. Degrowth would have to reverse this dynamic without undermining social wellbeing. This might involve being intentionally unproductive in some sectors, notably health, education or the arts, as Tim Jackson proposes.[2] Or leaving certain human and natural resources idle, taking them out of the accumulation circuit. Work-sharing, basic and ceiling income, carbon taxes or carbon caps are all institutions that redistribute surplus in an economy that no longer grows.

And yet, a post- or de-growth civilization would also have to rethink how to expend its surplus, however small that may be. And expend it in line with a new essence and a new purpose.

---

1 Polanyi, K. (1957). *The Great Transformation: The Political and Economic Origin of Our Time.* Beacon Press.
"Fictitious commodities", coined by Karl Polanyi, refers to those things such as land, labor, and money that exist regardless of market institutions (e.g. private property, interest, national banks, and taxation) but are nevertheless treated as commodities and traded. The result is that the social relationships and environmental resources that support the existence of these things become disembedded from market activity, leading to their eventual erosion.

2 Jackson, T. (2009). *Prosperity without growth: Economics for a finite planet.* Routledge.

10. *The Wolf of Wall Street* and the spirit of capitalism

Author's note: This is a very different essay in style than the ones before. I shift gears from a theoretical talk in a conference to a more passionate commentary about a movie that moved my emotions and mesmerized me: The Wolf of Wall Street. *I saw the film around the same time that I was reading David Harvey's* The enigma of capital, *and it struck me that the movie was capturing in visual form what the book was describing with theoretical concepts: the magic and folly of capitalism, the magic and folly of growth for growth's sake.*

The Wolf of Wall Street may well be the first film to really capture the spirit of late capitalism. "The enigma of capital," as David Harvey called it,[1] has eluded generations of intellectuals. With its relentlessly frenetic tempo, the movie reveals the brutal essence of capital: money in search for more money, faster and faster. Nothing more and nothing less.

Capitalism, Robert and Edward Skidelsky argue in *How much is enough?*, is "sense-less".[2] Jordan Belfort, the Wolf, played by Leonardo DiCaprio, is literally senseless, constantly high on drugs. Belfort embodies capital. Money circulates constantly through his hands. He sells, invests, makes profits, buys cars, helicopters and yachts, he crashes and sinks them, buys new ones, sniffs coke, pays prostitutes, invests again, makes more money, smuggles it out, throws it in the air. And on he goes. There is no sense in all of this, because circulating money is the sense. When the Wolf explains to his loony pack that everyone wants to get rich, one of them recalls an Amish who "just wanted to make furniture". The Wolf pauses, only for a moment. "What the heck… you don't want to make money? Who doesn't want to make money?" he yells to the rest. "You bet we want to make money," the loonies shout back. And that's the spirit of capitalism: make money, never stop to ask why. Life is better with money than without, right? A pagan tribe, Belfort's possessed partners beat their chests to the rhythm of money on the trading-floor in this memorable scene of the movie.

Early in the story an experienced Wall Street trader, played by Mat-

1 Harvey, D. (2010). *The Enigma of Capital and the Crises of Capitalism*. London: Profile Books.

2 Skidelsky, E., & Skidelsky, R. (2012). *How much is enough?: money and the good life.* Penguin UK.

thew McCounaghey, teaches young Belfort the tricks of the trade. The point is not to invest in something useful, he tells him. It's not even to make profits for clients. The point is to keep the client investing. Let them think they gain, but never let them cash out. Because then the whole thing becomes real and we are in trouble, he warns him. Isn't this unreal circulation what capitalist economies have come to be about? An endless collection of bubbles whose only purpose is the circulation of money, bubbles defended by those addicted to their commissions.

I am not thinking only of Wall Street here, or real estate. Vast, ever higher amounts of money circulate around spectacles, like professionalized sports, or the commercialized arts. But is a painting better or a football game more fun than 50 years ago? Or think of the endless resources devoted to the pursuit of the newest car, or the latest fad. Everyone might have a Ferrari one day, but then it will be the Fiat of its generation. Money keeps moving, senselessly. It has to move, economists tell us, so that the economy does not collapse.

The drug-fueled Wolf also moves fervently; if he stops, even for a single moment, he will collapse. Workers, academics, immigrants, and millionaires—we are all constantly moving, changing place, house or job, faster and faster, in order not to fall, dancing at the pace of the inaudible drumbeat of capital. Capitalism is not the well-intended plan that friends and foes see. The more frightening reality is that capitalism is a mad joke peddled by money-addicts with no clue of why they are doing what they are doing, other than that they are doing it and that they have to keep doing it. Unlike in the movie, there is no pilot in the cockpit of the crashing helicopter. It is Belfort driving.

The movie has no moral center, some critics charge; it glorifies greed. Writing for *Jacobin Magazine*, Eileen Jones expresses her disgust for Scorsese's "gleeful celebration of rich assholes."[1] Well, whether you see a celebration or an exposition of rich assholes depends on your perspective. Clever Scorsese is cashing out well on this ambiguity. I liked the movie, and so did a salesman who wants to hit it big like the Wolff. In my view, however, it is not Scorsese's own politics that matter. It is his indispensable attention to anthropological detail and his commitment to tell the story from the gaze of its heroes that allows this sharpest depiction of the grotesqueness of capitalism that cinema has ever seen. Scorsese's choice not to moralize is apt, because the problem of our society is not greed, it is capital and capital is what it is.

1 Jones, E. (2014). "Crocodile tears of the Wolf." *Jacobin Magazine, 14.*

Capital knows no moral limits. When Belfort's wife questions his profiting from poor people, he dumps her. When an FBI agent visits him, he tries to bribe him. Yet the paradox of the movie is that Belfort does not come out a "bad" guy. He is a likable sociopath. He is a sociopath, not because of an intrinsic psychological fault, but because he brings to a logical extreme what the system asks us all to do: endlessly pursue wealth. And he is magnetizing, like capitalism is. Even critics like David Harvey, like Marx before him, marvel with horrified admiration in front of the magic of capitalism and its relentless creative destruction.

The movie has no moral closure because capitalism is a drama that hasn't closed. Like Belfort himself, capitalism bubbles and crashes, but it comes out clean when the dust settles, preaching shamelessly what went wrong and how to fix it. The inconclusive smirk of the FBI agent who rides the shabby subway back home after indicting Belfort is in the face of all of us as we sit in our dilapidated public infrastructures contemplating the crisis. Happy that the monster stumbled; discontent that it didn't fall for good; and still possessed by its flashy magic.

"A genuine eco-socialism will be one that consciously decides, and plans for, living with enough; and one that collectively squanders the surplus of its production, removing itself from the circuit of growth."

Image: Leanda Xavian / Flickr

Part IV: (De)growth, capitalism, and (eco)socialism

11. Is there a growth imperative in capitalism?

Author's note: This and the next essay were written for the Entitle Blog *on the occasion of an essay by John Bellamy Foster that I was asked to comment upon for the Great Transition Initiative and a short exchange of emails I had with the author. In my reading degrowth is not only a critique of capitalist growth, but of all sorts of economic growth. This is less relevant in so far as capitalism is the only game in town. But it does become relevant once we start imagining alternatives to capitalism, or enacting concrete policies that are supposed to turn capitalism more "socialistic". The argument I build here and in the next essay is that socialist growth is an oxymoron: a socialism that pursues and produces growth ends up reproducing the dynamic of capitalism. Growth is unsustainable and undesirable not only under capitalism, but under any other conceivable social system.*

John Bellamy Foster recently published an excellent essay on "Marxism and Ecology: Common Fronts of a Great Transition".[1] Foster advocates a steady-state (eco)socialism. He argues that "a system of meeting collective needs based on the principle of enough is obviously impossible in any meaningful sense under the regime of capital accumulation." He continues: "capitalism as a system is intrinsically geared to the maximum possible accumulation and throughput of matter and energy". "Economic growth (in its more abstract sense) or capital accumulation (viewed more concretely)…cannot occur without expanding rifts in the Earth system." "Society, particularly in rich countries, must move toward a steady-state economy, which requires a shift to an economy without net capital formation".

In principle, I agree. Intuitively, and given our experience of capitalism, this makes perfect sense. Economic growth appeared under capitalism, and economic growth is almost 1:1 related to growth in material and energy use. But let me be a little bit more scholastic, with the intent of advancing and fortifying (rather than undermining) Foster's argument.

To begin with, I think we need to distinguish between different concepts that are mentioned in one and the same breath by Foster.

1. Throughput growth, i.e. growth in the use of energy and materials.

1 Foster, J. B. (2015). "Marxism and Ecology: Common Fonts of a Great Transition." *The Great Transition Initiative*. Retrieved from http://www.greattransition.org/publication/marxism-and-ecology

2. Economic growth, i.e. growth in GDP (or in some other conceivable index of the scale of productive activity).
3. Capital accumulation. From a Marxist perspective, we can define capital as money in search of more money through the production of commodities (the M-C-M' circuit) and capital accumulation as the process of reinvesting surplus value in further capital valorization cycles.
4. "Capitalism". Following Foster's Marxist approach (distinct from an institutionalist one, which would focus on private property, wage labor and credit institutions) we would define this as a system where the M-C-M' circuit is ubiquitous and dominant (Foster's "regime of capital accumulation"). Now, the vagueness in assessing the degree of "domination", obviously raises the difficult question of whether there are capitalist systems which are less capitalist or more socialist than others, or if and when a regime stops being a regime (in Cuba for example, certain parts of the economy do allow for M-C-M' circuits). This is probably why Marx avoided speaking of "capitalism". But without at least some reference, we cannot assess Foster's thesis that there is a growth imperative within capitalism.

Foster claims that capitalism is intrinsically geared to throughput growth. Or more precisely that: a) economic growth intrinsically brings throughput growth, and b) capitalism is intrinsically geared to economic growth. Let's consider each in turn.

Economic growth and throughput growth

I agree that economic growth comes with throughput growth and that there are no examples of absolute decoupling under capitalism. This is because production, alongside human labor, uses materials and energy. So-called "productivity increases" involve substitution of human work by fossil fuels (think of tractors).

A mainstream environmental economist however would counter-argue that it is possible (even if not achieved yet) to reduce material and energy use while sustaining growth, by becoming more efficient, by substitution (e.g. fossil fuels by renewables) and by structural change from primary production to high value services, whereby more value is produced without an equivalent increase in throughput (think of a Michelin star restaurant or an online company).

I would respond to the environmental economist that efficiency gains "rebound" (the "Jevons' paradox"),[1] since productivity gains are invested for more growth; that services embody lots of energy and materials which are imported in service economies often unaccounted for from other parts of the world; and that substitution, while plausible, would not sustain growth, because renewable sources (or nuclear energy) provide much less "net energy" (energy produced minus energy used for its production) than fossil fuels and hence productivity and growth will decline.

Notice though two things. First, my arguments are empirical. I can't provide an intrinsic "law" based on economic theory, which proves logically that growth and throughput will always be linked. Now Foster has elsewhere proposed "an absolute general law of environmental degradation under capitalism".[2] This basically posits that, propelled by competition, capitalists will seek to exploit the cheapest possible environments, and hence degrade them.

Note that Marxist "laws", such as the tendency of capital to exploit labor down to its levels of subsistence, are best understood as structural tendencies, "other factors being equal" conditionalities, rather than inevitable outcomes (and other factors are not equal since labor can organize and claim better conditions, productivity can reduce the costs of subsistence and give part of the gains to labor, and so on).

Similarly, if renewables become cheaper than fossil fuels, or if low material-input were to become more profitable than resource intensive activities, then in theory capitalism could decarbonise/dematerialize. I think this is unlikely, but I have no intrinsic law yet to offer.

Second, my arguments are not specific to capitalism, but apply to any conceivable alternative system; "green growth" in the terms that I reject it is unlikely, be it under capitalism or socialism (I will come back to this in the second part of my response). Absolute decoupling of economic from throughput growth has not been observed in either capitalist societies or any of the varieties of "actually existing socialist countries".

Capitalism's "growth imperative"

Foster's second argument is that capitalism is intrinsically geared to

1 York, R. (2006). "Ecological paradoxes: William Stanley Jevons and the paperless office." *Human Ecology Review, 13*(2), 143.

2 Foster, J. B. (1992). "The absolute general law of environmental degradation under capitalism." *Capitalism Nature Socialism, 3*(3), 77-81.

economic growth.[1] This depends on what we understand by "geared" and "intrinsic".

If we define capitalism as capital accumulation and capital accumulation as growth, then of course capitalism is intrinsically geared to economic growth. But this would be a semantic truism. And one that would fly in the face of evidence of the variable growth record of capitalist economies (unless we were to concede capitalism an economic supremacy that it doesn't merit, arguing that it is destined to always grow in the long-term, save for cycles and periodic crises).

As Piketty reminded us with citations from Austen and Balzac, capital in the 18th and 19th century was enjoying high rates of return (5%), while economies were stagnant.[2] Today, Greece has lost one third of its economy, but huge profits are still made. Capitalism is not doing well in terms of aggregate accumulation, but institutional changes under the dictates of the Troika expand capitalist institutions and the realm of M-C-M'.

How may this come to be? First, we know that the size of capital increases not only by producing surplus value, but also by dispossession and redistribution from labor to capital (austerity, etc). So, capital can grow without economic growth, at least up to the limit where labor is paid only its subsistence, a point from which most developed economies are far off.

Second, even if aggregate capital accumulation is malfunctioning and decreasing, some fraction of the capitalists will continue to invest money and make more money (profit). Profits may be reduced for some capitalists, but may well increase for others. Individual capitalists, propelled by competition, constantly seek to make profits; but this does not mean that they always achieve it. A stationary or shrinking economy where many individual capitalists make profit is perfectly plausible.

A mix of the two is what is happening in Greece. Capital accumulation continues with negative growth. First, austerity and enclosures redistribute value in favor of capital. And while oligarchs and the few capitalists who have managed to survive increase their profits, many other capitalists have seen their profits shrink or they have gone out of business.

By claiming that a steady-state or declining capitalism is plausible, I am not washing capitalism ideologically. My point is that there is no "in-

1 Harvey, D. (2010). *The Enigma of Capital and the Crises of Capitalism*. London: Profile Books.

2 Piketty, T. (2013). *Capital in the twenty-first century*. Belknap Press.

trinsic" law by which capitalism produces growth or does not survive if it fails to achieve it. A non-growing capitalism is a capitalism with an ugly face, which is indeed how capitalism has been in most periods and places. Bankruptcies, unemployment, shrinking living standards and enclosed commons, dispossessions, rising inequality.

How long can a capitalist economy withstand a Greek-style "Great Depression" before it collapses and becomes something else, better or worse? Probably not indefinitely; but there is no economic "law" suggesting that capitalism will naturally come to an end, independent of the agency of those who will struggle to transform it. And diagnosing a "law" does not tell us much about the direction and characteristics of the transformation.

In conclusion: there is no imperative in the abstract, but only in the concrete sense that capitalism becomes politically and socially unstable if it fails to produce growth and good conditions of accumulation. Growth defuses distributional conflict and makes the life of capitalists easier; this is why it is hard to imagine nations where powerful capitalist interests reign voluntarily pursuing degrowth or a steady-state. But as growth becomes harder and harder to get, and stagnation becomes the new norm, a counter-movement, the "social and ecological revolution by the … environmental proletariat" that Foster espouses, becomes more likely.

12. Socialist growth is an oxymoron

In the first part of this commentary, I argued that there is no necessary incompatibility between capitalism and a steady or declining economy. Such a state, unstable (and ugly) as it could be, would increase the likelihood of the rise of a social force that will transform and transcend capitalism. In this essay, I want to ask instead whether an end of capitalism would necessarily bring sustainable degrowth followed by a stable steady-state. Or, if not, under what conditions this may be possible.

Foster argues that socialism is more suitable than capitalism to a steady-state economy. But what is socialism? A system that is not capitalist is not necessarily socialist. Reducing the ubiquity of capital accumulation and surplus value—the M-C-M' circuit—(or eliminating it altogether?) is a necessary, but not sufficient condition for socialism.

One could argue in Marxist terms that a sufficient condition is the elimination of surplus value. Eliminating surplus value means eliminating exploitation with a collective appropriation of the surplus by those who produce it. Workers always produce more than the requirements for their mere reproduction. If they appropriate this excess (surplus) and use it to satisfy their human needs, then this does not become surplus value.

"Appropriation" cannot be literal, each and every worker appropriating the surplus of the factory or office that they happened to work in. If that was the case, then there would be rich workers from profitable factories, and poor ones from less productive ones. Appropriation and redistribution at some higher scale (region, nation, etc.) would be necessary and hence the onus would shift to the democratic process through which "workers" define collective needs and decide how to allocate the product and excess. Socialists' opinions differ on whether this is best done by a centrally planned economy, or by a more decentralized, participatory one.[1]

Would a socialist economy thus defined differ from a capitalist one in so far as the "growth imperative" is concerned? If the imperative is not axiomatic but contingent, as I've argued, then the answer is: it depends. A socialist economy without growth is less likely to be "ugly", given that there won't be bankruptcies, lay-offs, and the like. There will be no capitalists lobbying for growth.

On the other hand, if the socialist economy depends on international

1 See, for example, the debate between David Harvey and Simon Springer on anarchism and Marxism: http://progressivegeographies.com/2015/06/10/simon-springer-and-david-harvey-debate-marxism-anarchism-and-geography/

markets to finance its expenditures, or if its stability depends on output-fuelled arm races against capitalist competitors, then growth might be necessary. Importantly, if the legitimacy of the system depends on its capacity to deliver an ever-increasing output to satisfy ever-increasing material human needs, then lack of growth will also mean political and social instability.

One might argue that it is capitalism which creates artificial needs; without capitalism, needs will satiate. Satiation of needs however is not a principle that one will find in Marx or in much of contemporary socialist thinking, where needs are considered unlimited and calls for "acceleration" remain prominent.

Note also that there is no incompatibility between socialist economy thus defined and growth. Economic (and throughput) growth can well continue even in the absence of exploitation and capital accumulation. Growth can continue in so far as the workers refrain from consuming all of the product for the satisfaction of their immediate human needs, and instead invest it to increase production, to satisfy their higher needs of tomorrow.

Socialist growth isn't any greener

The process of surplus-(re)investment-growth[1] in a socialist economy is very similar to that of capital accumulation; the only difference is that since it is controlled by the workers themselves (and not by capitalists) and it is geared to their needs, then one could argue formally that there is no surplus value, and no capital accumulation (capital here understood in the Marxist sense of surplus value in movement, not in the standard sense of machinery and money, which obviously would increase). But there is economic and throughput growth.

This scenario more or less describes the "actually existing socialist" economies of the Eastern bloc, where there was lots of growth, though—formally speaking—no surplus value or capital accumulation. (The fact that these economies were probably not genuinely socialist, in the sense that a state bureaucracy took the place of capitalists, and drew surplus value from workers investing it without direct democratic control, does not negate the logic of my claim—that a collective, socialized control of surplus and investment can produce growth).

1 Marx, K. (1990). "Chapter Twenty-Four: Conversion of Surplus-Value into Capital" (B. Fowkes, Trans.) *Capital, Volume I*. Penguin Books.

I recently came across the notion of "socialist growth" in a book by the ex-leader of the French Communist party, Georges Marchais, written in 1973, called *The challenge of democracy*. In it, and responding to ecologists and the Club of Rome, Marchais argued that while capitalist (GDP) growth is bad because it destroys the planet for the needs of profit, without serving the needs of people, a different, "socialist growth" geared to the satisfaction of human needs would not have to be limited since it serves the real needs of the collective. And in his view, a case in point was the Soviet Union at the time, which was outperforming the West in terms of output, while serving the real needs of its citizens.

Marchais' view is not a relic of the past, save perhaps for his praise of the Soviet Union. In Spain, socialist and ecologically sensitive economists Vicenç Navarro and Juan Torres—the duo charged with drafting Podemos' economic program—have repeatedly written against degrowth in more or less the same terms as Marchais.[1] Let me unpack two arguments that they make in defense of a socialist green growth.

The first is that, unlike a capitalist economy, a proper socialist economy can grow and be green. In other words, it can better organize dematerialization and decouple economic growth from throughput. Their argument accepts that decoupling and dematerializing growth[2] is possible (the "green growth" thesis of environmental economics), but then adds that only a "rational", socialist system, not driven by profit is capable of bringing forward such green growth.

As I argued in the first part of this commentary, there are reasons why green growth is unlikely to apply to any type of economy, capitalist or socialist or else. It has to do with the material needs of economic expansion and the diminishing energy returns of renewable resources. I can't see how "rationality" will magically change all this. And this begs the question of what is "rationality" and to what extent a socialist system would be more rational, or more effective and inventive in driving technological change (assuming that there is such a techno-fix to environmental problems).

What ensures that the rational democratic outcome won't be a decision to increase material output now and care for the climate later? Or increase our material living standards by shifting their cost elsewhere?

1 Kallis, G. (2015). "Podemos party's plan to 'stimulate consumption' needs more ambition." *The Guardian*. Retrieved from http://www.theguardian.com/sustainable-business/2015/jan/15/spain-podemos-should-further

2 Foster, J. B., Clark, B., & York, R. (2010). "Capitalism and the Curse of Energy Efficiency: The Return of the Jevons' Paradox." *Monthly Review, 62*(06).

And why are we so sure that capitalism cannot turn "greening" into a profitable enterprise and put its irrationality to good use, if such greening is in principle technically possible?

The second argument is that a socialist economy would not care about GDP but about real human needs. GDP is an indicator that makes sense only in an economy based on profit since it is the aggregate of the accounting logic of individual firms. Hence a socialist economy could conceivably "grow" its own definition of wellbeing, while reducing throughput.

But this is a play of semantics. Of course, if we define the goal of the economy as the number of times we say good-morning to each other, we could make growth angelic at a stroke and decouple it from throughput. But this would be simply an accounting trick. The question remains what would happen to actual production and throughput. And beyond that, I can't see why a socialist economy should seek to grow the number of good-mornings geometrically to infinity. More seriously, I can't see why as eco-socialists we would care to salvage the idea of "growth"[1] (by adding the adjective socialist or otherwise), an idea that is so central to the imaginary of capitalism.

One could say that indeed the question of growth is irrelevant, and that a hypothetical socialist country would simply decide democratically on its needs and satisfy them, indifferent to the question of growth. Note, however, that to the climate or to the communities supplying primary commodities (often at the expense of their environments and health), it makes little difference if country X decides democratically or not that it needs to emit carbon or extract their materials.

Degrowing our way to eco-socialism

An eco-socialist response then can only be one that rejects the notion of (socialist) growth, and then argues that a socialist system could better organize a "prosperous way down", i.e. a degrowth in material and energy throughput to a steady-state.

This does not mean reducing each and every activity. It might mean increasing one activity (say trains or solar panels) while reducing and compensating with another (car production and nuclear power). Far from being indifferent to the question of growth, this calls for a conscious focus of the democratic process in the regulation of the social

1 Latouche, S. (2009). *Farewell to growth.* Polity.

metabolism[1] and the decline and stabilization of economic activity and throughput.

Capitalism is ill-suited for this since it is unstable in the absence of growth. But rather than a general invocation for an end to capitalism or a transition to socialism, this raises the concrete question of what specific institutions a post-capitalist economy will have and what desires it will privilege that will make it stable in the absence of growth. This is for me a core question for the economics of degrowth, or the economics of eco-socialism.

Further, if a socialist economy were to reach a steady state, it should eliminate not only surplus value, but also squander all excess from production above what is necessary for satisfying the basic needs of the producers. This is the argument we construct with Giacomo D'Alisa and Federico Demaria in the epilogue of our recent book on degrowth, benefiting from George Bataille's notion of "depense", or unproductive expenditure.[2]

In other words: to reach a "steady-state socialism", such as the one espoused by Foster, the collective appropriation of surplus is a necessary but not sufficient condition. A sufficient condition is that there is no excess or surplus reinvested into more production: all product should be consumed by the workers, now or later.

This, and only this, condition can satisfy Foster's "zero net capital formation" (capital here understood in the wider sense, and not the formal Marxist one). With zero net investment (which does not preclude reallocation of investment from some sectors/activities to others), the economy and its throughput will not grow, period.

One may claim that this idea of a steady state of zero accumulation and investment is the genuine vision of socialism (or communism). What I hope I have argued though is that this is only one possibility of how socialism may be conceived, indeed the one compatible with a steady-state eco-socialism. But there is another, actually dominant productivist vision, which sees human needs as insatiable and aims to satisfy them with the collective appropriation and re-investment of surplus to produce more and more ecologically in the future. This is a vision of socialism as a rationalized capitalism controlled by and for the collective.

---

1 Clark, B., & Foster, J. B. (2010). "The dialectic of social and ecological metabolism: Marx, Mészáros, and the absolute limits of capital." *Socialism and Democracy, 24*(2), 124-138.

2 D'Alisa, G., Demaria, F., & Kallis, G. (2014). *Degrowth: a vocabulary for a new era.* Routledge.

Zero accumulation/investment requires two things. First, that society accepts the principle of satiation of material human needs. We have a limited amount of material needs, though we can still flourish in qualitative terms developing arts, games, and other spiritual activities that are not materially intensive. And second, that meaningful and fun ways are collectively devised for the squandering of the unavoidable excess that human activity produces.

As Bataille argues, society and "the political" are concerned precisely around the question of squandering surplus. A society that only builds railways and solar panels is not a society worth living in. A society that builds railways and solar panels, but also wastes its excess in carnivals, maybe. Socialism from this perspective is not only the democratic control and planning of production but also the democratic control of the expenditure and destruction of surplus by those who produce it.

In conclusion: there is nothing intrinsic in socialism that will make it pursue degrowth and a steady-state economy. Yes, unlike capitalism there is nothing that makes a socialist economy unstable without growth. In addition, the democratic determination of production, with an eye on needs and not profits, makes it possible to degrow sustainably. But not necessarily.

Indeed, the long tradition of the idea of "socialist growth", and the insistence by socialist intellectuals that growth can be greened under socialism (in more or less the same terms as capitalist green growthers) shows that the imaginary of growth can well survive the end of capitalism, as it did survive it under "actually existing socialisms". A genuine eco-socialism will be one that consciously decides, and plans for, living with enough; and one that collectively squanders the surplus of its production, removing itself from the circuit of growth.

"Maybe to provoke Karl Marx, his father-in-law, Paul Lafargue once argued that the working class should not fight for the right to work, but for the 'right to laziness' that up to then was the privilege of capitalists only.... It is only through the reduction of wage labor that workers can finally set themselves free."

Image: "Het Luilekkerland" by Pieter Breugel the Elder

Part V: Politics and policies

13. Yes, we can prosper without growth

Author's note: this text was written in a concrete political context: the rise of Podemos in Spain and the opening up of its electoral agenda. We were often told as degrowthers that we have a very good critique of what is wrong with economic growth, but that we seldom offer proposals on what to do differently. This text was our effort as Research & Degrowth Barcelona to offer concrete policy proposals that a hypothetical New Green Left government in Spain could put in practice. I wrote the first draft in English and with my friends in R&D we improved and enriched the text, translating it into Spanish and publishing it in El Diario. *Without knowing that I wrote it in English, Mark Burton in Manchester translated the Spanish version back to English, producing a better version than my original. The English text was published by* The Ecologist, *and by Naomi Klein's "The Leap" website, where it received a lot of attention. It was subsequently translated and published in many foreign newspapers, including most notably* Libération *in France, and* Der Freitag *in Germany. Our proposals were not new, they have been around for a while; perhaps what is original is the new strategic orientation towards degrowth, or prosperity without growth. We were not naïve to think that these policies will be implemented tomorrow, and we did not really expect (although we perhaps over-optimistically hoped) that a party like Podemos would endorse them. Our point was to register them, and make clear that at least in theory, there are economic alternatives; whether they will ever be realized is a matter of social mobilization and radical political change, not a dearth of ideas. Friends from the Left of course criticized us for being utopian for thinking that reforms like these could ever be implemented within capitalism. We like to think of our proposals as non-reformist reforms; "reforms" that if they were to be implemented, the very contours of the system would have to change with them. And reforms that, simple and commonsensical as they are, expose the irrationality of a system that makes them seem impossible.*

In our recent book *Degrowth: A vocabulary for a new era* we argue that economic growth is not only becoming more and more difficult in advanced economies, but that it is also socially and ecologically unsustainable. The global climate, the welfare state, or social bonds that have lasted for ages, are all sacrificed in the name of appeasing the god of growth.

Like terminally ill patients, whole populations are asked to suffer without end, just so that their economies score a few extra decimals in the GDP scale, to sustain the profits of the 1%.

In theory, growth is needed to pay off debts, create new jobs, or increase the incomes of the poor. In practice, we have had decades of growth, yet we are still indebted, with our youth unemployed and poverty as high as ever. We were indebted to grow and now we are forced to grow to pay off debts.

Degrowth is a call to decolonize the social imaginary from the ideology of a one-way future consisting only of growth.[1] Degrowth is not the same thing as recession. It is the hypothesis that we can achieve prosperity without economic growth.[2]

In other words: that we can have meaningful work without the need for ever-lasting growth; sustain a functional welfare state without the economy getting bigger every single year; and increase equality and eliminate poverty, without having to accumulate more and more money each year.

Degrowth challenges not only the outcomes, but the very spirit of capitalism. Capitalism knows no limits, it only knows how to expand, creating while destroying. Capitalism cannot and does not know how to settle. Capitalism can sell everything; but it can't sell "less".

Degrowth offers a new narrative for a radical left that wants to go beyond capitalism, without reproducing the authoritarian and productivist experiences of real existing socialism (or what some may call "state capitalism").

A new Left, new in terms of ideas, but also in terms of the young age of its members, is rising in Europe, from Spain and Catalonia, to Greece, Slovenia or Croatia. Will that Left also be green and propose an alternative cooperative model for the economy inspired by the ideas of degrowth? Or will this new Left, like the new Left of Latin America, driven by the demands of global capitalism, reproduce the expansionary logic of capitalism, only substituting multi-national corporations with national ones, distributing somewhat better the crumbs to the populace?

Many people who are sympathetic to the ideas expressed in our book, tell us that even though the critique of degrowth sounds reasonable, its proposals are vague and, anyways, they could never be put into practice. It seems easier to imagine the end of the world, or even the end of capitalism, than to imagine the end of growth.

Even the most radical political parties do not dare to utter the "D" word, or at least question the desirability of growth. To break this spell

1 Kallis, G., & March, H. (2015). "Imaginaries of hope: The utopianism of degrowth." *Annals of the Association of American geographers, 105*(2), 360-368.

2 Jackson, T. (2009). *Prosperity without growth: Economics for a finite planet.* Routledge.

of growth, we at Research & Degrowth in Barcelona,[1] decided to codify some of the policy proposals that are coming out of the theory of degrowth, policies that are discussed in more detail in our recent book.

In what follows we present 10 proposals that we wrote for the context of Spain and Catalunya, and which we submitted to progressive political parties such as Podemos, the United Left, the Catalan Republican Left, CUP or Equo. The context to which these proposals refer to is specific; but with certain amendments and adaptations they are also applicable elsewhere and relevant for radical Left and Green political parties all over Europe.

1. Citizen debt audit. An economy cannot be forced to grow to resolve accumulated debts that have contributed to fictitious growth in the past. It is essential not only to restructure but also to eliminate part of the debt with a people's debt audit, part of a new, really democratic culture. Such elimination shouldn't be realized at the expense of savers and those with modest pensions whether in Spain or elsewhere. The debt of those that have considerable income and assets should not be pardoned. Those who lent for speculation should take the losses. Once the debt is reduced, caps on carbon and resources (see 9) will guarantee that this will not be used as an opportunity for more growth and consumption.
2. Work-sharing. Reduce the working week to at least 32 hours and develop programmes that support firms and organisations that want to facilitate job-sharing. This should be orchestrated such that the loss of salary from working less only affects the 10% highest income bracket. Complemented by environmental limits and the tax reform proposed below (see 4), it will be more difficult for this liberation of time to be used for material consumption.
3. Basic and maximum income. Establish a minimum income for all of Spain's residents of between 400 and 600 Euros per month, paid without any requirement or stipulation. A recent study suggests this is feasible for Spain, without a major

1 See our website, www.degrowth.org

overhaul of the tax system.[1] To finance the change, design this policy in conjunction with other tax and work reforms so that they increase the income of the poorer 50% of the population while decreasing that of the top 10%. The maximum income for any person—from work as well as from capital—shouldn't be more than 30 times the basic income (12,000—18,000 Euros monthly).

4. Green tax reform. Implement an accounting system to transform, over time, the tax system, from one based principally on work to one based on the use of energy and resources. Taxation on the lowest incomes could be reduced and compensated for with a carbon tax. Establish a 90% tax rate on the highest incomes (such rates were common in the USA in the 1950s). High income and capital taxes will halt positional consumption and eliminate the incentives for excessive earnings, which feed financial speculation. Tackle capital wealth through inheritance tax and high taxes on property that is not meant for use, for example on the second or third houses of individuals or on large estates.
5. Stop subsidizing and investing in activities that are highly polluting, moving the liberated pubic funds toward clean production. Reduce to zero the public investment and subsidy for private transport infrastructure (such as new roads and airport expansion), military technology, fossil fuels or mining projects. Use the funds saved to invest in the improvement of public rural and urban space—such as squares, traffic free pedestrian streets, and to subsidise public transport and cycle hire schemes. Support the development of small scale decentralised renewable energy under local and democratic control, instead of concentrated and extensive macro-structures under the control of private business.
6. Support the alternative, solidarity society. Support, with subsidies, tax exemptions and legislation, the not-for-profit co-operative economic sector that are flourishing in Spain and include alternative food networks, cooperatives and net-

1 Arcarons, J., Domènech, A., Raventós, D., & Torrens, L. (2014). "Un modelo de financiación de la Renta Básica para el conjunto del Reino de España: sí, se puede y es racional." *Sin Permiso*. Retrieved from http://www.sinpermiso.info/textos/un-modelo-de-financiacin-de-la-renta-bsica-para-el-conjunto-del-reino-de-espaa-s-se-puede-y-es

works for basic health care, co-operatives covering shared housing, credit, teaching, and artists and other workers. Facilitate the de-commercialisation of spaces and activities of care and creativity by helping mutual support groups, shared childcare, and social centers.

7. Optimise the use of buildings. Stop the construction of new houses, rehabilitating the existing housing stock and facilitating the full occupation of houses. In Spain those objectives could be met through very high taxes on abandoned, empty and second houses, prioritising the social use of SAREB housing (those falling under the post-crash banking restructuring provisions following the Spanish real estate crisis), and if this is insufficient, then the government could proceed with social expropriation of empty housing from private investors.
8. Reduce advertising. Establish very restrictive criteria for allowing advertising in public spaces, following the example of the city of Grenoble. Prioritise the provision of information and greatly reduce any commercial use. Establish committees to control the quantity and quality of advertising permitted in the mass media and tax advertising in accordance with objectives.
9. Establish environmental limits. Establish absolute and diminishing caps on the total of CO^2 that Spain can emit and the total quality of material resources that it uses, including emissions and materials embedded in imported products, often from the global South. These caps would be in CO^2, materials, water footprint or the surface area under cultivation. Similar limits could be established for other environmental pressures such as the extraction of water, the total built-up area, and the number of licenses for tourist enterprises in saturated zones.
10. Abolish the use of GDP as indicator of economic progress. If GDP is a misleading indicator, we should stop using it and look for other indicators of prosperity. Monetary and fiscal national accounts statistics can be collected and used but economic policy shouldn't be expressed in terms of GDP objectives. A debate needs to be started about the nature of well-being, focusing on what to measure rather than how to measure it.

These proposals are complementary and have to be implemented in concert. For example, setting environmental limits might reduce growth and create unemployment, but work-sharing with a basic income will decouple the creation of jobs and social security from economic growth.

The reallocation of investments from dirty to clean activities and the reform of the taxation system will make sure that a greener economy will emerge, while stopping to count the economy in GDP terms and using prosperity indicators ensures that this transition will be counted as a success and not as a failure.

Finally, the changes in taxation and the controls in advertizing will relax positional competition and reduce the sense of frustration that comes with lack of growth. Investing in the commons and shared infrastructures will increase prosperity without growth.

We do not expect parties of the Left to make "degrowth" their banner. We understand the difficulties of confronting, suddenly, an entrenched common sense. But we do expect radical left parties to take steps in the right direction, and to pursue good policies, such as the ones we propose, independent of their effect on growth. We do expect genuine Left parties to avoid making the relaunch of economic growth their objective. And we do expect them to be ready, and have ideas in place, on what they will do, if the economy refuses to grow. Is this a reasonable expectation in the current political conjecture of Southern Europe for example? Yes and no.

The draft economic policy of Podemos released in November (see chapter 14) has many elements that fit with the above agenda. The document does not set growth as its strategic goal. It omits any reference to GDP. It proposes to reduce working hours to 35, it sets a minimum guaranteed income for the unemployed, it calls for a forgiveness of part of household and public debt, and it promotes a shift of investments toward caring, education and the green economy, posing the satisfaction of basic needs through an "ecologically sustainable consumption" as its primary objective.

The policy could go further by shifting taxes from labor to resources, establishing environmental limits, controlling advertising, generalizing the basic income, and reforming the welfare state by thinking ways to universalize the solidarity economy that is thriving in Spain, providing viable and low cost solutions for health, care, or education.

In Greece, in contrast, huge overhanging debt and the need to escape the socially disastrous policy of austerity and structural adjustment imposed by the Troika makes it much harder to ignore growth.

Syriza rightly confronts austerity with a proposal to forgive part of Greece's public debt. Unfortunately though, the objective of such debt cancellation is seen as the relaunching of growth, with Syriza adopting

Joseph Stiglitz' proposal for a "growth-clause", whereby the remaining part of the debt will be growth financed.

Syriza proposes a European New Deal and espouses public investments that will spur growth in Greece, but unlike Podemos, it does not talk of a "green" New Deal, or about a shift from conventional to clean industries or from resource intensive sectors to caring and education.

Within the current conjecture of powers in Europe, the dictatorship of the markets and the fixation of Germany with austerity, even the Stiglitzian proposal of Syriza comes to pass as "radical" and stands slims chances of being realized, save for dramatic socio-political events in Greece and a political upheaval in the EU.

Assuming that Syriza were to implement its strategy one day, the question is what would it do if, even after a restructuring of debts, the professed growth was not to come.

Would it recoil into a left version of austerity as the "socialists" of Hollande did in France when faced with the same problem?

Would it pursue even more intensely the current extractivist model of development, exploiting the environments of Greece for resources, exports, and tourism, even though this would be against the wishes of its political base that is at the forefront of current struggles against extractivist projects?

Or would it stop and listen to its youth, which is involved in the thriving solidarity economy of Greece, and try to decipher and think about how to universalize these pre-figuring local experiments into something new for the national economy as a whole? Not an easy feat, but a radical left was never supposed to follow the easy path.

14. Spanish Keynesianism without growth?

Author's note: I wrote this piece at the end of 2014, and it was one more attempt to link some of the ideas coming out of the degrowth debate to a concrete political moment and task—the preparation of Podemos' economic program. Here I wrote for an international audience, and The Guardian's *"Rethinking prosperity" blog, but most of the ideas were already published in Spanish. The question that concerns this text is the same as the one in chapter 3. Can the New Left escape productivism and growthism, putting in practice a new imaginary of prosperity without growth? I argue that yes, it can, but no, it doesn't. Not yet.*

Austerity or stimulus? That is the question in the aftermath of the financial crisis—a question, however, that is past its expiry date.

Relaunching growth, be it through austerity or stimulus, may no longer be possible and is definitely not sustainable. The core question of our era is how to secure prosperity without growth. Don't expect much, though, from the conservatives or social liberals who rule. For them, abandoning the growth fetish is unthinkable. But will Europe's rising new left be different?

Spain's Podemos, a political party of 30-somethings from universities and the occupied squares, recently released its economic programme. The draft document by Professors Navarro and Torres does not call for prosperity without growth, but this may well be its outcome. Its aim, in fact, is to "stimulate consumption".

Yet, unlike Keynes, this is not any consumption. It is the basic consumption of those in need. Higher taxes await capital and top incomes, wage differences within companies would be capped, and a minimum income is guaranteed for those without work. If growth ends, securing a basic living for all out of the—still substantial—common wealth is vital. Without growth, redistribution is indispensable as otherwise wealth accumulates to those who already have more.

Prosperity requires what Naomi Klein calls the "selective degrowth" of dirty sectors and the flourishing of sustainable ones. Podemos' programme calls for a moratorium on Spain's notoriously corrupt mega-infrastructure projects and for a move to invest public funds in clean industries and renewable energy. It commits support to caring, education, and co-operatives. Without growth, these sectors have an advantage:

they do not require growing profits. The document also seeks to slow speculative capital and divert investments to small enterprises and the working classes with drastic banking reforms and a Tobin-like tax[1] on financial transactions and short-hold stock exchange.

The authors recognize that care or education might not increase GDP now. They are confident, though, that they will increase broadly-defined economic activity in the long run. I am skeptical that this is possible. But the proposals are good, independent of their effect on growth.

Yet if Podemos is to ignore GDP, as the report does, then it will need new prosperity metrics to evaluate its successes. And it should think more carefully about how it will maintain stability if economic activity refuses to increase.

Without growth and with work increasingly computerised and automated, workers become redundant. Correctly, the document proposes a 35-hour working week: in an economy that does not grow, more jobs can be created if each of us works less.[2] The support of caring and education is also right: these "less productive" activities are employment-intensive[3] while providing higher social value.[4]

But Podemos is wrong to replace its commitment to a Basic Income with a minimum income guaranteed only for those who cannot find work. A Basic Income secures a dignified life for all. A citizens' right, it removes the stigma of unemployment. It offers no disincentive against work as people receive it when they work too. But, unlike an unemployment benefit, you also get it if you want to work less, devoting more time to family, care, leisure, voluntary or political work. Studies show that a basic income of €400–€600 per person is feasible in Spain without radical changes in taxes.[5]

---

1 The Tobin Tax, named after Nobel Laureate James Tobin, originally described a tax on all currency exchanges for short-term investment purposes meant to limit exchange rates fluctuations and cushion small countries against global financial markets. However, the term has now come to refer to any kind of "Robin Hood tax" that penalizes short-term transactions, meant to reduce the impact of speculators on a country's markets and aid in redistributing wealth from the finance industry to the population.

2 Schor, J. B. (2012). "Exit Ramp to Sustainability: the plenitude path." *Revistes Científiques de la Universitat de Barcelona, 1.*

3 Jackson, T. (2009). *Prosperity without growth: Economics for a finite planet.* Routledge.

4 Graeber, D. (2014). "Caring too much. That's the curse of the working classes." *The Guardian.* Retrieved from https://www.theguardian.com/commentisfree/2014/mar/26/caring-curse-working-class-austerity-solidarity-scourge

5 Arcarons, J., Domènech, A., Raventós, D., & Torrens, L. (2014). "Un modelo de financiación de la Renta Básica para el conjunto del Reino de España: sí, se puede y es racional." *Sin Permiso.*

Without growth, debts cannot be paid. An economy cannot be forced to grow unnaturally to pay debts incurred to fuel a fictitious growth in the past; some debt has to be canceled. Whose debt will be forgiven is a democratic question. Losses should fall upon speculators, not small savers. Podemos' policy does call for civic deliberation to restructure and cancel Spain's debt, household and public, but it is mute on the specifics.

Debt cancellation may relaunch unsustainable growth, as in Ecuador. Time liberated from work and a basic income could go on televisions, gadgets and weekend trips by plane. Instead, Navarro and Torres aspire to an "ecologically sustainable" consumption. Unfortunately it is not clear how or why this will be the outcome of their proposals.

What will Podemos do if unsustainable growth recovers despite its intentions? Here Podemos should go further. First, it should set clear ecological limits, like caps on the carbon emitted and the raw materials used by Spain, including those embedded in imported consumer goods.

Second, it should curtail advertising, banning it from public spaces, like the recent decision made by the city of Grenoble.[1] Finally, to incentivise sustainable consumption, taxes should gradually shift from labor to resource use[2] in ways that benefit those with lower incomes and consumption. A carbon tax could be linked to the financing of a Basic Income.

Without growth, public revenues also stall. Podemos' economic policy document may commit to an efficient public sector, but other than the goodwill of uncorrupted newcomers, it offers no alternative to cuts, privatisation and outsourcing. An opportunity is missed here to link to Spain's flourishing co-operative economy, where groups organize affordable solutions for health, education, food, housing, or care themselves. These solutions could lower the costs of the welfare state and help reform it.

All in all, Podemos' policy takes us in the right direction. However, it could—and should—go further.

---

1 (2014, 26 November). "Grenoble: Europe's first ad-free city. *Euronews*. Retrieved from http://www.euronews.com/2014/11/26/grenoble-europe-s-first-ad-free-city

2 Daly, H. (2011). "What should we tax?" Retrieved from http://steadystate.org/what-should-we-tax/

15. The right to leisure

Author's note: this article was written for the Greek blog Greeklish.info*, where Greek intellectuals of the diaspora write about issues that concern Greece in Greek and English. Here I tried to make, in simple terms, the case for reduced working hours, a proposal that was flying in the face of the proposals of the Troika to the Greek government.*

We often talk about the New Deal but we tend to forget a more important reform under President Roosevelt during the period of the Great Depression. Roosevelt was the first to introduce the five-day workweek, reducing the weekly working hours from 48 to 40. It was a simple idea. If each of us works less, then there will be more work for everyone and unemployment will be reduced. Employers did not like this but accepted it when Roosevelt threatened them with worse measures. Studies by Neumann, Taylor et al, published in the *Economic Journal* and the prestigious *American Economic Review*, estimate that Roosevelt's policy created 1.1 million new jobs in the long-term (down from an initial gain of 2.7 million jobs), whereas monthly salaries were not reduced, i.e. the hourly pay increased. After the war, all advanced economies followed the example of the USA, establishing Saturday as a day off. So did Greece in 1982 in one of the first "revolutionary changes" of Andreas Papandreou's socialist government. I still remember how happy I was the day my parents told me that school would be closed on Saturdays.

Labor rights acquired since decades are under threat today. In August 2013, the Greek government introduced a bill that makes it possible for shops to operate on Sundays (the right for Saturday off has long since been lost) causing the reaction of the church. Judging also from news coverage, the return of a six-day workweek is part of the various packages negotiated between the Troika and the Greek government, even if "dressed up" in the more neutral terms of "flexibility" in working hours. Of course, in times of crisis and unemployment, flexibility means the right of the employer. The five-day workweek is already, de facto, in the a past for many employees in the Greek private sector who work many more than 40 hours a week without additional compensation. Taking the whole of August off is a distant memory for most employees, who nowadays can get a couple of weeks holiday at best.

These changes are supposed to take place in order to reduce labor costs and help the Greek economy become competitive again. There are two untold assumptions governing this idea. First of all, that the crisis in Greece is a result of low productivity making the Greek economy non-competitive. Secondly, that productivity will increase if working hours increase. Both of them are wrong, as we argue with Nicholas Ashford, Professor in MIT, in our recent article published in the European Financial Review.[1]

Firstly, the Greek indebtedness is a result of the cheap cost of borrowing after joining the euro, itself driven by the need for cheap money to keep the GDP growing. If Greece was the only indebted country in the West, we would say that this has to do with our undoubtedly low productivity. But, traditionally industrial Italy and the up-until-recently emerging powerhouse of Spain are also indebted. Both Italy and Spain have extremely competitive multi-national corporations. Ireland suffers from the same crisis of indebtedness as Greece, although as late as 2008 it was considered a miracle of productivity due to its transition to the information economy. Great Britain and the USA are also indebted. The bubble of easy money has nothing to do with the productivity of each country. Rather, this bubble was the temporary solution of the capitalist system in order to keep the abnormal growth rates needed for its reproduction. Indebtedness has nothing to do with the hard work or the laziness of the citizens of a country; otherwise the Japanese would not be in so much debt!

Secondly, contrary to arguments implying that Greeks are lazy and should work more, the most recent statistics of the OECD in 2008 (i.e. before the crisis), suggest that the Greeks already worked more hours than any other country of the 15 EU member states; each Greek worker worked almost 2100 hours per year compared to 1400 hours in Germany and the Netherlands, the two countries with the least working hours. Does this mean that Germans or the Dutch are lazy? Of course not. Development means liberating time from work for the people. Long working hours and cheap labor indicate underdevelopment and dependency, not economic competitiveness.

Our study with Nicholas Ashford reviews the state of the art in statistical studies, according to which countries with less working hours damage the environment less and have happier citizens (regardless of growth levels or other socio-economic differences). We found that the reduction of working hours not only opens new job posts but also frees time for creative activities, which improve the cultural level of a country.

1 Kallis, G., Kalush, M., O'Flynn, H., Rossiter, J., & Ashford, N. (2013). "'Friday off': reducing working hours in Europe." *Sustainability,* 5(4), 1545-1567, see also Chapter 16 in this book.

Free time breeds innovation and new ideas, political debate, artistic creation as well as social interaction and ties, necessary for healthy societies.

Economists, the guardians of neoliberalism, who disapprove of any and all concessions to workers, have a different opinion. They do not really care about issues like the environment, the mental health and life satisfaction of people or culture. They care about "the economy" and focus on how the reduction of working hours will lead to the increase of labor costs for firms. As costs increase, output will decline and so will jobs. Also as labor gets more expensive firms will have more incentives to substitute workers with machines, another avenue through which employment may decline. Indeed, studies that we cite in our work (see next chapter) confirm that in the long run the employment benefits from a working hour reduction evaporate, but some extra jobs will still remain (1.1 million in the case of New Deal down from 2.7). In simple words, if in theory the transition from the five-day to the four-day workweek were to create one new job per 5 employees, in fact there might be only 1 new job available per 30 employees. But even then, we are talking about one new job! The importance of this cannot be underestimated in a period of crisis when young people are in danger of becoming permanently unemployable. Even more so, since there are many other than economic benefits from a reduction of working hours.

Maybe to provoke Karl Marx, his father-in-law, Paul Lafargue once argued that the working class should not fight for the right to work, but for the "right to laziness" that up to then was the privilege of capitalists only. The forefather of the degrowth movement, Andre Gorz, developed this idea theoretically, arguing that socialism cannot come from the collective control of the means of production, since a certain degree of alienation of employees from their product and the administration of production is inevitable in complicated assemblages of production. It is only through the reduction of wage labor that workers can finally set themselves free. Keynes once had predicted that his grandchildren would work 15 hours per week thanks to upcoming technological progress. Many thinkers in the early 80s were also talking about the "end of work". The technological progress Keynes foresaw did materialize but the last two to three decades we have been working more and more. Why? Keynes could not have predicted the neo-liberal counter-offensive and the erosion of labour rights and of collective organization after the 1970s. Without a strong labour movement to demand less working hours, Roosevelt or the capitalists would never concede a share of their profits liberated as leisure for the working class. Profit-making rests on workers as much as possible for as little as possible.

Will Keynes' prediction become true one day? Will we benefit from technological progress and work less and less or will we return back to the 19th century with large numbers of people unemployed or employed in inhuman conditions while a few rich lazy ones enjoy leisure? In Greece, citizens, social movements, and even the church are raising their voices against the offense of capitalism on free time. How many hours will we be working in a few years? It depends on the success of their struggle.

16. Fridays off

Author's note: This is a more academic version of the argument of the previous chapter. I wrote it with my compatriot (Greek-American) Nicholas Ashford back in 2013 during my visit at MIT. It is based on a literature review that I conducted with Mike Kalush, Hugh O'Flynn, and Jack Rossiter back in 2012 as part of our final policy study for the masters in macroeconomics at Pompeu Fabra. (I wont forget the ashen faces of our professors when we were presenting our case that a four day work week will be good for the European economy.) Nicholas joined the team to help us prepare a draft for submission to the journal Sustainability. *He insisted on the point that reduced working hours should take place without a reduction in wages, increasing hence the wage per hour worked. In a context of crisis and attack on the working classes, this is an important point if there is to be a convergence between workers' and environmentalists' demands. Degrowthers often worry that without a concomitant reduction in wages, the liberated time will simply lead to more material consumption and stimulate more growth and more environmental damage. In this article we argue, that given constant wages, there is no reason why this would be the case, since demand and consumption would be constant too. Coupled with a green tax reform, the liberated time from work can be directed to more ecological activities. A stable economy without growth, in a context of rising productivity, is only possible if working hours decline.*

Three arguments have been offered in support of a reduced workweek:

1. Less hours worked by each currently employed worker means more hours available for the currently unemployed.[1] Work-sharing may allow an economy to maintain, or even increase the number of jobs, even when it does not grow.[2]
2. While productivity gains have historically resulted in reductions of working hours, this trend has stopped, or even been reversed, in the last 20 years in the U.S. and some European countries.[3] Some of these productivity gains could be rechan-

1 Schor, J., & White, K. E. (2010). *Plenitude: The new economics of true wealth.* New York: Penguin Press.

2 Jackson, T. (2009). *Prosperity without growth: Economics for a finite planet.* Routledge.

3 Lee, S., McCann, D., & Messenger, J. C. (2007). "Working time around the world." *Geneva: ILO.*

neled into liberated time and leisure for working people.[1]

3. Fewer hours worked may lead to less production, less consumption, and more free time for leisure. This will reduce environmentally-harmful activities and carbon emissions.[2]

However, economists have been skeptical of regulating working hours, and even more so, of reducing working hours. Their concern is that these may raise the cost of labor, suppressing output. In the long-term, it is argued, this can lead to less, not more work.[3]

In contrast, environmentalists enthusiastically endorse the proposal[4] because: first, it can secure employment without growth (argument 1) making economic restrictions in the name of climate change socially stable[5] and second, because it promises to reduce consumption (argument 3).

In this article we take a different approach than most economists and environmentalists. We argue that the economic, social, and environmental effects of any particular policy of reduced working hours are uncertain, and depend on contextual conditions, which we discuss below. Reduced working hours are likely to lead to some employment gains, especially in the short-term. Unlike some environmentalists however we advocate a reduction of the workweek to 4 days *without a change in weekly wages*; in other words, we call for an increase in hourly wages. If reduced working hours are to come at the cost of wages for currently employed workers, then this in effect is a proposal of making them poorer so as to save the environment, and giving them more leisure, when in effect what they need might be a sustainable earning capacity. Note that this form of work-sharing is effectively a wealth transfer within the working class, from the employed to the unemployed, and not a wealth transfer from capital owners and the wealthy to the working class. In the current financial crisis, the major problems are increasing unemployment, the decline in the earning capacity of workers, and the disappearance of

1 Skidelsky, E., & Skidelsky, R. (2012). *How much is enough?: money and the good life.* Penguin UK.

2 Coote, A., Franklin, J., & Simms, A. (2010). *21 hours: Why a shorter working week can help us all to flourish in the 21st century.* London: New Economics Foundation.
Schor, J., & White, K. E. (2010). *Plenitude: The new economics of true wealth.* New York: Penguin Press.

3 Fitzgerald, T. J. (1996). "Reducing working hours." *Economic Review-Federal Reserve Bank of Cleveland, 32*(4), 13.
Hunt, J. (1999). "Has work-sharing worked in Germany?" *The Quarterly Journal of Economics, 114*(1), 117-148.

4 Coote, A., Franklin, J., & Simms, A. (2010). *21 hours: Why a shorter working week can help us all to flourish in the 21st century.* London: New Economics Foundation.

5 Jackson, T. (2009). *Prosperity without growth: Economics for a finite planet.* Routledge.

large segments of the middle class. Below we explain why a reduction in working hours without wage losses might create more and better conditions of employment, and why, against common wisdom, it may also be good for the environment, provided other reforms are instituted as well.

Benefits for employment

In the current political climate in Europe, contrary to work-sharing, the tendency is to liberalize working time restrictions and to increase work beyond 5 days where necessary.[1] The rationale for this is partly that Europe is experiencing a crisis of productivity; by increasing hours of work (without increasing hourly wages proportionally), the less productive economies can become more competitive. Note, however, that in reality the most productive and wealthy countries are the ones that work less. As figure 1 shows it is not the lazy PIIGS (an acronym for Portugal, Italy, Ireland, Greece, and Spain, coined to denote the five Eurozone nations that were weaker following the economic crisis) that work fewer hours, but the productive German and the Dutch. This does not suggest that a nation gets more productive by working less. It suggests however that the more productive a nation gets, the more time it liberates for its workers. More leisure time has historically, at least in Europe, been a sign of progress and betterment. Working more may be a sign of economic and social regression. As noted in the previous chapter, there is also a historical precedent in reducing working hours during a crisis. In the wake of the Great Depression, US President Roosevelt introduced a massive program of work-sharing in 1933. By 1936 this became the law for a 40-hour workweek[2], which gradually became the norm for the rest of the developed world. The argument during the Great Depression, remarkably absent in the current crisis, was that this would generate more new jobs.

1 Traynor, I. (2012). "Eurozone demands 6-day week for Greece." *The Guardian*. Retrieved from https://www.theguardian.com/business/2012/sep/04/eurozone-six-day-week-greece

2 Taylor, J. E. (2011). "Work-sharing During the Great Depression: Did the 'President's Reemployment Agreement' Promote Reemployment?" *Economica, 78*(309), 133-158.

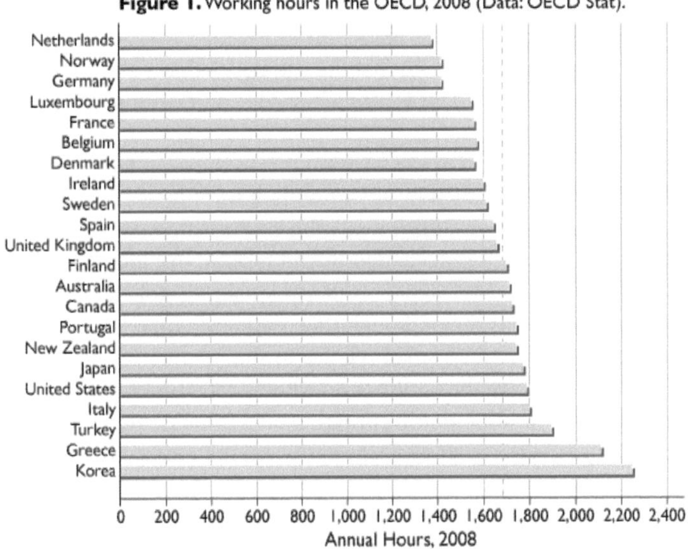

Figure 1. Working hours in the OECD, 2008 (Data: OECD Stat).

The argument is largely absent today because most economists in positions of influence have been convinced that work-sharing is bound to the "lump-of-labor fallacy". The fallacy is to think that the amount of available work in an economy is a fixed total. Indeed, the amount of work available changes as the cost of labor changes. A simple firm-level theoretical model can illustrate why work-sharing may backfire. Labor costs have both fixed and variable components, so any reduction in hours per worker increases the average hourly cost of production.[1] Fixed costs include those of training new workers, or social security contributions. The price of inputs climbs higher if a work-time reduction is accompanied by an increase in wage compensation per hour, either due to higher wages, higher fixed cost or higher coordination costs. This can be considered a direct tax on productivity. The conclusion is that reduced working hours reduce firm productivity, output, and hence employment, unless offset by significant reductions in wages (per hour) or counter-improvements in productivity.[2]

Yet this lump-of-labor criticism is partly a straw man. Serious pro-

1 Fitzgerald, T. J. (1996). "Reducing working hours." *Economic Review-Federal Reserve Bank of Cleveland, 32*(4), 13.

2 *Ibid.*

ponents of working hours reduction never claimed that there is a fixed lump sum of labor or that a reduction in working hours will lead to a 1:1 increase in employment.[1] What they argued is that work-sharing will reduce unemployment. This is a much milder proposition. Does it find support in the data?

Intuitively, we know that the transition from the 6- to the 5-day workweek was not accompanied by any unsettling work losses in most countries; rather the opposite. Still, it is possible that other confounding factors increased employment independently, and masked declines that resulted from work-sharing. An evaluation of work-sharing policies in Germany in the 1980's finds that although this produced employment gains of around 1.1%, it remained small relative to the "counterfactual" of 1.7% gains in the US during the same period without any similar policy.[2] Nonetheless, Germany's work-sharing program did produce employment gains even as it maintained monthly wage parity, i.e. it increased hourly wages. This according to the simple model presented above should have had dramatically negative effects on output and employment.

Studies from the employment effects of work-sharing during the Great Depression find that there were employment gains, even if smaller in the long term than anticipated by government. Indeed work-hour reduction during the Great Depression put 2.7 million back to work in the short-term. In the long-term the potential employment gains were offset by an increase in the wage rate, reducing the total gains to 1 million.[3] Still, there were an additional 1 million jobs. As Taylor's study concludes: "Work-sharing, through mandated shorter workweeks, can be an effective short-run tool in combating major episodes of cyclical unemployment." Even if work-sharing had only short-term benefits, these can still be important if they succeeded in keeping active a part of the population that might otherwise fall permanently out of the job market during a crisis. One of the greater risks with the current recession is that a considerable portion of the younger generations stays out of the labor force for such

1 Walker, T. (2007). "Why economists dislike a lump of labor." *Review of Social Economy, 65*(3), 279-291.

2 Hunt, J. (1999). Has work-sharing worked in Germany? *The Quarterly Journal of Economics, 114*(1), 117-148.

3 Taylor, J. E. (2011). "Work-sharing During the Great Depression: Did the "President's Reemployment Agreement' Promote Reemployment?" *Economica, 78*(309), 133-158.

prolonged periods that it might become permanently unemployable.[1]

In the simplistic world of the firm-level model, such sustained gains can only have been the result of counter-improvements in productivity (note that in a Keynesian model the benefits could also have come from the demand-side, the increase in employment and wages causing an increase in demand and output). An important question is the extent to which workers may become more or less productive by working less. For our purposes it is helpful to distinguish between improvements in labor productiveness (e.g. workers being more productive due to acquiring greater skills or due to less exhaustion), capital productiveness (capital becoming more productive through technological progress) and the substitution of labor by capital.[2] Whereas the first increases wages, the second and third suppresses wages and increases profits. Reduced working hours may increase labor productiveness by: reducing the exhaustion of workers in the workplace; concentrating work in the more productive parts of the day and the week (i.e. reducing the hours spent "hanging out" in the office); allowing a more flexible distribution of labor during peak demand hours; liberating time that can be invested in lifelong training and education; liberating time that can be invested in human and social capital; attracting creative workers from abroad who find appeal in a more favorable work-life balance.[3]

Plausibly, work-sharing can also reduce labor productiveness by: entry in the workforce of the less-productive workers; coordination, congestion and transaction costs (more workers per task); less time spent in skill-acquisition through work; loss of workers from abroad who find appeal in harder work—higher earning opportunities. From a firm perspective also the costs of labor may increase as a result of higher fixed costs (social security contributions), higher hourly wages and higher labor costs as unemployment declines.[4] In turn, rising labor costs may prompt substitution of labor by capital and/or energy, and increase in productivity without a rise in labor productiveness, resulting in a reduc-

1 Krugman, P. (2012). *End this depression now!* Norton & Company.
Lee, S., McCann, D., & Messenger, J. C. (2007). "Working time around the world." *Geneva: ILO.*

2 Ashford, R., Hall, R. P., & Ashford, N. A. (2012b). "Broadening capital acquisition with the earnings of capital as a means of sustainable growth and environmental sustainability." *The European Financial Review* (October-November 2012): 70-74.

3 Kallis, G., Kalush, M., O'Flynn, H., Rossiter, J., & Ashford, N. (2013). "'Friday off': reducing working hours in Europe." *Sustainability,* 5(4), 1545-1567.

4 *Ibid.*

tion of employment and wages in the longer term.[1]

The above analysis suggests that it is difficult to predict what will happen in any given case, since it is really hard to foresee how the above factors may play out. Even with reduced output, wages may even increase if reduced working hours increase labor productiveness sufficiently. One can adopt various mathematical formalizations and reductionist models with limiting assumptions to illustrate the conditions under which one or the other outcome might occur. We see little added value in this exercise. Historical observation can be a better basis for policy. History suggests initially large, and, over time, reduced gains in employment with sustained wages. Positive factors seem to dominate overall, but over time are dampened by the rising labor costs and the substitution of labor by capital. If this were the case for the reduction from 6 to 5 days of work, the question is whether it will hold for a further reduction to even less hours. Rather than ambitious proposals such as the 21-hour workweek,[2] we propose a more cautionary, learning-by-doing approach, reducing working hours first by one day, to 32 hours a week. The main attraction of this policy is the short-term boost of employment, even if all else fails.

The French adoption of a 35h workweek was for a while at best a temporary moderate financial success for most workers, but not successful for some, and it had mixed results on conditions of work and gender.[3] Hayden[4] provides a detailed analysis of the implementation of the shorter workweek with some wage retention that was accomplished by reducing the payroll taxes levied on employers. Thus, rather than wage parity maintained by transferring wealth from employers to workers, it was actually accomplished indirectly by transfers from the taxpayers to the workers. Even so, because of concessions in work-time flexibility of hours (including evening and weekend work) that could be demanded—on short notice—by employers of their workers in any particular week, the advantages of extra leisure time was compromised by uncertainty in time demands on workers, especially those that were lower-paid and

1 Rezai, A., Taylor, L., & Mechler, R. (2013). "Ecological macroeconomics: An application to climate change." *Ecological Economics, 85*, 69-76.

2 Coote, A., Franklin, J., & Simms, A. (2010). *21 hours: Why a shorter working week can help us all to flourish in the 21st century.* London: New Economics Foundation.

3 Ashford, N. A., Hall, R. P., & Ashford, R. H. (2012a). "The crisis in employment and consumer demand: Reconciliation with environmental sustainability." *Environmental Innovation and Societal Transitions, 2*, 1-22.

4 Hayden, A. (2006). "France's 35-Hour Week: Attack on Business? Win-Win Reform? Or Betrayal of Disadvantaged Workers?" *Politics & Society, 34*(4), 503-542.

less-skilled, as well as reductions in overtime pay. The overall level of employment was essentially unaffected.[1]

The case in favor of reduced working hours is stronger if one adopts a broader view of welfare that extends beyond purchasing power. A reduction of output and consumption is not necessarily bad, if Daly[2] is right, and economic growth in advanced economies has become uneconomical, i.e., it has more social costs than benefits. Reducing the deleterious effects of climate change is a good reason for reducing output. The question is whether output and consumption can be reduced while increasing welfare, what has been called "sustainable degrowth".[3] Liberating time from work for leisure is likely to increase welfare, not least by liberating time that can be invested in social, human, or cultural capital. At the individual level empirical estimates point to an inverse relationship between working hours and life satisfaction or happiness when other individual characteristics have been controlled for, with greater benefits for men.[4] Alesina et al.[5] use data on individual life-satisfaction from GSOEP, a German survey, and comparative national data for European countries from the Eurobarometer, in both cases finding that fewer hours worked are correlated with greater life satisfaction, controlling for other factors, such as income. They show that the negative relationship between hours worked across countries and life satisfaction holds for the international comparison after using collective bargaining agreements as an instrument, in this way addressing reverse causality concerns, i.e. the possibility that it might be happier people (or nations) that choose to work less. These empirical findings suggest that Europeans might obtain a higher level of welfare with fewer hours spent at work. The satisfaction from working less is likely to increase if there is coordination in the timing of the free days; people generally prefer to go on holidays together, or spend weekends together. This "social multiplier" effect [the utility of leisure

1 Estevao, M., & Sa, F. (2008). "The 35-hour workweek in France: Straightjacket or welfare improvement?" *Economic Policy, 23*(55), 418-463.

2 Daly, H. (2013). "A further critique of growth economics." *Ecological Economics, 88*, 20-24.

3 Kallis, G. (2011). "In defence of degrowth." *Ecological Economics, 70*(5), 873-880.

4 Pouwels, B., Siegers, J., & Vlasblom, J. D. (2008). "Income, working hours, and happiness." *Economics Letters, 99*(1), 72-74.

5 Alesina, A. F., Glaeser, E. L., & Sacerdote, B. (2006). "Work and Leisure in the US and Europe: Why so Different?" *NBER Macroeconomics Annual 2005, Volume 20* (pp. 1-100): MIT Press.

rising in the quantity of leisure consumed by peers[1]] might amplify the benefits of shortening the workweek from five to four days. It offers a basis for government intervention and for coordinating the liberated time around, say, an extra day off (e.g. "Friday off" or "Saint Monday"). Of course, the extent to which the newly adjusted weekly wage can provide an adequate access to essential goods and services will greatly influence the outcome.

In conclusion, a reduction in working hours with the maintenance of weekly wages could very well increase employment for previously unemployed people, as well as improve employment and living conditions for existing workers by increasing leisure without a loss in earning capacity. In a period of crisis where workers experience losses on all fronts, such non-monetary welfare gains are an extra reason for reducing working hours.

Benefits for the environment

The recent reincarnation of work-sharing proposals has come from environmentalists, but the environmental benefits of reduced working hours are not immediately evident. First, by tightening labor markets and increasing wages, more capital may substitute for workers, increasing energy and resource intensity.[2] Second, if work-sharing redistributes income and earning capacity to people with lower incomes, then consumption may increase given the increased propensity for consumption by low-income groups. Third, leisure is not necessarily environmentally benign. When Henry Ford gave Saturday off to his workers, his objective was that they buy more and travel with his cars, not that they consume less. It is not clear that if people got more free time and leisure; this would be directed to less resource-intensive activities. In general, leisure can be consumption-intensive and the leisure services offered by the market are resource intensive: if more leisure time is offered with no change in preferences, then resource consumption may potentially increase as a result. To put it metaphorically, the office lights may be off, but those of the hotel room will be on.[3]

None of the above outcomes is inevitable, however. First, if as a re-

1 Alesina, A. F., Glaeser, E. L., & Sacerdote, B. (2006). "Work and Leisure in the US and Europe: Why so Different?" *NBER Macroeconomics Annual 2005, Volume 20* (pp. 1-100): MIT Press.

2 Kallis, G., Kalush, M., O'Flynn, H., Rossiter, J., & Ashford, N. (2013). "'Friday off': reducing working hours in Europe." *Sustainability*, 5(4), 1545-1567.

3 *Ibid.*

sult of reduced working hours workers could become more productive (i.e. an increase in labor productiveness), then the increased wages need not lead to a substitution of workers by capital or energy. Also if energy and resource prices increase, due to natural or imposed scarcity (e.g. CO^2 caps) or green taxes, the inverse will be true, i.e. the relative cost advantage of employing workers over capital or energy will likely increase. Price volatility is important here. General price (market) volatility favors capital over workers, since it is less costly to leave a machine idle than fire workers in times of low demand, or hire less-productive contingent labor in times of increased demand. But if there is excessively high volatility in energy and trade (transportation) costs, then labor is likely to be more favored. The predominating effect may not initially be known.

Second, on the one hand, reducing working hours will reduce output and some consumption by previously employed workers, assuming unchanged labor productiveness. For the environment this may be good: less will be produced, and less will be available to consume. On the other hand, if more workers are hired, they will also increase demand and output and this may have the opposite effect.

Third, while the poor tend to consume a comparatively higher share of their income, the wealthier tend to save and invest a greater portion of it. It is not evident that decreased saving/investment is more environmentally beneficial than increased consumption by newly hired, and previously poor workers. If a reduction of savings leads to less extractive projects than otherwise would be the case, then the net environmental effect of less saving may be positive. More earning capacity for the poor through work-sharing does not necessarily lead to more use of environmental resources in the aggregate.

Fourth, it is unknown whether liberated time (for workers previously working five days) changes leisure-related consumption patterns in ways that are environmentally beneficial. One possibility is that the liberated time is directed toward low-intensity convivial activities (walking, reading, playing with friends). In addition, households scarce in time tend to use more timesaving appliances and technologies, which in general tend to be more environmentally intensive (even if more efficient per unit of product delivered). Transport and food preparation are two obvious cases where time compression is linked to more intense resource use. Fewer hours spent at work means reduced transport demand and reduced consumption (of energy, water, etc.) at the workplace.[1] Assuming that production and service facilities will also operate fewer hours, then reduced working hours are likely to lead to less energy spent on public and office buildings and a decline of commuting, which are sources of greenhouse gas emissions.[2] Of course, all these effects must be compared to the case of having a larger number of workers performing the work, with all their work-related costs and changes in their total consumption accounted for.

What does the empirical evidence show? There is tentative evidence suggesting that a decrease in working hours correlates positively with a reduction in ecological footprint and energy consumption per capita after controlling for factors such as labor productivity, labor participation rate, climate, and population.[3] These studies however do not control for inverse causality—that is, the possibility that it is, say, a degradation of the environment that makes people work more—or "omitted variable bias"—that is, a change in a third variable, such as wages, which affects both the amount of hours worked and the damage to the environment. The only study that has used methods better suited to reduce the error from these effects, with data for 29 high-income OECD countries, finds that shorter work hours tend to have lower ecological footprints, carbon footprints, and carbon dioxide emissions.[4]The tentative evidence therefore suggests that working hours correlate positively with ecological footprint and energy consumption per capita after controlling for factors such as labor productivity, labor participation rate, and climate.

If a working hours policy is accompanied by a policy of shifting taxes from labor to consumption (or energy, or pollution), then it is more likely that reducing working hours will be good for the environment. This will favor convivial over material consumption, as well as investment in

---

1 Kallis, G., Kalush, M., O'Flynn, H., Rossiter, J., & Ashford, N. (2013). "'Friday off': reducing working hours in Europe." *Sustainability, 5*(4), 1545-1567.
Knight, K., Rosa, E. A., & Schor, J. B. (2013). 12. "Reducing growth to achieve environmental sustainability: the role of work hours." *Capitalism on Trial: Explorations in the Tradition of Thomas E. Weisskopf*, 187.

2 This depends crucially though on the "social multiplier effect" and coordination between workers on common days-off; if with work-sharing there is no change in the actual hours and days that offices or shops are open, reduced working hours may lead to more employees, and hence more commuting, per hour worked.

3 Hayden, A., & Shandra, J. M. (2009). "Hours of work and the ecological footprint of nations: an exploratory analysis." *Local Environment, 14*(6), 575-600.
Rosnick, D., & Weisbrot, M. (2007). "Are shorter work hours good for the environment? A comparison of US and European energy consumption." *International Journal of Health Services, 37*(3), 405-417.

4 Kallis, G., Kalush, M., O'Flynn, H., Rossiter, J., & Ashford, N. (2013). "'Friday off': reducing working hours in Europe." *Sustainability, 5*(4), 1545-1567.

low-intensity over high resource-intensity projects.[1] Furthermore, the reduction of labor taxes will reduce the costs of labor making employment gains more likely.

Conclusion

Can a reduction of working hours provide for increases in employment and earning capacity and a healthier economy without leading to a growth of environmentally-damaging production and consumption? This article has revealed how complicated this question is. Predictions of policies that focus on working hours can only be made if we start with assumptions about how workers would use their free time (e.g. in environmentally friendly ways), what effects reduced hours will have on labor productiveness and labor costs, how wages/incomes and the number of workers employed would change, and how the implementation or enforcement of a work hour reduction might vary by industry, occupation, or firm size. In addition, the effects of a work hour reduction would depend heavily on union bargaining power and environmental and social policies, such as lifelong education programs or green taxes that might simultaneously be enacted to influence how workers use their additional free time and how firms and workers respond to the new limits on work hours. We conclude that mainstream economists and neo-liberal politicians who are eager to dismiss the reduction of working hours, or propose to increase them, are wrong, but that so may be those in the environmental camp who call for reductions in working hours without taking into account the effects that could make such policies ineffective and counterproductive to their own objectives.

Yet, beyond this complexity, there is a strong argument that in economies that progress technologically and in which capital gets more and more productive, workers should work less and less. However, in order to ensure that workers and poor people have the financial means to acquire an adequate supply of essential goods and services, either wages need to increase or workers and the poor need to be given access to capital ownership.[2] Prior to the burst of the financial bubble in 2008, this was happening less and less because the surplus was reinvested in new goods

1 Kallis, G., Kalush, M., O'Flynn, H., Rossiter, J., & Ashford, N. (2013). "'Friday off': reducing working hours in Europe." *Sustainability, 5*(4), 1545-1567.

2 Ashford, R., Hall, R. P., & Ashford, N. A. (2012b). "Broadening capital acquisition with the earnings of capital as a means of sustainable growth and environmental sustainability." *The European Financial Review* (October-November 2012): 70-74.

and more consumption, rather than more leisure and increases in wages. If economic output were not a goal in and of itself for a nation, then the main concern with reduced working hours, i.e. that it might reduce output, is not necessarily bad since workers may have the same earning capacity and more free time. In other words, productivity gains could be directed to free time and not further accumulation, which is damaging for the environment. The questions are: what will currently employed workers do with their liberated time, and what will newly hired workers consume? If material and energy-intensive goods and services are consumed, environmental gains may be limited. If more consumption results instead in convivial activities, then the net effect may be positive. Ecological taxes or investments in convivial infrastructures—such as, for example, playgrounds or public squares, or in educational and cultural activities—can further shift consumption in favor of low-intensity environmentally benign activities.

Simply mandating a reduction of working time is not sufficient. First, it is important to ensure with government policies that the reduction in working hours is not achieved at the expense of workers or the poor: reduction of working hours should come without a decline in wages. Second, given that more free time with equal wages may lead to more material consumption, additional policies are necessary to shift incentives in favor of convivial, environmentally friendly consumption. Finally, given that we live in a world that is far from optimal or ideal, any policy of reducing working hours is likely to have unintended and undesired effects. For example, if the policy is not implemented as well for service workers, then manual workers and public employees may lose as a result (emulating the case in France). Also if the policy leads to capital and energy substituting for workers, or if factories or services move elsewhere where workers are cheaper and work longer hours—or environmental concerns are minimized—then employment, wages, and environmental conditions stand to lose.

We propose therefore the reduction of working hours be implemented initially as an interim measure to relieve unemployment, and over time improved through trial and error as other structural changes (in taxation, increasing working and poor people's access to capital and also investment of convivial infrastructures) are instituted. An interim trial and error approach makes sense since, in a future of expensive energy, capital productiveness may decrease, not increase, and we might have to work more again, rather than less.

17. Barcelona's new commons

Author's note: This short piece was written for an editorial page for scientists at Catalonia's biggest newspaper La Vanguardia *(Neus Casajuana translated it to Spanish). The idea behind the editorial page was that scientists from Catalonia's Universities could share short insights from their own research. These editorials have a limit of 400 words, hence the brevity. In the article I argue that Barcelona en Comú, the radical left wing movement party that surprisingly won the city's elections, embodies the theory of the commons.* La Vanguardia *did not accept the article, and I submitted it to the Huffington Post where it was published and shared over 5,000 times. I was told that the newspaper was looking for something more "scientific" for this page, while my article was political.*

Barcelona has become Europe's capital of technological innovation. Barcelona en Comú also stands to make it a capital of social innovation. The theory of the commons is the most novel idea of the 21st century. Nobel laureate in economics Elinor Ostrom showed that the commons do not inevitably end up in tragedy and they do not have to be privatized or managed by the state. The communities she studied, more often than not, found ways to pool efforts together, devise their own institutions, and govern their shared resources sustainably.

Barcelona en Comú is all about reclaiming the city as a commons. Its program intends to recuperate water and energy services as a commons. It wants to institute a community currency and secure a citizens' income for all. It promotes the sharing of bikes and cars, and reclaims public spaces like the Diagonal Avenue to convert them into green commons, alongside a flourishing network of urban gardens. It wants to relocalize and grow a cooperative economy. It puts common care work at the center, increasing the number of guarderias publicas (public childcare centers). It sees culture as a commons and wants to make Barcelona a city of open software. And it wants to involve the public in municipal budgeting and auditing, as it involved it in the making of its electoral program.

If it succeeds in this, Barcelona may well become Europe's first genuine sharing economy. Economists' 19th century concern with how to produce more monetary wealth is obsolete. 21st century economics will be about how to prosper without growth. Advanced economies are facing a future of secular stagnation. Growth is not only harder to come by, but ecologically unsustainable, destroying the climate and ecosystems. Prosperity requires finding new ways to equitably share the abundant wealth that we already produce. Instead of Pharaonic infrastructures that damage the environment and drain the public budget, we need small and affordable interventions that make a city livable for everyone. In our research on degrowth we study the effects of innovative proposals from an ecological finance, to a basic income, a reduction of the working week or alternative money, and exchange and food networks.

It is exciting to live in a city where these novel ideas will be put into practice.

18. The "sharing" economy is not a commons

Author's note: This piece was inspired from discussions with my partner Amalia who was, at the time, doing a PhD in Media & Communication at the London School of Economics. Amalia was studying the formation of trust in the so-called "sharing economy". One of her interests was how companies like AirBnb mobilize a discourse of "community" and "sharing" as part of their business strategies, and more specifically, the role of this sense of community in building an environment of trust without which these platforms would never work. After I wrote the piece criticizing AirBnb and its discourse of a "sharing" community, I had several discussions with friends who were subletting their flats or apartments at AirBnb trying to explain to me why they do it, and justifying themselves. Well, they didn't need to do any explaining. I do the same. With my family back in Greece we offer both our summer home and our principal home in Athens on AirBnb. Without the income from AirBnb, my family would not be able to pay the increasing property taxes and maintain the houses, given the dramatic reduction in their pension. My point in the article was not a moralistic one blaming those who rent at AirBnb. My point was to understand AirBnb for what it is, i.e. not a sharing economy, but a major and super-profitable corporation (I guess this is a quite obvious point by now, though it was less so then; I remember a friend that I met in the degrowth conference in 2010 in Barcelona sending me an email telling me what an amazing sharing experiment AirBnb was, and encouraging me to "join" it). The problem is not in those of us who rent our houses at AirBnb. The problem is the system that makes it necessary for us to do so.

Over 300 thousand homes and rooms were rented out the previous year via the AirBnb website, hosting some 4 million people worldwide. When I decided to help my parents rent our vacation home in the island of Syros, I was shocked to find every second home in the vicinity of ours already posted on AirBnb. It wouldn't be a gross exaggeration to say that half of Greece this summer (2013) was up "for rent" on AirBnb's pages.

AirBnb, and other sites such as Uber—where drivers car-share with passengers for short routes in town—or, Greek-origin Cookisto—where amateur cooks deliver home-cooked meals—are part of a phenomenon that has been dubbed "the sharing economy". As the title of Rachel Botsman's book tellingly puts it, in this new economy "what's mine is yours".[1] I offer my house, and you offer yours. You cook for me, or I can cook for someone else. Use takes the place of ownership.

Instead of buying new consumer goods, in this "sharing economy" we supposedly collaborate to share goods that we already have, when we do not need them: from rooms, houses, cars and bikes, to appliances, drills, or even dogs (in BorrowMyDoggy). Of course, borrowing, lending and doing small favors are not new phenomena. What is new is the scale in which these can now take place. The new online social networking platforms allow exchanges not only between friends and neighbors, but between complete strangers, from different parts of the world.

As with everything new under capitalism, creation brings destruction. The new economy is disrupting existing industries. In June 2014, London grinded to a halt, due to a strike held by 10 thousand taxi drivers[2] who demonstrated with their vehicles in the city center against Uber, whose low prices are threatening to put them out of business. In theory, Uber drivers were supposed to be everyday people who decide to make an extra buck by taking a passenger with them in their rides. In reality, most drivers are former taxi drivers who are exploiting the legal gap and drive without having to pay for insurance or for a license.

For similar reasons, in New York or San Francisco, hoteliers accuse AirBnb[3] of unfair competition. Its hosts do not pay municipal taxes, do not have to meet expensive safety regulations, and can operate wherever they want, and outside the zones set out by planning authorities for tourism activities.

It is hard to sympathize with taxi drivers or hoteliers, or lament that the prices of these, often overpriced, services are going down as a result of the "sharing economy". However, there is a deeper issue at stake here. Laws and regulations exist for a reason. Municipal taxes finance the public infrastructure that is then used by tourists. Planning authorities limit the number of "rooms to let" or the taxis in a city, because otherwise life can become unbearable for the inhabitants of the city.

---

1 Botsman, R., & Rogers, R. (2010) *What's mine is yours: The Rise of Collaborative Consumption*. New York, USA: Harper Business.

2 Sparkes, M. (2014). "London cab drivers promise 'chaos' in strike over Uber app." *The Telegraph*. Retrieved from http://www.telegraph.co.uk/technology/news/10888838/London-cab-drivers-promise-chaos-in-strike-over-Uber-app.html

3 McGarvey, R. (2014, 2 July). "Airbnb smackdown: Hoteliers go to war and you are the winner." *Main Street*. Retrieved from https://www.mainstreet.com/article/airbnb-smackdown-hoteliers-go-war-and-you-are-winner

I have many friends in Barcelona who have experienced a total transformation of their apartment blocks, suddenly finding themselves alone within AirBnb rentals, unable to sleep from the parties of weekend travelers. Rental prices in the center of Barcelona are sky-rocketing, as owners find it more profitable to rent through AirBnb than lease their apartments long-term. New "entrepreneurs" raise real estate prices, renting apartments that they then sublet on AirBnb.

Zoning restrictions for new hotels was a key site of struggle for Barcelona's neighbourhood movements. But all this has now become irrelevant by the unregulated avalanche of AirBnb houses popping up literally everywhere and changing the form and composition of the city.

Regulatory authorities are slowly catching up. In Barcelona, municipal authorities fined AirBnb with the symbolic sum of €30 thousand for advertising apartments that did not have rental permits. After a public backlash against unregulated rentals in the neighbourhood of Barceloneta this August, with spontaneous citizens' protests, the municipality has started a door-to-door check, closing down rented apartments[1] that lack a permit. In New York, authorities have begun evicting people who sublet apartments that do not belong to them, whereas in San Francisco authorities file lawsuits against short-term rentals that violate the law.

AirBnb and other companies which have come under the attention of regulators, such as Uber, respond that over-legislation is threatening to kill innovation at its birth. If, in order to rent out a room or give a ride, one has to get a license like a hotel or a taxi, then these sharing activities become economically impossible.

AirBnb is running a huge advertising campaign in New York,[2] reminding New Yorkers of the benefits it offers to them, not least the income. Mobilizing their so-called "communities", companies like AirBnb or Uber are organizing counter-protests, involving their users. This discourse of "community" and "sharing" is instrumental not only for mobilizing people in regulatory battles, under the guise of a romantic battle for a different economy, but is also essential in building up a case, that these ventures are not like any other capitalist venture, and therefore merit a different treatment from the regulators. But is this so?

1 Pellicer, L. (2014, 16 July). "Barcelona's crackdown on Airbnb renters." *El País*. Retrieved from http://elpais.com/elpais/2014/07/16/inenglish/1405501012_966041.html

2 Gokey, M. (2014). "AirBnB's new ad campaign aims to convince New Yorkers it's good for their city." *Digital Trends*. Retrieved from http://www.digitaltrends.com/mobile/airbnbs-new-ad-campaign-new-york-city/

According to the advocates of the "sharing economy", the social benefits of their ventures are manifold. Firstly, environmental: rather than buying newly produced cars or blenders, one can rent and use the ones that are already available. More sharing means less new, environmentally damaging production, advocates argue. AirBnb houses consume less energy than hotels.

Secondly, the new economy increases socialization. Instead of staying at a corporate hotel, one can lodge at someone's home, meet their family and get acquainted with the habits of their country. No longer alienated consumers, we become "peers"; or "prosumers", people who both produce and consume, and in the process connect with each other.

Finally, there are the economic benefits. According to advocates, productive forces (e.g. unused houses or cars) that would otherwise remain economically inactive are put into circulation. The efficiency of the economy increases. The cost of services such as lodging or transport go down, while a new source of income becomes available to the financially-battered low and middle income classes. According to AirBnb, the average host in San Francisco (the city where the website began and has been operational for more years) earns roughly $9,300 each year.[1] It's no coincidence that AirBnb is now flourishing in crisis-hit southern Europe.

On the other hand, the case for a special treatment by regulators seems weak, if one considers other factors. First, AirBnb itself is a capitalistic corporation like any other, valued at $10 billion. Its profits—dozens of millions today—are forecast to reach an estimated $1 billion per year in the coming years. AirBnb is a company with only 600 employees (at the time of writing), with relatively low costs (related to software development and operation), but with a potentially huge market under its reach.

This is a company that can potentially control the global market for short-term rentals, charging a 10-15% commission in each and every exchange. Online social networks are not only bringing people from faraway together, but are also creating global markets, where only local segmented markets existed before. The profits from these markets are astronomical, unlike anything a real estate agent would ever dream of, and are concentrated in the pockets of a few entrepreneurs and venture capitalists, a phenomenon with probably little precedent in history. Tellingly, but somewhat exaggeratingly, this has led some to call companies like AirBnb, a "mafia of intermediaries".

1 Geron, T. (2012). "Airbnb Had $56 Million Impact On San Francisco: Study." *Forbes*. Retrieved from http://www.forbes.com/sites/tomiogeron/2012/11/09/study-airbnb-had-56-million-impact-on-san-francisco/

Second, most of the transactions taking place under AirBnb are pure rentals, involving money. It is a euphemism to call them "sharing" and hence argue that they should not be regulated or taxed. They are normal economic transactions. Where is the sharing in renting at AirBnb, and why is it "peer-to-peer" when you rent at AirBnb but not when you rent in the rental market?

In the rental economy of AirBnb a whole suit of small scale intermediaries are popping up, from those who rent houses and then sublet them through AirBnb, to companies who take care of everything that needs to be done for renting your house at AirBnb (from furnishing it, to managing the listing), for a cut on the deal. It's one thing to host someone in your home with the prospect of someday being hosted in theirs too, and another one to rent or pay to rent.

Third, and worst of all, under a rhetoric guise of "sharing", websites like AirBnb or Uber are creating a new informal economy of uninsured workers whose entire life is up for rent, from cars and homes, to their own hands available to perform chores for a fee in sites like "taskrabbit". Entire professions—cab drivers, cleaners, etc.—are passing into a new black market—unregulated, tax-free, and uninsured. And instead of (or alongside) the much-touted socialization and community, the result is the commodification of the final shreds of social life that had remained outside the economy.

Everything now is available for rent, at the right price; from empty rooms to an unused frying pan. Nothing any more is available for free. Hosting a friend at your house has an "opportunity cost", eroding the value of hospitality.

The rental economy of AirBnb is not the same as the real sharing economy of urban gardens, time banks, or couchsurfing, where users truly share their work, their resources, and their assets, without the intermediation of money—and crucially without profit. The rental economy is the inevitable—within capitalism—commodified version of the sharing economy. As the crisis opened opportunities for new forms of mutual aid and sharing, enterprises such as AirBnb saw the opportunity to monetise them and profit.

As for the environment, I am not sure that leaving nothing idle is all that good. The "sharing economy" mobilizes and puts everything into circulation, retaining, at all costs, an unsustainable consumption model. Uber's taxis constantly roaming around for clients; this is not my view of a sustainable future.

In conclusion: AirBnb is a rental intermediary. It is a capitalistic enterprise like any other and a very innovative and successful one at that. It should be treated, regulated, zoned and taxed as such. The same applies for those who profit from it. Exemptions could be made for those who do not use it professionally or do not make money from it (this can easily be ascertained by the frequency, duration and value of the services offered as the websites document everything).

Renting is not sharing: it should be regulated and taxed.

19. A Pope for degrowth

Author's note: This was my second attempt for a scientific opinion piece at La Vanguardia, *this time successful. I guess it is one thing to praise the Pope and another one Ada Colau.*

In his recent Encyclical on the environment, Pope Francis writes that "[it has become] easy to accept the idea of infinite or unlimited growth, which proves so attractive to economists, financiers and experts in technology. It is based on the lie that there is an infinite supply of the earth's goods, and this leads to the planet being squeezed dry beyond every limit." He concludes that "the time has come to accept decreased growth in some parts of the world, in order to provide resources for other places to experience healthy growth."[1]

This time the Pope has science on his side. Ecological economists have proven that the miraculous growth of the 20th century would have been impossible without the bonanza of cheap oil. Yet growth has costs. Studies of happiness and genuine progress confirm the Pope's claim that "the growth of the past two centuries has not always led to an integral development and an improvement in the quality of life."[2] Since the 1970s, in most advanced countries GDP has grown, but happiness and wellbeing have stagnated together with wages. Growth has become uneconomic, economist Herman Daly argues.

Climate change will be disastrous, scientists warn us, and there is no doubt that it is caused by the carbon our growing economies emit faster and faster. We can fantasize all we want about carbon markets, geo-engineering, or solar panels in Sahara, but up to now the only factor that probably reduces carbon emissions is de-growth.

Degrowth is politically impossible, I am often told. As the Pope puts it, "A politics concerned with immediate results, supported by consumerist sectors of the population, is driven to produce short-term growth." Yet it is more than that. Lack of growth in economies that are designed to either grow or die can be catastrophic. But it doesn't have to. There are alternatives for "prosperity without growth": sharing work, instituting a basic and a maximum income, reallocating public resources and investments, taxing carbon not work, capping carbon emissions, or limiting

1 Francis, P. (2015). "Laudato si: On care for our common home." Retrieved from http://w2.vatican.va/content/francesco/en/encyclicals/documents/papa-francesco_20150524_enciclica-laudato-si.html

2 *Ibid.*

the creation of money by private banks.

Many non-believers would agree with the Pope that "[i]t is a return to that simplicity which allows us to stop and appreciate the small things" and that "[s]uch sobriety, when lived freely and consciously, is liberating."[1] Creating the conditions in which more and more people can live simple and fulfilled lives requires transformative political change. And an end to the self-destructive pursuit of more and more growth.

1 Francis, P. (2015). "Laudato si: On care for our common home." Retrieved from http://w2.vatican.va/content/francesco/en/encyclicals/documents/papa-francesco_20150524_enciclica-laudato-si.html

20. A society without growth: The planet of *The Dispossessed*

Author's note: In 2012, the Centre for Humans and Nature invited a group of ecological economists, myself among them, to write a short essay responding to the question "How can we create a successful economy without economic growth?" A few years back, my Berkeley friend and colleague Lee Worden had introduced me to the world of Ursula Le Guin, and I was always struck by the similarities between the anarchist planet of Anarres in her novel The Dispossessed, *and the visions of the future pre-figured in the degrowth literature. After I wrote this essay I decided to conduct more serious research on Le Guin, and I found out that there is a huge amount of literature written on her work, and* The Dispossessed *more specifically, including treatises on the ideas of the book about environment, scarcity, or growth. None other than Andre Gorz had also noted that Anarres is one of the liveliest depictions ever written of an ecological anarcho-communist society with all its seductions and snares. My thoughts on the novel and on the radical geographies that it is pre-figuring were published in a joint article with Hug March in the academic journal of the American Association of Geographers.*[1] *It is one of my articles I am most proud of. This blog piece is a simpler and earlier version of the full article.*

Disciplined as a scientist, my imagination is poor. Listing the various proposals that are springing up from the degrowth movement and pretending that they form a coherent vision would not be sincere. It would also be boring. Let me then describe the vision of someone with a richer imagination.

Welcome to Anarres, the planet of "the dispossessed" in Ursula K. Le Guin's award-winning (social) science fiction of the same name.[2] After a revolution in the Earth-like planet Urras, revolutionaries organized a mass exodus to settle the nearby planet Anarres. But it is a barren, dry place:

1 Kallis, G., and March, H. "Imaginaries of hope: The utopianism of degrowth." *Annals of the Association of American Geographers* 105, no. 2 (2015): 360-368.

2 Ursula K. Le Guin is one of the most prolific and successful science fiction writers. Her fantasy of alternative social worlds is not coincidental: Le Guin is the daughter of one of the founding fathers of modern anthropology, Alfred Kroeber.
Le Guin, U. (1974). *The Dispossessed*. New York: Harper & Row.

> Humans fitted themselves with care and risk into its narrow ecology. If they fished, but not too greedily, and if they cultivated, using mainly organic wastes for fertilizer, they could fit in. But they could not fit anybody else in. There was no grass for herbivores. There were no herbivores for carnivores. There were no insects to fecundate flowering plants; the imported fruit trees were all hand-fertilized.[1]

On Anarres, wind is used to produce energy. Water and heat are scarce and economized with great care. Nothing goes to waste; everything is recycled.

Settlers brought with them values that helped them survive in this limited biosphere. Mutual aid through sharing and giving are the organizing social principles. There is no private property on Anarres. People "have," they do not "own." "Egoizing" is a major curse and "profiteering" from exchange is considered the ultimate anti-social behavior.

In Anarres there is a patchwork quilt of small urban centers with peripheral settlements. Each settlement follows the principle of an "organic economy," aiming to survive to the extent possible with its bioregional resources—the water, wind, and soil in its vicinity. When this is not enough, resources move between locales according to need. There are no borders on Anarres, nor local identities; individuals can—and constantly do—move between settlements. No need, therefore, to capture and control resources or cheat about your needs.

The scarce amenities in the towns are shared. There are no private houses, but dormitories with common rooms that house four to five people each. There are also single rooms for couples or families that prefer privacy. There are big dining commons organized by each dormitory or run by worker cooperatives, and professional associations for their workers. There are plenty of open public spaces and playgrounds, with dry sand, of course. The little water is shared in public baths, where people meet and socialize daily. People move using electric trains and small buses. There are plenty of bicycles and a few cars that are shared by all citizens. Traveling takes days, and so does communication by post. Manufacturing workshops are located in the towns, their doors open to the main squares of the cities.

Production is organized in voluntary cooperatives and associations. Each individual has the freedom to associate with or start her own productive enterprise. There is no profit to be made or property to be capitalized and, hence, no incentive to expand beyond what gives everyday

1 Le Guin, U. (1974). *The Dispossessed*. New York: Harper & Row, page 186

satisfaction and fulfillment. Every ten days, each Anarresti must devote one day to communal work. People work six to eight days of every ten, for four to seven hours a day. Working is voluntary, but almost everyone works, as there is little else to do and strong contempt for those who don't. A central computer matches workers' preferences for job placement with the needs of different cooperatives. People specialize, developing their own skills, but also contribute regularly to common tasks of cleaning, building, and maintaining public infrastructure. Every four years, an Anarresi has to spend six months reforesting the desert or accomplishing some other major public work. There are no wages. The basic needs of food, housing, heating, and transport are collectively provided; people use their creativity to provide for the rest. Resource allocation is coordinated by a central committee with subdivisions in the various settlements. It provides food directly to the dinner commons and organizes the construction of public works. The members of the committee are drawn by lottery, while more permanent members are democratically elected; none stays in power for an extended period of time.

Arts, pure sciences, and the humanities thrive on Anarres. Since there is no profit to be made or intellectual property, there is no applied science, and productive technology has no reason to advance. Anarresi brought with them technology, equipment, and advanced knowledge from Urras. They have preserved and renewed these resources but have not expanded them.

Anarres has no military or police. What, then, holds it all together? No one threatens to invade Anarres, as there is nothing to gain and no one wants to live there. As there is no property, there is also no theft. The community contains the occasional individual violence. Make no mistake; there are plenty of indirect punishments and sanctions for anti-social behavior, and a strong communal ethic and set of norms keeps everyone in line. Those who free-ride and "egoize" or who wish to own things are ostracized from the community. They are free to move out of the town, but if they want to own, they are on their own—no collective provisioning exists for those that the Anarresi call "privateers."

Life is hard, dirty, and frugal by Urras' standards. But the Anarresi have one another and are connected by their common past and fate. In good years, there are plenty of festivities to burn and enjoy the surplus (there is no accumulation for investment on Anarres). In bad years, though, when the drought hits, rationing applies and people may be posted to jobs they hate. The Anarresi very seldom go hungry, but when they do, they go hungry all together.

Anarres is not an Eden. Everything is transparent on Anarres, and there is no hiding from the gaze of others unless by departure. Anarres is not a place for the secluded, the lonely, or the individualistic. For those ostracized, Anarres is hell. And for those wishing to differ and push the frontiers of knowledge or of their individual creativity, Anarres can be stifling. Power has been horizontalized, but unavoidably, some individuals have gotten privileged access to the core institutions of distribution. And with every drought, bureaucracy expands and eats more and more of the scope for voluntary association. There is no police force or physical violence, but rather a brutal, invisible mental police, a common rationality, and a network of norms that makes everyone stick to their duty even when they think they are free. But everything is also up for grabs. Permanent revolution is the motto of collectives that emerge to openly criticize centralization, the Central Committee, and the emerging elites in order to create their own alternative structures.

Is Anarres a utopia or a dystopia? Is it a degrowth vision? Is it a future that appeals to me, or is it a post-apocalyptic landscape that I predict Earth is heading toward?

The achievement of Le Guin is that she presents neither a utopia nor a dystopia. She describes an alternatively organized human society as is, with its goods and bads, or snares and seductions as Andre Gorz called them.[1] Science fiction is not predicting where we are heading, or dictating where we should go; it opens up possibilities to our imagination. Le Guin welcomes us to think how our life could look if we did not have property, money, or government and if we had to live within ecological limits. The point is not that we should live without money or property or to predict that we are heading toward an ecological catastrophe. The point is simply to force us to think the unthinkable. And having "seen it" in our minds, to consider again what we could change now, without boundaries to our imaginations.[2]

Many of the ideas Le Guin weaves together—worksharing; reduced work hours; co-housing, transport, and consumption sharing; horizontal and direct forms of decision-making; ecological limits and bioregionalism; open borders; cooperatives of production and consumption; tech-

1 For a more academic discussion of Le Guin's approach, underlying politics, and contribution, see: Davis, L. and P. Stillman, Eds. (2005). *The new utopian politics of Ursula K. Le Guin's The dispossessed.* Lexington Books.

2 For an excellent academic treatise of utopian thinking and its role in politics and current debates over socio-ecological alternatives, see Harvey, D. (2000). *Spaces of hope.* University of California Press.

nological preservation rather than advancement; frugality and festival destruction of surplus—feature in degrowth debates.[1] Some are already practiced; in Barcelona, where I write, we have an excellent municipal system of bikesharing and a thriving sector of producer-consumer organic food cooperatives. The people who took to the squares of Barcelona in the 15M (or "occupy") movement called for direct democracy and practiced horizontal forms of decision-making. I do believe that the future of a prosperous non-growing economy passes inevitably through such initiatives and reforms, even if the end result cannot—and does not need to—look exactly like Anarres.

Is Anarres an appealing future? For those practicing degrowth in various eco-communes and co-housing initiatives in Europe and the Americas, there must be something strikingly familiar to life on Anarres.[2] Despite what to others would seem to be hardship, they enjoy the way they live, as do the people of Anarres. Ultimately, the beauty of Anarres is in the eye of the beholder. Having gone through the 350 pages of the novel, I side with the protagonist, who at the end prefers to live and fight for change on Anarres rather than on Urras. You should read, think, and decide for yourself.

---

1 After reading *The Dispossessed*, I came upon a footnote in a book by eco-philosopher André Gorz, considered one of the intellectual referents of the degrowth movement, who also thought that Le Guin's Anarres is the most lively and fleshed out description he had seen of a frugal, non-growing, non-hierarchical society. Interestingly, Gorz was rejecting in his essay an Anarres-type possibility of a drastic simplification of contemporary complex societies. He called instead for radical eco-social-democratic reforms within the current mode of organization, confining capitalist relations to a limited sphere of industrial production.

2 Cattaneo, C., & Gavaldà, M. (2010). "The experience of rurban squats in Collserola, Barcelona: what kind of degrowth?" *Journal of Cleaner Production, 18*(6), 581-589. Lietaert, M. (2010). "Cohousing's relevance to degrowth theories." *Journal of Cleaner Production, 18*(6), 576-580.

"If Egypt started with one cubic meter of possessions and grew them by 4.5% per year, by the end of its 3,000-year civilization, it would need 2.5 billion solar systems to store its stuff."

Image: Shawn Clover / Flickr

Part VI: Conversations

21. The degrowth debate

Author's note: Below are comments from well-known scientists and intellectuals who participated in the discussion on my essay about degrowth (chapter 2) hosted by the Great Transition Initiative. The mission of GTI's platform is to trigger and host critical discussions. There were fourteen different responses to my essay. Here, shortened versions of some of these responses are presented, followed by my rebuttal.

Fourteen responses to "The degrowth alternative"

Nicholas Ashford

I must confess that I had expressed to Giorgos Kallis at the second Degrowth Conference my concern that the term "degrowth" would probably be received negatively before its positive aspects were appreciated. I also do not agree that sustainable development is an oxymoron; it is sustainable growth that is an oxymoron, following on the important distinction Herman Daly draws between growth and development. For my part, a movement described as "confronting growth" might have accumulated less baggage in achieving that change. I am not yet willing to forgo sustainable development as a unifying all-encompassing construct.

Since writing my book *Technology, Globalization, and Sustainable Development: Transforming the Industrial State*, I have come to believe that "Transforming the Industrial State" would have better been the title, rather that the subtitle—and that it would better describe the degrowth movement. Some critics of the degrowth movement bemoan the fact that there is much there on what things have to change, but not much of a blueprint for how to change things.

We all know that products and services that are not only subsidized, but also do not include in their price the full environmental, social, and economic costs that they impart on the economy and individuals, are examples of distortions and negative externalities that result in too much being produced or offered. That is why either investment for the public good needs to be a willing cultural norm of a society, or government laws, regulations, and programs need to be fashioned to correct the fact that there are those who are deprived of essential goods, services, education, and employment because they are unable to pay for them.

When van den Bergh offers that we ought to be concerned with what changes we want rather than focusing on growth per se, he has a point. Regarding Giorgos Kallis' essay, as a practical matter, I am not convinced whether we will ever achieve a "viable" "alternative to capitalism" or "an exit from the economy," but capitalism within limits and with a more human face with attention paid to the redistribution of economic and political power could be achieved. Fostering a deeper understanding of options for the industrial state is the place to begin. I would not join the doomsayers that say we are on the road to destruction, but we have been on the road to fracturing and dividing society along economic and political fault lines and hollowing out the middle class—and that is not a very pretty sight. The expansion of Northern-style growth in the Global South (and population growth too) may very well dwarf anything that can be done soon enough in the North. That is why we must engineer a different model for the South to emulate and provide financial and technical assistance in its global adoption. Confronting growth and transforming the industrial state could unite us in that effort.

Maurie Cohen

I have long found it striking—and Kallis' essay reminded me of this fact—that those of us who work primarily in the English language face a major obstacle in envisioning alternative futures. This situation is clearly demonstrated in discussions about degrowth where the very point of departure is an inelegant interpretation of the French word décroissance. And it gets worse with the importation of terminology like dépense (French for "financial outlay" but often used colloquially to suggest "unproductive expenditure"), ubuntu (a Nguni Bantu word meaning "human kindness"), and buen vivir (a Spanish expression that is much more evocative than its English near-equivalents, "good life" and "good living"). Linguists call these terms loanwords, and they have become essential to the English language discourse which has required still further enlivening through the invention of phrasing such as "illth" (conceived by ecological economist Herman Daly) and "commoning" (coined by historian Peter Linebaugh).

What might we construe from these etymological twists? Language mirrors the predominant system of societal organization, and as neoliberal economics (and politics) has seeped further and further into our collective consciousness, we—and especially those of us in the English-speaking world—have lost our ability to communicate proficiently about a world without growth. If we struggle to find the vocabulary, how can we express ourselves so others will comprehend? Such circumstances, it seems to me, evoke our deeply impoverished state of affairs. Even the words that we do have at our disposal to describe conditions of sufficiency—frugality, prudence, thrift, parsimony—have become so toxic in popular usage that careful scholars set them to the side.

Further, while I acknowledge that the notion of degrowth is, as Kallis says, "not synonymous with recession or depression," proponents of the concept could be more assertive in tackling the actual challenges of presently contracting economies. Such engagement would help to bring degrowthist thinkers into closer debate with mainstream macroeconomics. And there is, as any reader of the daily news will realize, no shortage of useful cases. The Japanese economy has been ebbing now for more than a generation. Significant parts of Europe have again tipped into "negative growth" (itself a quite curious expression), and countries like Russia and Argentina are reliable examples to consider. While I fully understand that degrowth (in its unadulterated form) suggests a process of purposefully planned contraction, we are unlikely to encounter such a situation given current growthist commitments. This recommendation suggests a need for greater pragmatism among members of the degrowth research community.

Finally, for all of its talk about system transformation, my reading of the work on degrowth finds it to be insufficiently systemic. Degrowth cannot be simply about the activation and veneration of small-scale experiments, as useful as they may be as proof of concept through practical demonstration. In the contemporary reductionistic world, few people understand the interconnections among, say, the energy subsystem, the financial subsystem, and the agricultural subsystem, but in actual practice all of these spheres are tightly coupled. It is futile to talk about establishing, for instance, 100% reserve requirements for banks without working through the impacts that such a move would have on other subsystems (and how they would respond in kind). Most conventional academics can perpetuate this conceit because they rarely step out of their siloed disciplinary neighborhoods, but visionary thinkers focused on system change of vast socio-technical systems—as I presume is the case for the vast majority of degrowthists—need to be better on this score.

Herman Daly

I would like to thank Giorgos Kallis for cogently summarizing the current thinking of the "degrowth movement." The discussion has been stimulating, and I will mostly build on points also made by others.

1. One welcomes a strong and youthful voice from Europe in opposition to growthism. Their goal of getting off our suicidal growth path and reducing our ecological footprint to a sustainable level, justly distributed, is one I enthusiastically support, and I wish them more success in promoting it than others of us have had to date.
2. The name "degrowth," as others have suggested, is infelicitous, but it is hard to change names once something has begun. Neither positive nor negative growth is possible in the long run. A steady state can at least last for a long time, although not forever.
3. Degrowth currently pays too little attention to population growth, and this is especially the case if population growth arises from net immigration, as is the case in Western Europe and the US. In the past, some degrowth writings have seemed to advocate a policy of open borders, although a reasoned case was not attempted. It would be good for them to be explicit about such a fundamental policy position. Globalization erases national boundaries to movement of goods (free trade) and capital (free capital mobility), and increasingly to people as well (free migration). Kallis discusses problems of "global governance" without really offering a position for or against globalization as a driver of growth. I see global governance as requiring a federation of nations. But if goods, capital, and people cross national borders at will, then nations are basically dissolved as political units, and there is nothing left to federate—just post-national corporate feudalism in a global commons. Most likely, the degrowth advocates are trying to develop a consensus among themselves on these difficult and divisive issues, and understandably have not yet arrived at one.
4. On the vexed issue of absolute decoupling, ecological economists see GDP as fairly tightly coupled to throughput and loosely coupled to welfare, while neoclassicals believe that GDP is only loosely coupled to throughput but tightly coupled to welfare. There is clearly room for empirical work here. However, I think basic policy does not much depend on the results. We should limit throughput first and foremost. If GDP coupling is loose, that makes things politically easier, but if it is tight, welfare can still increase since it does not depend much on GDP anyway, beyond a basic sufficiency.

In the US and Western Europe, GDP growth is as much a measure of increase in illth as of increase in wealth. Just distribution and efficient allocation should be the policy focus, not growth in scale of the macroeconomy, which should shrink for a while. This would seem to be consistent with the degrowth view.

Al Hammond

Bending the direction of growth is not only feasible, but to some degree likely; decoupling from the economic engine of capitalism and from growth (in some sense) is not. Indeed, far from facing a resource crisis, we are drowning in cheap resources—oil, natural gas, sunlight. Moreover, it seems quite clear that the on-going and accelerating pace of science and technological change may be one of the best hopes for shaping the direction of growth. Within twenty years, we will likely have grid scale batteries and solar devices above 35 or 40% efficiency. We will likely have synthetic biology so powerful that we can not only increase food yields but also nutritional content as well as transform many chronic diseases. We may even have workable fusion energy sources, thanks to high temperature superconducting magnets. And we will have mobile access to unlimited information and computing power—which, with a little luck, will translate into really effective self-education systems available to everyone. To me, that education revolution and the spreading transformation of the role of women (it is not yet 100 years since women became legal citizens of the US and could vote) are the really big—and the really hopeful—transition drivers for the next 50 years.

I speak in part based on a current project that I am doing with MIT that has provided a look into where science can go/is going. Unless you are paying very close attention, it is really hard to grasp how rapidly the frontier of knowledge is advancing in dozens of fields. So if we avoid a global war or similar total breakdown of society for another three to four decades, I think it likely that the weight of informed opinion in the world will in fact drive change in more positive directions. For one quick example, who would have guessed that the acceptance of gay marriage in the US has spread even more quickly than the change that made cigarette smoking socially unacceptable two decades earlier? This is an example of what I have called the soft variables that can change far more rapidly that the hard variables of energy and infrastructure.

This is overly condensed—the more detailed and subtle version of the argument is not short—but I suggest we look for ways to bend the curve, not break it.

Michael Karlberg

A more coherent conceptual framework for the economy is clearly needed to inform direction and decision-making by both governmental regulators and self-regulating market actors. In this context, the semiotics of degrowth are limited because it connotes a limiting negative vision (what not to do) rather than a generative positive vision (what to do) for the economy.

There is, of course, a need to translate metaphorical concepts into actual economic policies and practices, and that is not simple work. But that work can only proceed, and will only motivate action, move populations, and attract institutional support, within a coherent conceptual frame. I doubt degrowth provides an adequate overarching frame in this regard.

Rajesh Makwana

This is an excellent article on the immensely important issue of degrowth, with a comprehensive overview that avoids focusing only on local-scale solutions to global-scale problems. Clearly, the vision and principles underpinning the degrowth perspective can contribute much to the discourse on planetary limits and the urgent need for a new paradigm for economic development—especially since it is inherently a political perspective that directly challenges neoclassical economics.

However, in relation to the debate on how to facilitate a great transition, I think the issue of degrowth is likely to be a red herring. As a popular framing that can mobilize a global citizens movement or enable system change on the scale needed, degrowth is limited. Apart from concerns around what might (paradoxically) still need to grow in a degrowth society, which might even include GDP, a key concern is its negative and unappealing framing. In an interconnected world, any great transition can only happen if it is underpinned by broad principles that have real transformative potential and can mobilize support on a scale never before achieved. Almost half the planet still lives in two-dollar-a-day poverty, and this number increases dramatically if we shift the poverty line upwards. The demand for degrowth is not likely to appeal to the poorest and most disenfranchised—those who will benefit the most from a great transition, and whose support is therefore essential in the creation of a "movement of movements."

I suggest that the concept and practice of sharing could be used to reframe the degrowth debate, as it embodies critical concepts such as redistribution and participation while also alluding to the need to live within the constraints of "one-planet living." For example, we could talk about the creation of a "sharing society," "sharing the Earth," or even "shared planet economics." This more positive framing lends itself to an important debate on sufficiency—the ethic of "enough" versus the materialistic culture of "more." It also speaks to the many sharing-related reforms that must be part of any transition to a degrowth society (some of which Kallis mentions in his essay)—from redistributing wealth, power, and jobs to sharing knowledge, land, and natural resources. In particular, the frame of global sharing lends itself to the growing recognition that humanity must work together on an international scale if we are to create the conditions to thrive peacefully on a planet with finite resources.

As for the central problem of economic growth, rather than promoting degrowth as a policy framework or a collective demand, the aim should perhaps be for governments to simply deprioritize the pursuit of GDP growth so that it is no longer considered a panacea for prosperity. Instead, public policy should be geared towards more appropriate goals and indicators that focus on the attainment of economic, social, and cultural rights within an overarching global framework of planetary limits. But as Kallis rightly points out, this paradigm shift will not be possible until governments find more effective ways of cooperating on global issues and reforming systems of global governance so that they are far more inclusive and democratic than is currently the case.

Mary Mellor

I welcome particularly two aspects of Kallis' paper: the attention to care and the need to work at other levels as well as the local.

I want to begin with a few points on care:

1. I don't think many degrowthers realize how heavy a burden care work will be without domestic equipment—cookers, washing machines, hot water, vacuum cleaners, etc. This is not an argument to keep them, but domestic work is going to take a lot of the day. In most communities, this falls to women. I am troubled by how much attention in the literature is

given to welcoming increased leisure time by male authors.
2. Health care and other public services are not easily localized—specialist care and specialist training in particular.
3. The local has often been oppressive for women: a lot of gender equality was about breaking free.
4. On a more positive note, there is no reason why a provisioning economy could not be built on care as a source of wealth; while de-growing in resource terms, we could grow in care terms.

The key is where money enters the economy. At present, new money emerges through a commercial circuit of investment/loans profit/repayment and trickles out to public services. My proposal is to expand the public money circuit (public money creation—public/social expenditure—retrieval through taxation). If this were directed to education or care, that would become the source of wealth, with money trickling out to the commercial sector. Quantitative easing shows how easily monetary authorities can create new money; they just need to give it to the people not the banks. What neoliberalism calls a deficit is better thought of as surplus public expenditure, money in circulation not extracted through tax. This debt-free money can be used for the exchange of use value.

Robert Paehlke

I very much appreciated Giorgos Kallis' piece and the resultant discussion. My take on economic growth is somewhat different from what Kallis articulates. In broad terms, if degrowth means comfort with slow growth, I welcome it, but I do not think that economic contraction is either necessary or likely.

I am agnostic about economic growth measured monetarily so long as growth in energy and use of raw materials is reversed. I accept studies by the Wuppertal Institute suggesting that this is possible. I think it could be achieved using "throughput" taxes on energy and material inputs and waste outputs. Such a view is a very long way from neoliberal approaches to economic policy, but it does leave some room for economic growth and for some form of capitalism. Would successfully capping energy and material throughputs halt economic growth? In the end, I am open to the possibility of what Herman Daly calls "angelized" GNP. That is, declining material throughputs do not exclude the possibility of slowly growing economies, at least for the next twenty to fifty years.

Some products, services, and sectors would, of course, shrink significantly—including mining, fossil energy, airline travel, cross-planetary shipping of heavy, low-cost goods, and the like. Other relatively benign sectors would not be severely impacted (though they would adapt by shifting towards new production methods, more durable products, and recycled inputs). The third category is where things get interesting. Again, my take differs somewhat from that of Kallis. He sees local food, renewable energy, and human-to-human care as within the degrowth paradigm. I would add to his list other sectors including new media. Kallis sees these undertakings as often demonetized and not-for-profit undertakings. I see them as just as often entrepreneurial, usually small-scale.

The way I have come to understand this "new economy" is not as anti-capitalist, or degrowth. It is a new economic realm that provides meaningful work often where it is desperately needed—among the young. Those involved are open to earning a good living, but are equally intent on balancing that objective with socially and environmentally-minded considerations. On a more theoretical plane, I have come to distinguish between the established corporate-dominated economy and new entrepreneurship led by environmentally and socially mindful organizations.

Will the net result of these many shifts be growth or degrowth? I am agnostic; I just do not think we can know in advance. We know that many large corporations will be challenged and some will disappear. Capitalism itself (in some form) may well, however, survive. The speed at which entrepreneurs can adapt is important to changing an economy. Our greatest challenge is to find ways to keep large corporations from almost literally owning governments and blocking needed changes. If allowed to innovate and adapt, humans are very good at finding alternative ways to meet human needs, and even human whims.

Richard Rosen

If "degrowth" is the answer to the question of what the economies in fairly rich countries should do in the near future, then we are asking the wrong question. We need to take a much more nuanced view about what sustainable development (not sustainable growth) should imply for the economy in both the near term and the longer term. Thus, if "degrowth" means that the GDP should go down over the next few decades, then we need to take an analytical approach based on a more disaggregated view of the GDP.

I think it is clear that, even in rich countries, some components of the economy, such as education, health care, elderly care, and the arts, need to go up significantly. This is true also for organic food production, especially for nourishing foods that many poor people in rich countries cannot currently afford. We must take the impact of income inequality in rich countries into account in our approach to "degrowth." For the rest of the world, the above sectors must increase even more rapidly.

A better way to look at the desirability of GDP growth or decline would be to consider which sectors of the GDP need to grow, which should decline, where and when throughout the world, and for how long. What the net effect on global GDP will be year-by-year over the next few decades is anyone's guess, but it does not really matter as long as people lead ever better and more sustainable lives, and if the world's ecological systems can be restored to health quickly enough to save most disappearing species and to prevent significantly more climate change.

In addition, I feel that the term "degrowth" is most unfortunate from a political perspective, for it is more likely to turn people off from supporting the valid aspects of the politics behind it than to turn them on. Since, by far, most people in the world do not have enough of many goods and services necessary for an adequate and sustainable life, the term "degrowth" will surely convey the intention that they will never be able to have such a life. Yet, given what I have said above, this turnoff is totally unnecessary, and inaccurate besides, relative to what needs to be done. It would be much easier to reach people politically if we make it clear that we need fewer of the "bad" things the world currently produces and more of the "good" things. Then we could focus on the important debate, which is what are the "bads" versus the "goods," how much of each does each region want or need, and how do we get to these goals.

Tilman Santarius

I have enjoyed both Giorgos Kallis' essay and the stimulating debate. Two issues seem particularly interesting to me.

First, the debate seems to mirror an interesting transatlantic distinction: Why is it that the degrowth debate is so "European"? To be sure, a number of scientists and NGO representatives in the US support degrowth, and there are some very good publications coming out of the US. Yet overall, it seems to remain a rather small niche here. In contrast, degrowth on the other side of the Atlantic is highly en vogue. Most degrowth-related publications nowadays come from "old Europe," and at last year's Degrowth Conference in Leipzig, the 2,700 participants from all over the continent broke records.

Second, whether we can remain agnostic to growth, or support continued (green) growth, all depends on the issue of decoupling. Is it possible to decouple (gross national) income from energy and resource consumption? The literature conventionally distinguishes between absolute and relative decoupling. Yet I think for industrialized countries with high ecological footprints, this question has become obsolete. Relative decoupling is not an option anymore, because we are already living in overshoot (however, the concept of relative decoupling might still be valid for poor and resource-low countries). Absolute decoupling might not be enough either, if energy and resource use only slowly declines, e.g., proportionally to GDP growth. We need to reduce resource use and greenhouse gas emissions by a factor of ten in less than four decades. Industrialized countries, therefore, actually need "radical absolute decoupling": if GDP keeps growing by, say, 3% per year on average, resource and energy use must decline several times more steeply than GDP goes up.

I am not sure if there are any degrowth supporters who demand to start shrinking the economy immediately. Rather, as Giorgis Kallis has pointed out, degrowth is a vision, a paradigm shift. This paradigm shift starts from the fact that radical absolute decoupling is by and large utopian. To be sure, this does not make the task at hand any easier. If growth rates fall below 3% on average, current systems of pension funds, public spending, financial markets, etc., have to be rethought. The challenge is tremendous. The transition toward environmental sustainability requires much more than environmental policymaking.

Alas, what is a viable alternative if radical decoupling doesn't work? "Green growth," selective/smart growth, etc., would have been great concepts back in the 1980s. Too bad that it is already 2015, and that ecological footprints have been rising and rising and rising. Standing close to the edge of the precipice, merely walking slower, smarter, or with environmentally sound shoes, won't do.

Anders Wijkman

Being a follower and supporter of Herman Daly for many years, and being active in the leadership of the Club of Rome, I am of course very much in agreement with the view that infinite growth on a finite planet is not possible. However, going back to the *Limits to Growth* report in 1972, it is important to note that what the report primarily did was not question growth per se, but rather the growing footprint of humanity.

At that time, the footprint was within the planetary boundaries. But developments since have led to overshoot and an increasingly risky situation in terms of climate change, overuse of central ecosystems, resource depletion, and loss of biological diversity. Most of the overshoot is due to wasteful lifestyles in industrialized countries. Poverty is still rampant—more than 3 billion people live on less than 2 US dollars a day.

To do away with poverty will require energy and materials. The North-South tension around these issues should not be underestimated. I have participated in quite a number of conferences on resource efficiency in recent years, where the hostility from Southern participants has been obvious. A more resource-efficient economy is seen by many as a threat to their development.

The discussion must take this into account and avoid language that will polarize the debate.

Technology can and will help enhance resource efficiency. The rapid technology shift—the digitization of the economy—offers a lot of opportunities. The same goes for advances in energy technology, in particular solar energy and energy storage. But technology alone will not suffice. We need redistribution of wealth and income, and we need a shift in values, thus leaving behind a culture dominated by excessive consumerism. But to achieve that under the motto of "degrowth" is, in my opinion, going to be very difficult.

As Tim Jackson writes in *Prosperity without Growth*, "[g]rowth is environmentally unsustainable, but degrowth is socially unstable." We have built a society where growth is necessary—whether we talk about corporations, employment, taxes, government budgets, financial markets, or pension funds. Society in general is dead against degrowth.

But there is another aspect, more on the level of the individual. Most people want things in which they are involved to grow, and definitely not the opposite. Growth is not negative per se. What is negative is when growth is only appreciated and measured for its quantity, not its quality. A major problem—something we have discussed for decades, but with no change happening—is how we measure growth. GDP is definitely not a good indicator for measuring wealth. On the contrary, there are many shortcomings. The fact that we do not assess annually how the stock of natural capital develops is a disaster.

We want many things to grow—public transport, renewable energy, health, education, natural capital, etc. By replacing GDP with a set of welfare objectives, including a stable climate and healthy ecosystems, we would start moving in the right direction.

By changing business models—offering services instead of selling more stuff; moving towards a circular economy—we would move the business sector in the right direction.

So there are indeed positive things we can do to start changing course. Such changes would be of a positive nature and not—like degrowth—be perceived by the public at large as negative. Dr. King did not have a "nightmare"; he had a "dream."

Change, in my opinion, can only be brought about through a narrative that is positive. And that narrative has so far been missing.

So instead of a degrowth campaign, I would urge us to develop together a positive narrative where growth and development are discussed in qualitative rather than quantitative terms. Part of that narrative, no doubt, will have to be to curb energy and material throughput. But the strategy has to recognize the dangers in the short term of degrowth—"socially unstable" according to Jackson—and the importance of charting out a transition course that is credible over the long term.

Response: In defense of the degrowth alternative

Degrowth is a "missile concept" to open up a debate silenced by the "sustainable development" consensus. The lively debate triggered by my viewpoint suggests it is doing well. Here I will respond to five overarching critiques, clarifying and advancing the case for degrowth.

Degrowth is subversive

The first critique is that degrowth signifies a "limiting negative vision" (Michael Karlberg), a nightmare, rather than a dream (Anders Wijkman). This depends on the eyes of the beholder. For the 3,500 participants at the degrowth conference in Leipzig, growth is a living nightmare and degrowth, the dream. Degrowth unsettles the commonsensical gaze which sees growth as good. Growth has more social costs than benefits, as Herman Daly documents. It brings us closer to climate disaster, as Kevin Anderson and Naomi Klein show. Then why do we still have to protect it as a positive vision?

For two reasons, suggest some commentators to my essay. The first is that degrowth scares many people who still think that growth is good. The second is that "the system is dead against degrowth" (Anders Wijkman). Well, if our role as scientists and educators were to please the public opinion and cater to the powers that be, then the earth would still be flat. Degrowth, as Serge Latouche puts it, is an atheist claim against the secular god of Growth. Growth has been substituted for religion in modern societies, providing meaning to all collective endeavours. Degrowth is intentionally subversive; it inverses what is seen as good and bad. "Degrowth" initially may not sound nice in this or that language. The point is to make it sound nice. If I judge by a recent article in *The Guardian*, which argues that degrowth is a "cute word," then we are succeeding.[1]

Degrowth is not an ultimate objective. "Sharing," "commons," or "conviviality" are positive visions used by the degrowth community. Yet if these futures are to come, they will come with a dramatic reduction of material and energy throughput and a radically "simpler way" of living. The fixation with Growth is the main obstacle to a great transition. Overcoming the fear of degrowth, and turning the grief of living with less into joy is a first step.

Fewer of the bad things + more of the good ones = Degrowth

The second criticism, expressed by Rich Rosen and many others, is that it is not growth per se that is bad, but the current un-economic growth. Care, renewables, and organically-grown food will need to grow in a Great Transition; we need "fewer of the 'bad' things...and more of the 'good' things," Rosen argues. Who would disagree? Problems start when what we think is good, others think is bad. Liberalism, embodied in consensual notions such as "sustainability," professes an apolitical neutrality to competing interests. Degrowth, instead, is a partisan claim: these things that typically count as "Growth" (highways, bridges, armies, dams) are bad for "us" degrowthers. Things that are considered anachronisms in the arrow of progress—communal institutions, fresh local food, small cooperatives, or windmills—are good. Perhaps degrowth is an imperfect term for signaling this. Still, it is better than neutral terms like "sustainability," or "transition" on its own, which are apolitical and can be appropriated for anyone's cause.

Another problem with "the good things argument" is that it is couched in growth terms. 2% annual growth doubles a "thing" every 35 years. If Egypt started with one cubic meter of possessions and grew them by 4.5% per year, by the end of its 3,000-year civilization, it would need 2.5

1 Poole, S. (2015, 30 January). "Steven Poole: beware growthspeak." *The Guardian*. Retrieved from https://www.theguardian.com/books/2015/jan/30/steven-poole-growthspeak-general-election-looms

billion solar systems to store its stuff. Perpetual growth, even of organic food, is an absurdity. It is time to abandon the idiom of growth and focus on good things that need to flourish to a quantity and quality sufficient for satisfying basic needs.

I doubt that the economic conversion that Rosen advocates, and with which I concur, could sustain growth. If it could, then this means that absolute decoupling—whereby the growth of economic activity continues and resource use declines—would be possible. Tilman Santarius and Ernst von Weizsäcker in their commentaries explain why this is unlikely. Let me add three more reasons.

First, a renewable economy will produce less energy surplus (energy return on energy investment) than the fossil fuel economy. An economy with lower energy surpluses will be more labor-intensive, and hence smaller.

Second, a static, disaggregated snapshot of the economy is misleading. It might appear that more GDP from renewables, education, and health and less from the military equals net—and "angelized"—GDP growth. This is wrong. Solar panels, hospitals, or university labs are end-products in long chains utilizing primary and intermediate inputs that are energy and resource-intensive. With the danger of overstretching my examples, Britain's emblematic National Health Service was subsidized by oil secured with arms through the Suez.

Third, a transition from, say, a resource-intensive economy of SUVs to a "weightless" economy of Priuses and Kindles would reduce throughput, but only for a while. Once the transition is complete, any further growth of the Prius-Kindle economy, however resource-light, will still grow throughput.

Herman Daly is right that there is "room for empirical work here." I am willing to follow Bob Paehlke and be "agnostic" about the effects on GDP of a shift to "good things." I am not sure, however, that "what the net effect on global GDP will be year-by-year...does not really matter as long as people lead ever better and more sustainable lives" (Rich Rosen). "We" might wish to be agnostic, but the conservatives who defend the vested interests that feed on growth are not (witness the reactions to climate legislation). Also, "we" might not care whether GDP rises or falls, but in the world we live in, GDP falls are problematic (witness Greece). If a Great Transition is to take place, then we have to contemplate the institutions and socio-political processes that will make the degrowth that may come with it socially sustainable.

Beyond GDP means beyond Growth

The third critique is that the problem is GDP, not growth. If we could only measure the goods an economy provides, say "massages," and count out at the bads, say "oil spills," then there would be no reason not to want growth.

First, perpetual growth, of whatever, even of an "angelized" GDP, is an absurd objective. I do not look forward to an Earth with people frantically giving enough massages to satisfy 2.5 billion solar systems.

Second, GDP counts what counts for the current economic system: capital circulation, whatever its source. The decision of the EU to count drugs and prostitution in GDP, but not unpaid care work, is illustrative. GDP counts total monetized value. This is what feeds corporate profits and public coffers, and this is what governments want to secure and stabilize. The metric is an epiphenomenon; it is the result of the social system, not its cause. This is why GDP persists despite criticisms from prominent economists.

I agree with Bob Nadeau that mainstream economics with its reductionist obsession with maximizing a homogeneous quantity called utility (aka "money") is part of the problem. Yet I would go further. The emergence and entrenchment of the neoclassical orthodoxy has to be situated within its social context: the triumph, first, of growthism and, then, of neoliberalism. Maximizing money is what the system cares about. As Serge Latouche puts it—tellingly, if somewhat exaggeratedly—economists are the priests of the religion of growth. A different type of economics will be part and parcel of a transition to a different social system.

"We" should degrow, but not so that "they" grow.

Commenting on my essay, many argued that degrowth is irrelevant for the great part of the world still living in poverty. The argument is that while "we" (wealthy, overfed Northerners) may have to degrow, "they" (poor, underfed Southerners) still want and need to grow. This is the most powerful discourse that perpetuates the ideology of growthism. It has to be discarded.

We all—to some degree, or at some periods—feel like "Southerners." My Greek compatriots tell me degrowth is not for us, for we are now poor and in crisis. The 99% in the US has good reasons to believe that it is the 1% that has to degrow so that it can grow. Even when millionaires are surveyed on how much money they need in order to feel economically secure, they typically state twice what they already have, irrespective of their actual income. Positional comparisons drive and perpetuate the quest for growth. Economic insecurity, at all levels of income, makes everyone run faster and faster so as not to fall. And economic crises, when standards of living suddenly fall and insecurity intensifies, are the moments where the quest for growth reappears most forcefully, but this time as a progressive cause. There will never be a time for degrowth.

The people on this planet, perhaps a majority, who lack access to basic goods, such as water or public health, deserve them, and this might entail higher energy and resource use. This need not be couched though in the absurd terms of growth. It is a matter of redistribution and sufficiency. "We" need to degrow so that "Southern" cosmologies and political alternatives closer to the spirit of sufficiency (such as Sumak Kawsay or Ubuntu) can flourish. Southern alternatives are colonized intellectually by developmentalism and materially through the extractive industries that, in the name of growth, bring destruction and poverty.

I propose the same logic for countries in economic crisis. We do not need to grow our way out of economic crisis in Greece. We need to come up with alternative models of sufficiency rooted in Greek tradition, materialized into institutions that will let us prosper without growth.

I am wary of those talking in the name of others reminding me that unlike what I—an elite intellectual—think, "poor people" (sic) dream of plasma TVs and Ferraris and we can't deny them their dreams. Most people that I know, including myself, do indeed have materialistic dreams: our positional societies force those on us if we are to remain its dignified and secured members. Fortunately, we also have a longing for a simpler life, for community, friendship, and many other needs that collide with the imaginary of growth. The question is how to change social structures and institutional contexts so that it is these latter aspirations that come to be fulfilled and not our worst acquisitive desires.

A transition beyond growth is a transition beyond capitalism

Capitalism is an ensemble of property, financial, and exchange institutions that create relentless competition, forcing enterprises to grow or die. The surpluses generated by this dynamic are constantly reinvested into further growth. A society without growth may still have markets, forms of private property, or money. But as Edward and Robert Skidelsky put it, an economic system which does not grow and in which capital no longer accumulates is no longer capitalism, whatever one might want to call it. Property, credit, or employment institutions will have to be reconfigured in radical ways so as to make the system stable without growth. Proposals such as a basic citizen's income or the public control of money are such radical reforms.

Benign enterprises such as Mondragon or Novo Nordisk, which combine economic with social and environmental considerations "are the rare exceptions," as Allen White notes in his commentary, for a reason. In a capitalist economy, the bottom line is profit. Environmental and social concerns can be accommodated by few players who can increase their market share by cashing in on socially-responsible consumers. As George Monbiot put it, capitalism can sell many things, but it can't sell less.

If the corporation signifies the globalized growth economy, the sharing cooperative is the emblem of a localized degrowth economy. Bob Paehlke argues that sharing enterprises that he knows do not necessarily espouse degrowth values, and they seek some profit. My argument was not behavioral, but structural: in an economy that will no longer grow, worker or consumer cooperatives, which do not depend on perpetually growing profits, have a natural advantage. Some sharing enterprises have features that make them apt for a degrowth transition. Not all. I distinguish the sharing economy from the "rental economy"[1] of AirBnB and similar capitalistic corporations, which, however innovative, reproduces rent-seeking and the dynamics of perpetual surplus creation.

A sidetrack on population and immigration

I consider Herman Daly my intellectual mentor, even though I haven't met him. I agree in almost everything with him minus his stance on immigration. We have exchanged emails, and I owe him a more "reasoned case," as he asks in his commentary. Here are a few thoughts.

First, if our concern is planet Earth, and not the forests and rivers that happen to be within the borders of our "imagined" national community (to borrow a term from Benedict Anderson's classic), then immigration is good. Resources are used much more efficiently in advanced economies. For a given income, more resources will be saved by letting people come where efficient technologies are used, than by waiting for their economies to grow and become more efficient.

Second, immigration and remittances are a fast and resource-efficient mechanism for the global "contraction and convergence" of income be-

1 See Chapter 18 in this book.

tween North and South that Herman Daly espouses.

Third, there is no evidence that nations with more people or more immigrants damage their environments more. Population, affluence, and technologies affect one another in complex ways. Labor and resources are partly substitutes; a slowdown of population growth in rural India may lead to intensifying use of pesticides and gasoline-fueled tractors. What is worse for the environment is anyone's guess. Infinite population growth is impossible within a limited planet or nation, but feedbacks ensure that population will not grow indefinitely. In Europe, and increasingly in Asia, fertility is in decline and population is bound to peak.

Fourth, immigration to advanced economies is capitalism's response to the shortage of cheap labor for menial jobs due to declining population growth and the rising education standards of natives. Undocumented, unsecured immigrants keep labor costs low. I am concerned, like Herman Daly, with the prospects of a "post-national corporate feudalism." The response however is not to protect the immigrants from exploitation by blocking them out. Immigration is the result, not the cause, of the problem—namely globalization and the relentless need of capital to grow. It is the cause that has to be fixed, not the effect.

Finally, people do not leave their birthplaces and risk their lives in the Mediterranean Sea for fun or out of greed. They do it because conditions home are insupportable. The colonial wars waged by the North to secure its resource supplies, and the ecosystem degradation wrought by its overconsumption, have something to do with it. There is a humanitarian case to be made that the North should host the socio-environmental refugees that it has helped produce in the South.

In conclusion

Anders Wijkman invoked Tim Jackson's dictum that "growth is environmentally unsustainable, but degrowth is socially unstable." Curiously, it was invoked against degrowth, insisting on a one-way future where we will make growth sustainable, by a technological or social miracle. One commentator (Al Hammond) was thrilled by a near future of hydroponics, synthetic biology, fusion, and supercomputer power. Count me out. The point of my original piece was that such a future is unsustainable, unnecessary, and undesirable (at least by those of us who consider ourselves degrowthers). Technological fixes shift costs to others, to the environment, and to future generations, at an ever-grander scale. Climate change is the legacy of our past technological achievements. I read

Tim Jackson differently. Given that further growth is unsustainable, we have to bring forward the systemic and institutional changes that will make degrowth stable.

22. Will trees grow in a degrowth society?

Author's note: Andy Stirling, a professor at the University of Sussex, is one of the most distinguished sustainability scientists of his generation. Stirling was a long-time environmental activist before joining the Science Policy Research Unit at Sussex, and his research focuses on international environmental governance, power relationships, and science policy. Andy attended a talk I gave in the University of Sussex in February 2015 hosted by the STEPS Center and the Center for Global Political Economy. Between April 2015 and March 2016 I was based at SOAS, London, sponsored by a Leverhulme visiting professor grant. Andy's response to my talk was posted on the STEPS Center's website in three parts, titled, "Outgrowing the twin simplifications of growth and degrowth." The following is an excerpt from his articles, edited for flow, followed by my own rebuttal.

Outgrowing the twin simplifications of growth and degrowth (Andy Stirling)

I recently had the privilege of hearing a great talk by Giorgos Kallis. His topic was the "degrowth hypothesis"—around which an important global activist-academic movement is currently (rather ironically!) undergoing burgeoning growth.

"Degrowth" involves a powerful critique of the supposed need for continuous economic growth. Recognising the massive global destruction and injustice caused by growingly unequal consumption, the degrowth critique instead envisages a general contraction in the overall scale of economic activity as measured not by social values in general, but by narrow monetary value in particular.

So why then—despite my respect for this analysis and many of those who propound it—did I find myself with such an ominous feeling about what it all entails? Notwithstanding the richness of the discussion at this seminar, what came over most strongly, was a sense of momentous self-defeat. The apparent error is both strategic and tactical: in substantive analysis as well as practical impacts.

These are strong words. So, there's a duty to explain. Though far from original, the central neglected question is very simple. Surely it all depends? Growth … or degrowth … in what?

What kind of degrowth?

Giorgos ably demolished the contrived and politically expedient monetary constructs around which he rightly argued most current capitalist notions of growth are fabricated. But not all forms of capitalism are equally obsessive about money as the sole arbiter of value. And systems other than capitalism have also shown themselves to be highly susceptible to the cult of economic growth.

This said, Giorgos rightly argued—like other degrowth analysts—that the practices and institutions that shape the apparently natural clarity of monetary metrics are actually highly conditioned in order to reinforce existing structures of privilege and power. Without the enormous infrastructures within which these economic metrics are shaped and given meaning, abstract notions like economic surplus, monetary value, financial accounting or gross domestic product would all be very nebulous.

Of course, this tyranny of money is far from abstract in practice. It is imposed by many kinds of coercive power and hard structure—and (ultimately) by threat of organized violence. This is why the associated political forces are so oppressive of the people they marginalise and disappropriate—and all those held in thrall by fear of such exclusion. Any realistic understanding of the world must acknowledge this. Again, Giorgos put the case very compellingly.

But in an increasingly unequal world, it is extremely important to gain a realistic understanding of the underlying political dynamics. Currently hegemonic notions of growth are enforced with such assertiveness, not because monetary value is a self-evident physical quantity. Nor even is money a direct proxy for the material manifestations of harm.

Instead, in ways that Giorgos also underlined well, it is arguably inequality itself that forms a major factor in the forces that shape the institutions that determine monetary values—and the growth they denominate. These forces reflect specific kinds of powerful interests, which stand to benefit from reducing diverse social values to a far narrower monetary form. It is only in this way that social dynamism and diversity can become tractable to appropriation by the most privileged interests.

Focus on economic value

In other words, the monetary values that the economic growth dogma asserts so emphatically must always be made to grow, take the magnitudes they do, in large part precisely to allow the accrual of inequalities in favor of the structures and interests that shape them. In this perniciously regressive sense, actively-pursued inequalities are a driver as well as a consequence of patterns of growth.

In seeking to support and reinforce these political dynamics, no force is stronger than the shaping of cognition itself. So, strong pressures arise to build public understandings that the only imaginable growth is that measured in prevailing (highly politically contingent) definitions of economic value.

After all, no cage is more inescapable, than that which leads the caged to believe "there is no alternative". So it would be a triumph for the prevailing hegemony of this stand-alone, one-dimensional economistic notion of value, if even the criticisms are defined by the same parameters!

And this is a key reason why the "degrowth critique" seems to me to be so problematic. As presented by Giorgos and others, it can (despite best intentions) too readily act to further concentrate attention disproportionately on the very quantities it aims to target—material consumption and economic value. And this problem is compounded in the way the term "degrowth" also appears to conflate problems with solutions—appearing to criticise general growth of all and any kinds.

Far from subverting the prevailing hegemony of monetary value, then, seeing degrowth this way actually risks reinforcing it. By eliding the undoubted negativities of narrow economic growth with growth in all other kinds of social values, it is as if all growth is necessarily denominated in money. Or it implies that if some aspect of positive societal growth is measurable in money, then this too is bad.

These impressions risk subconsciously entrenching precisely the kinds of "no alternatives" fatalism that the hegemony itself imposes—feeding rather than resisting underlying dynamics of inequality.

Pluralities of growings

It is odd that the thrust of Giorgos' lecture concentrated so exclusively on a single narrow material dimension of growth – as denominated in monetary value. This is because, like other proponents of such narrow definitions of degrowth, he made it very clear that there are plenty of other social values that can be much more positive and progressive than the monetary metrics around which currently dominant global capitalism obsesses so regressively.

For instance, Giorgos rightly pointed very clearly to the massive potential to improve current worldwide levels of "happiness" and "longevity". In other words, even for him, there is a progressive imperative that at least these additional kinds of values – and their associated enabling cultures, institutions and practices – actually grow.

This is a crucial point. To Giorgos' mention of happiness and longevity must be added other social values like equality, health, wellbeing, justice, sustainability, care, liberty, fulfilment, education, human flourishing and quality of life. In empowering communities to define their own values, many more arise. And each of these progressive values might meaningfully be hoped to grow.

Lived social experience of many of these qualities – and their opposites! – is at least as concrete as the complex and ambiguous abstractions that underlie and constitute monetary values. Although money values are ostensibly precise, the underlying patterns of material production that they supposedly reflect, are actually far more ambiguous and perspective- and structure-dependent.

Had many of these other kinds of social values been the focus of so much elite attention over the centuries, then cultures, institutions, practices and methodologies could surely have grown around these to yield the same impressions of concretely precise quantification. Modern economic institutions are not the only ways to formalise social value.

The power of values

It was spuriously rigid assertions of values like "grace", "nobility", "piety" – or "comradeship" – for instance, that helped enforce equally stark forms of privilege and oppression in different times and places. That these values might be regarded as meaningless outside of their cultural contexts, in no way diminishes their potency – like money values – to shape dynamics within their political settings.

Nor are the pluralities of connotations of growth restricted to diverse kinds of social values beyond monetary value alone. Even in the narrowly restrictive terms measured by material consumption or monetary value, positive progress towards more just and sustainable societies will necessarily entail exponential rates of growth in particular practices, technologies and sectors.

Progressive areas for growth

Depending on context, then, progressive areas for material growth may include: peaceful dispute resolution; open source seeds; ecological farming; collective land tenure; co-operative enterprises; renewable energy; community utilities; grassroots innovation… and so on. For anyone interested in progressive transformations to just and sustainable societies, all these need to grow massively.

The point here is not that any one of the many possible counterfactual value metrics associated with such transformations would somehow automatically be progressive. Given a chance, forces of incumbent power and privilege will (and do) exercise their expedient pressures on the constituting of all kinds of social value – including "justice" or "happiness" as well as any kind of technology or practice. How regressive or emancipatory any given frame might be, depends more than anything else, on the emancipatory qualities of the political environment within which it grows.

So, there seems an obviously less oppressive way to engage with growth, than the current singular material parameterisations shared both by proponents and (sadly) many degrowth critics alike. This is, to open up more diverse appreciations for the many kinds of possible ways and values that societies might grow… and the radically different ways of growing. It is in enabling associated plural spaces for political creativity, contestation and experimentation, that hopes for emancipation lie.

Nor does this argument need to be wholly accepted, for key features of the current polarised growth/degrowth debate to radically change. So why do discussions like the one I witnessed, tend to remain so neglectful of these implications? It seems there may sometimes be more specific blinkers in play – like the comforting allure of performing a self-conscious critical identity?

For a beleaguered left, this may be understandable. But the struggle for emancipation from injustice and environmental destruction is too serious a responsibility to succumb to this kind of self-indulgence. The issues around degrowth are too important to be reduced merely to a slogan.

Toward transformations

Of course, this is not what Giorgos himself did. It is in indirectly highlighting plural ways of living and working more lightly on the earth and with each other, that the degrowth analysis is most inspiring.

In various parts of this literature, what is really advocated under the simplistically reductive banner of "degrowth", are profoundly progressive political transformations towards radically more just and sustainable societies. I admire these ambitions and stand in strong solidarity.

But it is precisely this shared commitment that makes me worry very deeply about whether the narrowly negative framing of "degrowth" – parameterised in similar terms to economic growth itself – is the best way to advocate this diversity of possible (and essential) kinds of growth.

Outgrowing the Growth/Degrowth Trap

Like others in this field, Giorgos repeatedly insisted (without qualification) that it is a necessary consequence of growth in general and of any kind that it entails impossible aspirations to infinity – and so come up against the resulting inevitable, uncompromising discipline of material limits.

This is certainly true of unqualified neoliberal visions of economic growth. But it can only generally be so for all kinds of growth, if these are also seen as one-dimensional, quantitative and unending. And this would also be ironically similar to the mindset that drives the oppressive reductions of the monetary growth hegemony itself. As elsewhere in politics, it appears that polarised oppositions can share more in common than they think!

It was actually very clear in some of the examples of contrasting non-material and non-monetary social values that Giorgos mentioned, that growth can be a far more nuanced and subtle process than this dismal zero sum calculus suggests. But he did not explore this. So beyond the challenge of plurality of values, the degrowth critique also seems in danger of neglecting the multiple complexities of what it can mean to "grow".

Does growth have to be limited? When it comes to crucial human values like health, equality, wellbeing, justice, sustainability, care, liberty, fulfilment, education, flourishing and quality of life (for instance), the orientations, constitutions – and so denominations – of growth are not just plural (as discussed in my last post), but also necessarily contextual, relational and ever-changing. They involve disparate topologies as much as different scales of change.

Yet "growth" is nonetheless still an appropriate word for these more complex phenomena. It is in these multidimensional terms, after all, that people speak colloquially of "personal growth" or the growth of relationships, or communities, or solidarities. When told to "grow up" by one's friends, they do not mean "get taller"! They are talking about patterns, not magnitudes. Why, then, must even critical notions of growth be reduced to such a singular uni-dimensional material economistic form?

To be fair, it is clear that Giorgos, like colleagues, is very well aware of all this. In the lecture and subsequent questions, the discussion was quite nuanced on this point. Yet the central account of degrowth nonetheless repeatedly emphasised that any kind of growth must necessarily imply some impractical infinite imagination.

And it was repeatedly asserted that any kind of growth seen in these terms, must unavoidably incur the stern discipline of its own purely scalar limits. Again, it seems complexities evaporate – the similarities with neoliberal-style insistence on a singular uncompromising "bottom line" is oddly insidious!

Growth in patterns

In reality, both natural and social worlds are replete with examples of modes of growth that defy these restrictive imaginations. For further examples: What about growth over time in patterns – like those in: Connections among neurons? Co-evolutions between species? Experiences of individuals? Empathies in relationships? Networks within communities? Sensibilities in art movements? Knowledges in traditions? New values in cultures?

None of these are simply scalar or reducible to single metrics. They are topological not scalar. And to recognise this implies no denial of hard biophysical limits or the scalar dimensions of growth where topologies are clear. They are, quite simply, different. So, it is this recognition, not only of pluralities but also different modalities, of growing, that a narrow scalar notion of degrowth risks suppressing.

So – despite the imperative to curb devastating current impacts of growth in quantities like carbon emissions or material consumption – the static notion of a singular scalar limit is fundamentally inappropriate to many other kinds of growth. "Limits" have no necessary meaning for topological growth. What counts as growth in patterns depends on context. And devils are in details.

Again then: why such serious neglect in the narrow degrowth argument of these more complex and diverse possible dimensions, topologies and dynamics of growth? The point of this query is not to dismiss all forms of singular quantification in any kind of context. What it urges instead, is contemplation of the need for pluralities of measures – each transcending the limits of others.

By simply flipping from overly narrow notions of "growth" to similarly constituted – equally restrictive and uncompromising scalar – ideas of "degrowth", prospects for progress can be more thwarted than enabled.

Seeking alternatives

Taken together with the problems discussed in the two earlier blogs, then, these are the reasons why I think it is necessary to challenge the degrowth critique – despite my solidarity with so much that drives it. I believe the implications of these criticisms are both momentous and very practical.

By implying that the only alternative to a supposedly singular growth is an equally restrictive and similarly-constituted scalar kind of "degrowth", an underlying impression is given that perhaps unintentionally entrenches the hegemonic pressure that "there is no alternative". This in turn risks engendering counterproductive reactions.

So, by simply inverting the terms of its target, a narrow "degrowth" critique risks counterproductively reinforcing the prevailing hegemony of monetary value in current real world- politics.

What is striking about all this, is that alternatives are so clear. Instead of half empty, the glass of political possibilities is half full! It entails no compromise on powerful critiques of existing impoverished notions of growth in carbon-dependent, consumption-addicted, pathologically-unequal current capitalist societies, to demand that growth of any kind be – not indiscriminately denied – but radically redefined and pluralised. There is a need to outgrow the current growth debate.

Of course, many concrete implications for positive kinds of action are shared with those that arise from narrow notions of degrowth – and which the degrowth community has done much great work in supporting. But the efficacies of these actions, their practical political prospects, and the risks that they might be subverted, may all be significantly improved by more plural understandings of growth.

Sustainable Development Goals

The Sustainable Development Goals (SDGs), for instance, offer a current pragmatic example of one place to start. Despite many flaws and undue compromises, many SDG indicators define multiple nonmonetary quantities that even high-level global governance institutions are emphasising must grow. Here is a chance to harness "the civilizing effect of hypocrisy", that a narrow emphasis simply on "degrowth" might miss.

So it is not a pipedream to argue that new ways of thinking, speaking and acting about growth can be radically more plural and complex than monetary values alone. The choices lie not just in "growth or degrowth", but in vibrant democratic struggles for "many-growths".

Nor does this necessarily mean repudiating all kinds of material growth. For excluded communities and marginalised kinds of green infrastructure, material – and economic – growth is essential. So, a many-growths approach need not necessarily imply (as degrowth does) rejecting growth as measured in narrow economic terms.

Instead, a many-growth analysis means reshaping and balancing activities measured in conventional economic terms, with radically more prominent and dynamic diversities of cultures, institutions, practices – and metrics – constituting far richer pluralities of social values than the money or material consumption on which current capitalist appropriations depend. Indeed, by opening up wider political spaces, this plurality itself is a driver of potentially empowering disruption.

And these alternative strategic possibilities also seem to offer important tactical benefits. There are plenty of political constituencies who are alienated by perceptions of an implied indiscriminately narrow "degrowth" critique. Rightly or wrongly, suspicions about simplistic rejection of any kind of growth may have a disabling effect on movements for sustainability and social justice.

Rather than losing any possibility of mobilising these allied interests, alternative forms of pluralistic many-growth critiques of narrow monetary hegemony offer a firmer basis for the kinds of broad alliances that are always needed for effective progressive transformation.

Not just "growth" or "degrowth"

So here at the end, I appreciate and agree with Giorgos' own underlying optimistic spirit. In fact, it is this positive progressive energy that I think the narrow degrowth critique actually risks eroding. The choice is not just between "growth or degrowth" on some notionally singular, expediently-imposed scale favoured by the regressive forces being challenged.

What must be resisted is the impoverished starkness of this restrictive one-dimensional choice itself. Progressive politics needs to move more fully out of the straightjacket of narrow economic growth – not by inverting it, but by pluralising it. What is needed is not degrowth, but outgrowth.

Response: Why we need degrowth (Giorgos Kallis)

Andy Stirling's intervention on the occasion of my lecture at Sussex is much appreciated. I am particularly thankful for his constructive engagement and the collegial tone of his comments and critique.

Andy argues that "the choices lie not just in growth or degrowth, but in vibrant democratic struggles for many-growths". But I think there is confusion here regarding my argument. What I criticized was the idea and practice of "economic Growth" (growth with capital G), which has come to have a very concrete meaning and material effect. I am not against any and all "growths" in general, such as the growth of kids into adults or of seeds into trees.

Andy points to many things that would need to "grow" even after we abandon Growth: "equality, health, wellbeing, justice, sustainability, care, liberty, fulfilment, education, human flourishing and quality of life". Also "connections among neurons, co-evolutions between species, experiences of individuals, empathies in relationships, networks within communities, sensibilities in art movements ..."

I honestly fail to see why Andy insists to frame these aspirations in terms of "growth". Equality has to be achieved (or approximated), not grow; same for justice, sustainability or liberty. Fulfilment, "human flourishing", and experiences to "grow"? In what sense? In all these domains we are talking of qualitative changes, patterns of emergence, change and evolution (that Andy knows much better than me), not growth. The co-evolution between species is not a "growth" phenomenon in any meaningful sense of the term. And a Picasso is as good as a Goya which is as good as an ancient Greek or Egyptian sculpture; in what sense is it meaningful to talk about "growth" in art?

"When we say grow up, we do not mean get taller", Andy comments. Precisely: trees or children do not need to grow at a compound rate of 2-3% per year *ad infinitum*. And happiness or wellbeing have an upper limit of... "10". Again, what I criticized in my talk and what we criticize as a degrowth community is capitalism's need for limitless Growth (the aggregate of what each individual firm needs in order to stay competitive in a capitalist economy). David Harvey argues that this is the most lethal of capitalism's contradictions. I would add that it is the most lethal threat for humanity's flourishing in this planet.

Unsustainability and growth

Andy argues that "like others in this field", I repeatedly insisted without qualification that unsustainability is "a necessary consequence of growth in general and of any kind, that it entails impossible aspirations to infinity—and so come up against the resulting inevitable, brutally-material limits".

First, I didn't criticize "growths" in general and of any kind; I am not against the growth of certain types of renewable energies or of social security provisions; but again, only "up" to a level, not their compound growth ad infinitum.

Second, as I argued in more detail for the Great Transition Initiative (see previous chapter), the "growths" of the things and services that "we" (ecologists of the Left) would like to see are unlikely to lead to aggregate GDP growth because they are bound to decrease productivity; and this is fine, as long as we prepare to manage without growth and change institutional structures accordingly. The "Sustainable Development Goals" Andy applauds shy away from dealing with the radical social reorganization that will be necessary in order to flourish in a world without growth and with radically less material and energy use.

Third, I did not talk only of "material limits"; the growth of any magnitude at a compound rate quickly escapes toward infinity, which is an absurd proposition. If someone doubts that, check the math.[1] Economic growth will soon come to an end (if it hasn't already)—be it because of ecological limits, or, as Harvey argues, because of the impossibility of finding ever-new outlets for investment.[2]

Finally, when I said that I am against any type of growth, I meant any type of economic Growth, be it green, immaterial, angelic or socialist; all these visions of growth that share the notion of a constant annual rate of growth and declare no end, are absurd.

Andy argues that this critique applies only to "unqualified neoliberal visions of economic growth". No, it is certainly true of all visions of economic Growth—neo-liberal, Keynesian, social-democratic, green or socialist. It is certainly true of all political projects that do not have a clear vision of when "enough will be enough". I am not aware of any definition

1 Rowan, M. (2014, 27 February). "We need to talk about growth. (And we need to do the sums as well)." Retrieved from http://persuademe.com.au/need-talk-growth-need-sums-well/

2 Harvey, D. (2014). *Seventeen contradictions and the end of capitalism*. UK: Oxford University Press.

of economic Growth other than in terms of economic activity without an upper limit; the growth of neurons or empathy is not economic Growth.

Growth and other systems

As Andy notes, "systems other than capitalism have also shown themselves to be highly susceptible to the cult of economic growth." I believe the reference here must be to the Soviet bloc and not to pre-capitalist formations, or indigenous civilizations, since to my knowledge the latter did not have a cult of growth.

One might debate whether "socialist" systems were truly not capitalist (or state capitalist in the sense that a state elite accumulated surpluses which it invested for further growth), or to what extent they were caught in a competition for growth with capitalist economies given the arms race.

It is beyond doubt, though, that the invention of economic growth is an invention of capitalism; it is both an ideology and a phenomenon that appears with its emergence. Previous civilizations did not see their production, consumption and exchange as a unified "economic system", nor did they perceive that such a system needs to accelerate the circulation of goods and services. Andy comments that "not all forms of capitalism are equally obsessive about money as the sole arbiter of value". Maybe so; I imagine the reference is here to Scandinavian capitalism or post-war UK labor. But no variant of capitalism that I know rejected the pursuit of economic growth and limitless expansion.

A network of ideas

Andy raises the importance of the "force … of cognition" and makes the valid point that degrowth risks reinforcing the prevailing hegemony by defining its critique in the same parameters of uni-dimensional value. I have debated in detail the cognitive aspects of degrowth with Kate Raworth and the discussion that ensued (see next essay in this book) is as good as any of our academic articles.

The misunderstanding with Andy seems to be partly from the fact that his main interaction with the degrowth literature was through my lecture. In my lecture, I made very clear that I restrained my ambition to a "ruthless critique" of the ideology of economic Growth. Hence I critiqued economic Growth in its own absurd mono-dimensional terms. Given that I had 40 minutes and I wanted to instill one "take home" message, I didn"t get into the details of the alternatives that are being promoted in the degrowth literature, alternatives however that can flourish only once we free our imagination and structures from the mono-dimensional pursuit of GDP growth. In our recent book, we provide a "garden" of alternatives (hence the book cover) and a range of inspiring signifiers from "commons" and "conviviality" to "depense" and "care". Degrowth is a network of ideas, not the mono-dimensional inverse of growth.

Uncomfortable critiques

Finally Andy referred to "the comforting allure of performing a self-conscious critical identity" and the responsibility for all of us to not "succumb to this kind of self-indulgence". He qualifies that this comment is not directed to me, but since it is directed to my friends and colleagues in the degrowth community, I cannot let it pass (more so I cannot see why I would be the only one from the degrowth community to be exempt).

First, I am not so sure what is comforting about going against the grain and criticizing explicitly economic growth and capitalism. Certainly being part of a community helps you not get scared; living in the EU also helps, at least for the moment (growth critics and ecologists in other parts of the world, including democracies like India or Turkey do not have this privilege). But rest assured: there is nothing comforting or indulgent in listening to a best-selling radio talk-host from the US directly citing from our book and labeling degrowthers (which also includes President Obama…) as enemies of the nation who want to end the American dream.[1]

Second, I don't think my students stand a better chance of building an academic career by being proponents of degrowth, rather than doing neat economic models or writing about more innocuous stuff such as "sustainability".

Third, I really admire the courage of "growth objectors" who block coal power plants or new airport highways; there is nothing indulgent in spending months if not years of your life in prison.

1 Levin, M. (Producer). (2015, 13 August 2016). "Mark Levin explains the degrowth movement." Retrieved from https://www.youtube.com/watch?v=lTLWuJVMoIA

Are the Sustainable Development Goals a source of hope?

Finally I am not sure how "the Sustainable Development Goals ... offer a current pragmatic example of one place to start" (Andy's words). Sustainable development is an empty signifier which has been with us for two decades, during which time there has been an unprecedented process of environmental de-regulation and a backtrack in each and every environmental front (typically in the name of the economy and its growth).

How is it not comforting to stick with this outdated, non-conflicting, depoliticizing (in the sense that it hides genuine antagonisms about the kinds of worlds we want to live in) agenda that has no real effects, and which has been fully assimilated by the establishment?

If this exchange has given the impression that I and Andy stand on opposite fronts, let me make clear that this is not the case. We both agree that Growth is not the way to go, and we both envision a future of equality where care, solidarity, justice, social networks and the commons flourish.

Andy recognizes that the "tyranny of money is far from abstract in practice. It is imposed by many kinds of coercive power and hard structure—and (ultimately) by threat of organized violence". Given such a formidable force to confront, the degrowth community needs the intellectual resources and help of people like Andy and his contribution in order to decolonize society's imaginary from the Growth fetish. I am not sure that pointing to the obvious fact that many things might have to grow, once we abandon Growth, is the best way to help.

23. Is degrowth a compelling word?

Author's note: Continuing along the lines of Andy Stirling's critique that the word "degrowth" is misleading, this chapter includes two further critiques on the cognitive aspects of the term. The first critique comes from Brian Dean, who writes from the perspective of cognitive framing, a field which seeks to explore how people react depending on how a concept is presented. Foremost in this field is the work of George Lakoff, who has recently published a book called Don't think of an elephant![1] *and has also written extensively about how environmental movements have been presented. Brian Dean is a disciple of Lakoff and runs a blog called* News Frames, *wherein he publishes thought-pieces on current topics, providing helpful insight on how activists can better present their claims to the public. The following piece deconstructs the term degrowth, and explains why it is problematic. The second piece is by Kate Raworth, an economist at Oxford University's Environmental Change Institute. She is known for her contribution to the planetary boundaries literature, and is currently writing the book* Doughnut economics: Seven ways to think like a 21st century economist, *to be published by Random House. I met Kate during my Leverhulme year in London and she invited me to give one of the opening lectures for the 2015 edition of Oxford's masters in Environmental Change and Management. Kate liked my arguments about degrowth, but she too was not convinced by the term itself. In December 2015, we debated the usefulness of the word "degrowth", hosted by Duncan Green's popular Oxfam blog,* From Poverty to Power. *My response partly accounts for some of the criticisms levied by Brian Dean as well, or at least shows how his framing of the issue failed to change the synapses in my brain.*

"Degrowth"—a problematic economic frame (Brian Dean)

The term "degrowth" is increasingly used to designate a sort of environmental movement. And while it may be an effective label to unite people with similar views, it ignores pretty much all the advice from the

1 Lakoff, G. (2014). *The All New Don't Think of an Elephant!: Know Your Values and Frame the Debate*. Chelsea Green Publishing.

field of cognitive framing on building popular alternatives to conservatively-framed "common sense".

I touched on this in an earlier post on economic "growth" framing.[1] Reaction to that post was mixed—some people "got" it; others seemed to think I was talking just about language. We have to remind ourselves that cognitive framing is about how we think—how we form worldviews. Ideas, beliefs and impressions which have been reinforced in our neural circuitry over decades, thanks to constant cultural repetition, cannot be undone simply by using a language of opposition (with some exceptions[2]).

With that in mind, here are some pointers on the problems with "degrowth", starting with "growth" basics.

"Growth" frame basics

- "Growth" of "the economy" is what George Lakoff calls an ontological metaphor. In plain English, this means we think about the unthinkable (e.g. immeasurable complexity) in terms of "entities or substances of a uniform kind".3 Thus, the diverse activities of millions of people are aggregated into a single entity called "the economy", with a uniform attribute of "growth".
- This metaphorical framing has some important downsides (as some economists have realized, at least since the establishment of Gross Domestic Product as a "measure"). For example, the crude binary logic of"growth"/"no-growth", as if "the economy" has only two ways to go. Also, the dangerous illusion of uniformity in the aggregate measure of "growth", as if different "economic activities" (with irreconcilable measures) can meaningfully be lumped together in a single quantitative measure.

1 Dean, B. (2014). "The economic "growth" frame – and its opposition." Retrieved from https://newsframes.wordpress.com/2014/08/27/economic-growth/

2 In some cases, direct opposition seems the only way to go. When slavery (for example) is directly opposed, the slavery frame is, of course, activated and reinforced in our brains. Does that undermine the anti-slavery cause? Clearly not when slavery is already widely conceived as immoral and unacceptable. But what about before that point in a given society? You might want to ponder the differences between something like slavery and something like "growth" of "the economy"—in terms of conceptual metaphor and level of abstraction. Also, consider my article on Antiwork. Am I contradicting myself by using a term that opposes work? Or is the idea of negating all work so obviously ludicrous, that I must be attempting some sort of "guerilla ontology", simply to provoke thought/debate?

3 Lakoff, G., & Johnson, M. (2008). *Metaphors we live by.* University of Chicago press, p. 25.

- "Growth", as metaphor for the increasing "sum" of diverse human activities, excludes qualitative differences. It thus conflates life-nurturing and life-destroying activities (both of which may count as "growth"). Qualitative frames (e.g. for differentiating types of activity creating well-being or environmental damage, etc) are diminished in cognitive importance by a repeated focus on "growth".
- "Growth" overwhelmingly tends to be conceptualised as natural and good, while lack of growth is seen as bad and unnatural. This is universal, deep-rooted, and unlikely to be reversed by promoting "degrowth" as a good, or by analogies with special cases where growth is seen as bad—e.g. growth of disease.
- Market ideology and the Protestant work ethic mutually reinforce the notion of "growth" as outcome of (and moral reward for) "efficiency", "discipline", "productivity", "hard work", etc. This moral framing system is deeply rooted in our culture.

Problems with "degrowth"

- "Degrowth" isn't a different frame from "growth"—it entails the same set of conceptual metaphors: an entity ("the economy") with a single aggregate measure ("growth"), and the implication of a top-down policy whose primary objective is to increase or decrease/stabilise "it". Both "growth" and "degrowth" are single, quantitative ends for "the economy".
- Although direct negation (e.g. as "degrowth" negates "growth") may appear to logically undermine a frame, it activates the frame in our brains, strengthening its physical, neural basis. And, by a process which cognitive linguists call "mutual inhibition", alternatives to the frame are inhibited by continual focus on its reinforcement/negation.
- The "growth"/"degrowth" frame of an aggregate quantitative measure, usually at a national level, reinforces both market capitalist and conservative nationalist conceptual schemas.
- Nationalist schemas include the Nation as Person metaphor in thinking about "national interest". In conservative framing, this means competition between nations, in which "national interest" (i.e. economic health and military strength) is about aggregate maximisation of wealth and power. This ties in with (mutually reinforces) national economic "growth" (i.e. "growth"/"degrowth"

framing).

In short, the way we think about "the economy" in terms of "growth" is reinforced in important respects by the "degrowth" vs "growth" narrative—including inhibition of alternative frames. And in what might be called conservative "felt" common sense (which is widespread as a result of cultural repetition of the economic "growth" and market frames over decades), "degrowth" will be "felt" as deeply unnatural, nefarious, and weakening to the nation.

If the penny still hasn't dropped for "degrowth" campaigners, I recommend they read, and carefully ponder, Lakoff's paper, "Why it matters how we frame the environment."

Never accept the right's frames—don't negate them, or repeat them, or structure your arguments to counter them. That just activates their frames in the brain and helps them.[1]

Postscript

A few responses I've had indicate a confusion between criticism of the "growth" frame and opposition to "growth" itself (as a believed reality). It's akin to confusing the map with the territory. Both respondents were quick to insist that they criticised the frame (i.e. the inadequacy of the aggregate "growth" metaphor), but then immediately contradicted themselves by insisting on opposing "growth" as if it were a tangible reality. I think this contradiction results because thinking in terms of conceptual metaphor is a new approach—we can easily slip back into reifying old frames if we're not paying attention (especially with well-established frames such as "growth").

1 Lakoff, G. (2014). *The all new Don't think of an elephant!: Know your values and frame the debate*. Chelsea Green Publishing.

Why degrowth has outgrown its name (Kate Raworth)

Here's what troubles me about degrowth: I just can't bring myself to use the word.

Don't get me wrong: I think the degrowth movement is addressing the most profound economic questions of our day. I believe that economies geared to pursue unending GDP growth will undermine the planetary life-support systems on which we fundamentally depend. That is why we need to transform the growth-addicted design of government, business and finance at the heart of our economies. From this standpoint, I share much of the degrowth movement's analysis, and back its core policy recommendations.[1]

It's not the intellectual position I have a problem with. It's the name.

Here are five reasons why.

1. Getting beyond missiles.

My degrowth friends tell me that the word was chosen intentionally and provocatively as a "missile word" to create debate. I get that, and agree that shock and dissonance can be valuable advocacy tools.

But in my experience of talking about possible economic futures with a wide range of people, the term "degrowth" turns out to be a very particular kind of missile: a smoke bomb. Throw it into a conversation and it causes widespread confusion and mistaken assumptions.

If you are trying to persuade someone that their growth-centric worldview is more than a little out of date, then it takes careful argument. But whenever the word "degrowth" pops up, I find the rest of the conversation is spent clearing up misunderstandings about what it does or doesn't mean. This is not an effective advocacy strategy for change. If we are serious about overturning the dominance of growth-centric economic thought, the word "degrowth" just ain't up to the task.

2. Defining degrowth.

I have to admit I have never quite managed to pin down what the word

1 Kallis, G. (2015). "Yes, we can prosper without growth: 10 policy proposals for the New Left." *Common Dreams*. Retrieved from http://www.commondreams.org/views/2015/01/28/yes-we-can-prosper-without-growth-10-policy-proposals-new-left

means. According to degrowth.org, the term means "a downscaling of production and consumption that increases human well-being and enhances ecological conditions and equity on the planet." Sounding good, but that's not clear enough.

Are we talking about degrowth of the economy's material volume—the tonnes of stuff consumed—or degrowth of its monetary value, measured as GDP? That difference really matters, but it is too rarely spelled out.

If we are talking about downscaling material throughput, then even people in the "green growth" camp would agree with that goal too, so degrowth needs to get more specific to mark itself out.

If it is downscaling GDP that we are talking about (and here, green growth and degrowth clearly part company), then does degrowth mean a freeze in GDP, a decrease in GDP, being indifferent about what happens to GDP, or in fact declaring that GDP should not be measured at all? I have heard all of these arguments made under the banner of degrowth, but they are very different, with very different strategic consequences. Without greater clarity, I don't know how to use the word.

3. Learn from Lakoff: negative frames don't win.

The cognitive scientist George Lakoff is an authority on the nature and power of frames—the worldviews that we activate (usually without realizing it) through the words and metaphors we choose. As he has documented over many decades, we are unlikely to win a debate if we try to do so while still using our opponent's frames. The title of his book, *Don't think of an elephant!*,[1] makes this very point because it immediately makes you think of a you know what.

How does this work in politics? Take debates about taxes, for example. It's hard to argue against "tax relief" (aka tax cuts for the rich), since the positive frame of "relief" sounds so very desirable: arguing against it just reinforces the frame that tax is a burden. Far wiser is to recast the issue in your own positive terms instead, say, by advocating for "tax justice".

Does degrowth fall into this trap? I had the chance to put this question to George Lakoff himself in a recent webinar. He was criticizing the dominant economic frame of "growth" so I asked him whether "degrowth" was a useful alternative. "No it isn't", was his immediate reply, "First of all it's like "Don't think of an elephant!"—"Don't think of growth!" It means

1 Lakoff, G. (2014). *The all new Don't think of an elephant!: Know your values and frame the debate*. Chelsea Green Publishing.

we are going to activate the notion of growth. When you negate something you strengthen the concept."

Just to be clear, I know that the degrowth movement stands for many positive and empowering things. The richly nuanced book *Degrowth: A vocabulary for a new era*, edited by Giacomo D'Alisa, Federico Demaria and Giorgos Kallis, is packed full of great entries on environmental justice, conviviality, co-operatives, simplicity, autonomy, and care—every one of them a positive frame. It's not the contents but the "degrowth" label on the jar that makes me baulk. I'll adopt the rest of the vocabulary, just not the headline.

4. It's time to clear the air.

Just for a moment let's give the word "degrowth" the benefit of the doubt and suppose that the missile has landed and it has worked. The movement is growing and has websites, books, and conferences dedicated to furthering its ideas. That's great. These debates and alternative economic ideas are desperately needed. But there comes a time for the smoke to clear, and for a beacon to guide us all through the haze: something positive to aim for. Not a missile but a lighthouse. And we need to name the lighthouse.

In Latin America they call it buen vivir which literally translates as living well, but means so much more than that too. In Southern Africa they speak of Ubuntu, the belief in a universal bond of sharing that connects all humanity. Surely the English-speaking world—whose language has more than one million words—can have a crack at finding something equally inspiring. Of course this is not easy, but this is where the work is.

Tim Jackson has suggested prosperity, which literally means "things turning out as we hope for".[1] The New Economics Foundation—and many others—frame it as wellbeing.[2] Christian Felber suggests Economy for the Common Good.[3] Others (starting with Aristotle) go for human flourishing.[4] I don't think any of these have completely nailed it yet, but they are certainly heading in the right direction.

1 Jackson, T. (2009). *Prosperity without growth: Economics for a finite planet.* Routledge.

2 NEF. (2015). "Well-being." Retrieved from http://www.neweconomics.org/issues/entry/well-being

3 ECG. (2016). *Economy for the Common Good.* Retrieved from https://www.ecogood.org/en

4 Wikipedia. (2016). "Eudamonia." Retrieved 14 August, 2016 https://en.wikipedia.org/wiki/Eudaimonia

5. There's too much at stake, and much to discuss.

The debates currently being had under the banner of degrowth are among the most important economic debates for the 21st century. But most people don't realize that because the name puts them off. We urgently need to articulate an alternative, positive vision of an economy in a way that is widely engaging. Here's the best way I have come up with so far to say it:

We have an economy that needs to grow, whether or not it makes us thrive.

We need an economy that makes us thrive, whether or not it grows.

Is that "degrowth"? I don't actually know. But what I do know is that whenever I frame it like this in debates, lots of people nod, and the discussion soon moves on to identifying how we are currently locked into a must-grow economy—through the current design of government, business, finance, and politics—and what it would take to free ourselves from that lock-in so that we can pursue social justice with ecological integrity instead.

We need to reframe this debate in a way that tempts many more people to get involved if we are ever to build the critical mass needed to change the dominant economic narrative.

So those are five reasons why I think degrowth has outgrown its own name.

I'm guessing that some of my degrowth friends will respond to this blog (my own little missile) with irritation, frustration or a sigh. Here we go again—we've got to explain the basics once more.

If so, take note. Because when you find yourself continually having to explain the basics and clear up repeated misunderstandings, it means there is something wrong with the way the ideas are being presented.

Believe me, the answer is in the name. It's time for a new frame.

You're wrong Kate, degrowth is a compelling word (Giorgos Kallis)

My friend Kate Raworth "cannot bring herself to use the word" degrowth. Here are nine reasons why I use it.

1. Clear definition.

"Degrowth" is as clear as it gets. Definitely no less clear than "equality"; or "economic growth" for that matter (is it growth of welfare or activity? monetised or all activity? if only monetised, why would we care?). Beyond a critique of the absurdity of perpetual growth, degrowth signifies a decrease of global carbon and material footprint, starting from the wealthy.

The "green growth camp" also wants such a decrease, but it argues that GDP growth is necessary for—or compatible with—it. Degrowth, not: in all likelihood GDP will decrease too. If we do the right things to thrive, such as capping carbon, if we transform the profit economy to one of care and solidarity, the GDP economy will shrink. Kate too calls for "an economy that makes us thrive, whether or not it grows" and to "free ourselves" from the growth "lock-in". The Germans named this "post-growth" and I am fine with it. But somehow it beautifies the scale of the challenge: reducing our energy or material use in half and transforming and stabilizing a shrinking (not simply "not growing") economy. With its shock element "de"-growth reminds that we won't have our cake and eat it all.

2. Right conversations with the right people.

Know this feeling "what am I doing with these people in the same room"? Hearing the words "win-win" and looking at graphs where society, environment and economy embrace one another in loving triangles as markets internalize "externalities" (sic)? Well, you won't be invited to these rooms if you throw the missile of degrowth. And this is good. Marx wouldn't be concerned with sitting at the table with capitalists to convince them about communism.

Why pretend we agree? I've never had a boring or confusing conversation about degrowth (witness the present one). Passions run high, core questions are raised (did we lose something with progress? what is in the past for the future? is system change possible and how?). But to have these conversations you need to know about—and defend—degrowth.

3. Mission un-accomplished.

Kate asks us to imagine that the "missile" "has landed and it has worked". Problem is the missile has landed, but it hasn't worked, so it is not yet "the time to move on". Microsoft spellcheck keeps correcting degrowth into "regrowth". Degrowth is anathema to the right and left. Economists turn ash-faced when they hear "degrowth". Eco-modernists capture the headlines with a cornucopian future powered by nuclear and fed by GMOs. A recent book calls degrowthers "Malthusians", eco-austerians and "collapse porn addicts". A radical party like Syriza had as slogan "growth or austerity". The ideology of growth is stronger than ever. In the 70s its critique was widespread, politicians entertained it and at least economists felt they had to respond.

4. There is a vibrant community and this is an irreversible fact.

In Barcelona 20-30 of us meet frequently to read and discuss degrowth, cook and drink, go to forests and to protests. We disagree in almost everything other than that degrowth brings us together. In the fourth international conference in Leipzig, there were 3500 participants. Most of them were students. After the closing plenary, they took to the shopping streets with a music band, raised placards against consumerism and blocked a coal factory. Young people from all over the world want to study degrowth in Barcelona. If you experience this incredible energy, you find that degrowth is a beautiful word. But I understand the difficulty of using it in a different context: half a year a visitor in London and I feel I am the odd and awkward one insisting on degrowth.

5. Why do we always have to be positive?

I come from the Mediterranean. Progress looks different; civilization there peaked centuries ago. Serge Latouche says that "degrowth is seen as negative, something unpardonable in a society where at all costs one must 'think positively'". "Be positive" is a North-American invention. Please, let us be "negative". I can't take all that happiness. Grief, sacrifice, care, honor: life is not all about feeling "better".

For Southerners at heart—be it from the Global North or South, East or West—this idea of constant betterment and improvement has always seemed awkward. Wasting ourselves and our products irrationally, refusing to improve and be "useful", has its allure. Denying our self-importance is an antidote to a Protestant ethic at the heart of growth. Let's resist the demand to be positive!

6. I am not a linguist.

Who am I to question Professor Lakoff that we can't tell people "don't think of an elephant!" because they will think of one? Then again, a-theists did pretty well in their battle against gods. And so did those who wanted to abolish slavery. Or, unfortunately, conservatives for "deregulation". By turning something negative into their rallying cry, they disarmed the taken-for-granted goodness of the claim of their enemy. The queer movement turned an insult into pride. This is the art of subversion. Is there a linguistic theory for it?

This is different from what Lakoff criticized US democrats for. Democrats accept the frame of Republicans, providing softer alternatives ("less austerity"). "Green growth" is that; degrowth is a subversive negation of growth: a snail, not a leaner elephant.[1] *The Guardian*'s language columnist Steven Poole finds degrowth "cute".[2] When most people agree with him, and find the snail cute, we will be on the path of a "great transition".

7. Cannot be co-opted.

Buen vivir sounds great. Who wouldn't like to "live well"? And indeed Latin Americans took it at heart: the Brazil-Ecuador inter-Amazonian highway with implanted "creative cities" in-between is a program for "buen vivir"; Bolivia's nuclear power programme is part of a plan for buen vivir; and a credit card in Venezuela is called buen vivir. Which reminds me of "Ubuntu Cola". No one would build a highway, a nuclear reactor, issue more credit or sell colas in the name of degrowth. As George Monbiot said in one of his texts, capitalism can sell everything, but not less.

Could degrowth be coopted by austerians? Plausible, but unlikely; austerity is always justified for the sake of growth. Capitalism looses legitimacy without growth. By anti-immigrants? Scary, but not impossible,

1 Poole, S. (2015, 30 January). "Steven Poole: beware growthspeak." *The Guardian*. Retrieved from https://www.theguardian.com/books/2015/jan/30/steven-poole-growthspeak-general-election-looms

2 *Ibid.*

it has been tried in France. This is why we cannot abandon the term: we have to develop and defend its content.

8. It is not an end.

It is as absurd to degrow ad infinitum as it is to grow. The point is to abolish the god of Growth and construct a different society with low footprints. There is a "lighthouse" for this: the Commons.[1] A downscaled commons though. Peer-to-peer production and the sharing economy use materials and electricity too. Degrowth is a reminder that you cannot have your cake and eat it all, even if it's a digitally fabricated one.

9. Focuses my research.

I make an effort arguing with eco-modernists, green growthers, growth economists, or Marxist developmentalists about the (un)sustainability of growth. This persistence to defend degrowth is productive: it encourages research questions that no one else asks. Sure, we can in theory use fewer materials; but then why do material footprints still grow? What would work, social security, money, look like in an economy that contracts? One who is convinced of green growth won't ask these questions.

Kate is not; she agrees with our 10 degrowth policy proposals[2]: work-sharing, debt jubilee, public money, basic income. Why in the name of degrowth though she asks? Because we cannot afford to be agnostic. It makes a huge difference, both for research and design, whether you approach these as means of stimulus and growth anew or of managing and stabilizing degrowth.

Degrowth remains a necessary word.

1 Helfrich, S., & Bollier, D. (2014). "Commons." In G. D'Alisa, F. Demaria, & G. Kallis (Eds.), *Degrowth: a vocabulary for a new era.* Routledge.

2 Kallis, G. (2015). "Yes, we can prosper without growth: 10 policy proposals for the New Left." *Common Dreams.* Retrieved from http://www.commondreams.org/views/2015/01/28/yes-we-can-prosper-without-growth-10-policy-proposals-new-left

24. Will degrowth be voluntary or involuntary?

Author's note: Brian Davey is the author of the book Credo: Economic beliefs in a world of crisis. *A long-time community organizer, he is also involved with the think tank Feasta and currently lives in Nottingham, UK. Davey wrote an in-depth review of the book I co-edited,* Degrowth: A vocabulary for a new era. *The following is an abridged version of that review, followed by my response. Davey also wrote a final response to my review, available at the* Feasta *site.*[1]

A very optimistic version of Degrowth? (Brian Davey)

... I think the book ought to have explored whether degrowth will mainly be an involuntary process. Let me try and explain what I see as being the difference.

By "voluntary degrowth" I mean a vision for the future that is promoted because it is regarded as preferable to a growth economy. It is preferable, for example, because it encompasses a number of proposals for change that get no attention in the growth economy where more output is seen as the solution for all problems. An example would be Ivan Illiich's tools for conviviality—creating the kind of tools that would make possible "space for relationships, recognition, pleasure and generally living well, and thereby, reducing the dependence on an industrial and consumerist system" as Marco Deriu explains in his chapter. Thus what I might term "voluntary degrowth" is a mainly French idea that is sometimes termed "décroissance conviviale", a cultural and social critique of society—an alternative "imaginary" of how society might be.

By "involuntary degrowth" I mean a view of the future that the production economy will contract anyway, whether we like it or not, perhaps in a chaotic fashion, perhaps through collapse, so that the task of the degrowth movement is to prepare for, and ameliorate, that contraction as best as we can. It is not so much communities and societies making a choice against growth—but communities finding means to cope with

1 Davey, B. (2015). "Brian Davey responds to Giorgos Kallis on Degrowth." *Feasta*. Retrieved from http://www.feasta.org/2015/01/14/brian-davey-responds-to-giorgos-kallis-on-degrowth/#comments

difficulties that they will inevitably face when the economy contracts anyway. For example the Transition Movement (that is barely mentioned in this book) has had an idea that "energy descent" is going to happen in the near future and that it is an urgent task to prepare communities so that they will be able to cope.

Now in trying to cope with this process that people like me think will happen anyway the Transition Movement have had a strong idea of making the most of the situation. They have wanted to "make a virtue out of necessity" and to look for the silver linings around the storm clouds. There is the suggestion that people might be surprised to find that the quality of life might actually be better. The Transition Movement thus works toward the revival of community, relationships, and different kinds of creativity too. The kinds of projects advocated for—like urban gardening—are the same as for décroissance conviviale. However, the starting point is not a choice for a different kind of society compared with the growth economy—as much as it is making the best of what will happen in the difficult conditions associated with future contraction.

To my mind it is a weakness of this book that it does not draw out and emphasise these distinctions enough. In fact different kinds of future are possible. Thus we can consider the possibility that involuntary degrowth happens (in the sense of a contraction of material production) but not quickly enough to reduce carbon emissions at an adequate pace. In this situation, cap and share to speed up the pace of emissions reduction—and voluntary degrowth of material production, would still be needed to speed up the involuntary contraction.

Reducing the allowable extraction of fossil fuels in order to leave most fuels in the ground would degrow the economy. However, on its own this is unlikely to be enough to avert runaway climate change. That's because CO^2 is already over the limit and any more will add to the danger. So a lot of CO^2 will have to be taken out of the atmosphere. This is another urgent future task. However, any draw-down of CO^2 will probably only be possible, if at all, by extensive land reclamation and re-vegetation, locking up the CO^2 in biomass—using ecological design methods (like permaculture). In my view draw-down or sequestration ought to be another idea with a chapter. It isn't. There is no consideration of enhancing carbon sinks.

One way of summarising these points is to say that the editors have drawn together a mainly optimistic version of degrowth. It is not a view that I share. I find it interesting to contrast the approach of the editors with the attitude of Dennis Meadows, a surviving member of the *Lim-*

its to Growth study of 1972. Meadows stopped believing that humanity would be able to adequately respond to the limits to growth crisis in the 1990s and feels that a collapse is now inevitable.

Graham Turner, an Australian academic, has now done 30- and 40-year follow-ups to see how the business as usual predictions of the 1972 *Limits to Growth* computer model compare with what actually happened. He concludes that they are pretty much on target—and that the turning point will occur in 2015.[1]

The distinction between voluntary and involuntary transitions matters. Without a transition that is at least partly involuntary it is highly unlikely that sufficient people will voluntarily adjust their lifestyles in the directions that degrowthers see as vital. At the same time what we are describing an unpleasant historical epoch in which death rates will be rising.

Risk aversion, prospect theory and the collapse of lifestyle packages

Daniel Kahneman's "prospect theory"[2] is an idea absent from this book. It shows that people organize their lives around what he calls "reference points" and are very "risk averse" when it comes to retreating away from those reference points. A reference point might be something like the income level to which one has grown accustomed and therefore the amount that one spends in day-to-day life, the expenditure associated with a lifestyle that is more or less adjusted to the income. My interpretation of this is that a fall in income is not welcome not only because one has less but because the organisation, the management of life's details, must be adjusted so as to create an adjusted expenditure pattern and this requires thought and attention. One spends less money but spends more time thinking about what one spends money on. This is unwelcome extra mental effort. For a significant change one must adjust a whole pattern of hourly, daily and weekly purchases with possible consequences for habitat, relationships, routine transport arrangements etc.

It is all very well to write, as the editors do in their epilogue, that scarcity is social, and that society can produce more than enough for our basic needs—but that does not address the main issue that people worry

1 Turner, G. M. (2012). "On the cusp of global collapse? Updated comparison of The Limits to Growth with historical data." *GAIA-Ecological Perspectives for Science and Society, 21*(2), 116-124.

2 Kahneman, D., & Tversky, A. (1979). "Prospect theory: An analysis of decision under risk." *Econometrica: Journal of the econometric society*, 263-291.

about when they manage their day to day lives. This is how to maintain their "lifestyle package" in sufficient balance so that their lives are not at risk of descending into chaos. Most individuals whose lives are in balance will be living in a set of circumstances where their income is more or less appropriate to match their habitat needs, which must match their relationships (accommodation suitable to living with their partner and dependents). These must match their job with its income—and with its time and travel commitments. These must match their job skills and domestic commitments. There is mental and emotional work involved in balancing one's life and it is scary if it seems like unravelling.

The biggest fear is of a generalised life crisis in which all of these things unravel together. For example, because they lose their job a person might find that they cannot service their debts (mortgage) or pay the rent and thus lose their accommodation. During the stress and practical chaos of this their relationships might break apart. During the last crash many ended up homeless living in tents or cars on their own. Many people also lost their minds—i.e. became totally disoriented, extremely emotional, and unable to function.[1]

The practical projects as "lifeboat arrangements"

The point about a generalised crisis is that large numbers of people could find themselves in situations like these—and thus need the urban farms, the food co-ops, the repair and maintenance workshops, the back to the land projects, the alternative currencies as "lifeboat" arrangements to keep them afloat. They will need these kind of projects to give them new social relationships and enable them to begin again, to regain confidence, to "recycle their lives". It seems implausible to me that most people will join these projects and organize their lives around them as a choice of rejection of the growth economy—although some will. It is however not implausible that if and when the growth economy is breaking down that people will join these projects. (I have seen how valuable a community garden can be for people who have mental health problems.)

Until a generalised breakdown occurs most people will remain too tightly tied into the economic mainstream. When a breakdown does occur, however, the times will be very dangerous and the projects must

1 See my paper produced for Economic De-Growth for Ecological Sustainability and Social Equity, Paris, 18/19th April 2008 at http://events.it-sudparis.eu/degrowth-conference/en/themes/. I did not attend this conference because, not being an academic, I could not afford to.

be there ready to include and support people. This is because it is when all their options seem bad that people lose their risk aversion and are prepared to take gambles—like for example betting what little they have left or, in a more fundamental sense, gambling with their life by joining a criminal gang or an extremist movement.

Resilience—another missing word

The word to describe this set of issues is "resilience". Unfortunately resilience is another missing concept in this book. Resilience is about how much stress an individual's "lifestyle package" or a community or a society can take and still function before it breaks down catastrophically. It is about the tipping points or thresholds within systems that reflect their levels of complexity and interdependence.

This ought to have been clear from the chapter by Sergio Ulgiati on "Entropy" which is about what role low entropy energy has in the maintenance of systems. The availability of low entropy energy in economic and social systems is not just in order to be able to produce enough "stuff". The conversion of energy in "hub interdependencies"—in transport systems, transactions and financial systems, computer controlled production systems, and global supply networks is used to maintain the continued functionality of an immensely complex set of organisational structures. If the energy is not there then the complexity degrades—systems cease to function—the organisation falls to bits.

The crucial issue here is: how resilient are these interrelated structures to disruptions in hub interdependencies brought about by energy and resource supply shocks? Systems can cope with reductions in inputs of energy and other resources up to a point but beyond that point they may break down completely. When organisational arrangements break down altogether nothing at all may get produced because workers are unemployed, production systems stand idle, banks are bust, nothing moves. There would not be stone age levels of production but no production at all. Gar nicht. Rien du tout. Res en absolute.

Here's a quote from a colleague in Feasta, David Korowicz, which reveals the issue at stake:

> In September 2000 truckers in the United Kingdom, angry at rising diesel duties, blockaded refineries and fuel distribution outlets. The petrol stations' reliance on Just-In-Time re-supply meant the impact was rapid. Within 2 days of the blockade starting approximately half of the UK's petrol stations had run out of fuel and sup-

> plies to industry and utilities had begun to be severely affected. The initial impact was on transport—people couldn't get to work and businesses could not be re-supplied. This then began to have a systemic impact.
>
> The protest finished after 5 days at which point supermarkets had begun to be empty of stock, large parts of the manufacturing sector were about to be shut down, hospitals had begun to offer emergency-only care, automatic cash machines could not be re-supplied, and the postal service was severely affected. There was panic buying at supermarkets and petrol stations. It was estimated that after the first day an average 10% of national output was lost. Surprisingly, at the height of the disruption, commercial truck traffic on the UK road network was only 10-12% below average values.[1]

It will be noted here that 10 to 12 % less commercial truck traffic and British society was about to fall to bits. It is easy to imagine particular kinds of emergency where the "life style package" of a lot of people would disintegrate.

Climate change, climate policy, overshoot, involuntary degrowth, collapse, risk aversion, inertia, resilience…here are a whole series of concepts and words that in my view ought to have appeared in the vocabulary but did not.

A French book written in English?

The degrowth book is a collection of 51 very short essays, almost all of which are by academic authors—16 of whom are at the University of Barcelona. Although it is claimed to be the first comprehensive collection about degrowth in English it is very much a southern European academic view of what degrowth means. This is reflected in the choice of topics by the editors who have clearly been very influenced by thinkers on the French left. Thus, to my mind, many chapters sit uneasily alongside the chapters by some of the English and American authors, some of whom have started from a different pre-analytical framework. I have no problem with a book whose authors start from different points but it places a particular responsibility on the editors to give the reader some orientation to the differences. It makes me wonder what the English and American authors have made of the parts of the book that they had no

1 Korowicz, D. (2013). "Catastrophic shocks through complex socio-economic systems: A pandemic perspective." *Feasta*. Retrieved from http://www.feasta.org/wp-content/uploads/2013/07/Catastrophic-shock-pandemic2.pdf

hand in writing.

This brings me to one of the words that do appear in this book and one in particular that the editors seem particularly keen on—that word is "dépense". This concept is discussed more than any other by the editors, particularly in their epilogue where the authors break into French slogans in their last two sentences:

> Vive la décroissance conviviale. Pour la sobriete individuelle et la dépense sociale.

With social dépense so clearly highlighted it is obviously important to understand it. If the idea is to be "operationalised" we need to know how to recognize "dépense" when we see it. In fact I've been left feeling that I am unclear what it means.

Part of the problem for me with understanding "dépense" is that it is another word coming out of the French tradition with which I have not been familiar. When the word "dépense" is left in French and not simply translated as "expenditure" then the reader is left assuming that it has a more complex meaning which I need to make some more effort into getting a grip on.

Unfortunately after a lot of work I am still not completely sure that I have understood what the word means. Nor am I sure that I have understood how the dépense chapter author, Onofrio Romano, and the editors want the word to be understood in the context of degrowth—because this is not necessarily identical to the way Bataille understood it. What follows is my attempt to convert the idea into a terminology that would make some sort of sense to me but I am not completely sure that I have got it right.

Underlying the motivational foundations for the ideology of growth is the mainstream economics idea of scarcity. If there can never be enough goods and services to meet human needs it seems to follow that the more we produce the better. Here is the simple case for growth. It would therefore be understandable if advocates of degrowth were drawn to Bataille who turned the scarcity idea on its head—the problem for the economy in his way of thinking is not how to deal with scarcity but how to deal with "excess".

According to Bataille, there is a "superabundance of energy" and more than enough to meet the basic material needs for organisms/humans. That part of work using energy to meet these basic needs which enable us to survive can be regarded as "servile:" serving and merely re-creating our animal existence. It is when we are deciding what to do with the surplus, which is more than we need for very basic needs, that we enter a realm of freedom where we are truly exercising our freedom in "forms of energy beyond the servile".

For Romano, and for the editors, here is a key concept that they want to put at the heart of "degrowth". Scarcity, the editors assure us, "is social. Since the stone age we have had more than we need for a basic standard of living."

The problem is that, instead of staying with our basic individual standards of living and democratically organising how we are going to "waste" the surplus together, for non servile purposes that develop our humanity, we have accumulated and invested the surplus in new technologies that expand production even more. We have thereby grown the capacity of "the economy" to produce ever more until it is threatening the eco-system. At the same time we have privatised and individualised the process of waste making of the surplus. "Given the individualisation of society, single individuals take on the burden of waste through small trade offs: from perverse sexuality to alcoholism, gambling and flashy consumption".[1]

The alternative then is guaranteeing a modest living for all individuals and socialising "dépense", the non productive use of society's surplus.

This superficially attractive idea could perhaps alternatively be expressed like this: if we want to stop growing we must stop accumulating productive capital. (Creating more technical devices and infrastructures that convert energy while turning more throughputs into what eventually become larger waste streams). With a modest income most individuals would not have enough to save and any surplus would go to democratic institutions to dispense—though not on anything productive that would grow the economy. According to the editors:

> Our message to the frugal ecologists is that it is better to waste resources in gold decorations in a public building or drink them in a big feast, than put them to good use, accelerating even more the extraction of new resources and the degradation of the environment. It is the only way to escape Jevons' Paradox. Accumulation drives growth, not waste. Even in a society of frugal subjects with a downscaled metabolism, there will still be a surplus that would have to be dispensed, if growth

1 Romano, O. (2014). "Dépense." In G. D'Alisa, F. Demaria, & G. Kallis (Eds.), *Degrowth: A vocabulary for a new era* (pp. 86-89). New York and London: Routledge.

> is not to be reactivated.[1]

I think that I get the main drift of the argument here but I am not absolutely sure I have understood it fully. This is partly because I am not sure that is meant by the word "energy"—is it the same energy that is actually becoming scarce because of peak oil or is there a looser use of the word? I am also not sure that I have understood partly because there is an implicit psychology under the analysis that I don't get either. For example, Romano argues that "individualised dépense" does not happen on an adequate scale:

> A large amount of energy remains unused, it continues to circulate and to stress human beings. Lacking tools of deliberate and symbolic catastrophe (i.e. the ritual collective dépense) the inhabitants of growth societies begin to dream them and to desire a "real" catastrophe.[2]

What seems to be being said here is not only that dépense is a means to dissipate resources so that they are not accumulated economically but also that dépense has a function in the management of mass emotion. If I have got that right then what is being described here is what therapists call "catharsis"—the release, and therefore relief from, strong emotions which would otherwise be channelled into real destruction.

How do you operationalize dépense?

If I have understood these ideas correctly then what opens up for me is a huge number of questions. For example how is the social depense to be organized/administered? How is it to be decided, and by whom, what is an acceptable level of basic provision and what is to be destroyed as "excess"? How is "excess" to be identified and then "socialised" prior to its "waste" in a useless fashion? I suppose that by guaranteeing a basic income and a maximum income and then taxing all the rest away that one could say that that rest was "excess" but would the authors really want to spend this excess without any investment whatsoever? For example all buildings as well as other forms of public infrastructure would be depreciating as they always do—should provision be set aside to main-

1 D'Alisa, G., Demaria, F., & Kallis, G. (2014). *Degrowth: a vocabulary for a new era.* Routledge, p. 218

2 Romano, O. (2014). "Dépense." In G. D'Alisa, F. Demaria, & G. Kallis (Eds.), *Degrowth: A vocabulary for a new era* (pp. 86-89). New York and London: Routledge.

tain their upkeep and replacement? "Growth" can happen because when equipment needs replacing and the replacements are "upgrades". Where does that fit into dépense?

Further to that, what exactly is "dépense sociale"? On the last page the editors give a list of examples—collective feasts, Olympic Games, idle ecosystems, military expenditures, and voyages to space—and they refer to pressure on democratic and deliberative institutions choosing between these.

I will put aside at this point the question of what an "idle ecosystem" is and raise some other points instead. The implicit faith in the ability of "democratic and deliberative institutions" to be able to stand up to the military industrial complex and prevent it claiming the surplus surprises me. Given the pre-existing power structures it would be very surprising if the idea of individual sobriety and social dépense did not to turn into the latest version of bread and circuses. The masses would have, at best, a very basic standard of living while the political elite would organize banquets in honor of the latest head of state, rope everyone into large scale theatrical events with everyone wearing a uniform and carrying torches while they listen to rants from their betters. Alternatively resources could be "wasted" in jolly festivals in which "civil people" (who are obedient) are entertained while those who are disobedient and uncivil, and thus "obviously" the cause of all the problems in society, are put in the center of ampitheaters and torn apart by lions. This would be wonderfully effective in channelling and managing mass emotions and getting rid of the surplus too. Wouldn't these qualify as social dépense? They appear to have done in the thinking of George Bataille for whom socialised dépense also included human sacrifices organized by the state in the Aztec empire.

In conclusion

It seems important to me to know whether degrowth is a voluntary or an involuntary process and to build that distinction into the vocabulary about it. If it is a voluntary process then certain things follow—like the need to know how it is going to be driven/motivated and administered, at what pace and in what manner, in order to respond to the climate crisis. It is also possible that even if degrowth is involuntary because of energy descent, it may not be fast enough. To address this, degrowth could be driven by climate policy by reducing the amount of fossil fuels allowed out of the ground.

To the extent that degrowth is an involuntary process then another set of issues arise—will the society and economy withstand the process without catastrophic breakdowns and what can the many kinds of projects and policies described in this book do to make energy descent a survivable process for the population? A great many people will be finding that their lifestyle packages are severely stressed and breaking apart and this will generate a great deal of fear and "negative" emotions.

Notions like "dépense" are useful for drawing attention the fact that "surplus resources" can be "invested" in things that have consequences for mass emotions and therefore for social stability or conflict. However, one must ask how much "surplus" or excess there will be on the way down given that energy descent is likely to take society through a variety of thresholds and tipping points and be an exceedingly bumpy ride. It is true that to "invest" resources in "capital accumulation" might in theory start the economy growing again—but only if new energy sources were found.

Growth is unlikely in a society where energy inputs are rapidly shrinking. Instead, what is needed for the resources that are there is investment in the community level projects and activities which help people cope—a direct investment in the lifeboat projects as I have called them. There is a danger that the rather vague call for "socialised dépense" can be interpreted as a support for state centralisation of the remaining surplus—for the maintenance of remaining resources in the hands of the military, the state bureaucracy, and privileged insiders whose claim to maintain "order" in difficult times is also buttressed by the use of resources to display their power and add theatrical embellishment to their authority. I don't think this would be a very good idea....

In defense of a Mediterranean spirit (Giorgos Kallis)

Dear Brian,

Thanks a lot for your thoughtful and in-depth review of our book. I really appreciate that you did put the time and effort to read it so closely and engage critically with its content and arguments. Your criticisms are all well reasoned and based on a sound understanding of what we were trying to do, even though I don't always agree with you and feel we write from slightly different perspectives.

Yes, there is a difference between what you call "involuntary" degrowth and what we see as a "politicized" take on degrowth. Note, we never used the term "voluntary", not even in our entry on simplicity. "Political" in Castoriadis' terms means the pre-paradigmatic view that humans make their own history, and they are not subject to immutable, outside forces that pre-determine their fates, and to which the best that they can do is adapt. "Political" means also an attention to distributional issues and an avoidance of generalized "we"s. "We" will not suffer all the same from climate change and "we" have not contributed the same to the problem. Richard Branson for example has contributed a lot with air and space travels to climate change, and he is well insulated in his gated estates from any future climate and social calamities.

In this respect, we do have a problem as you correctly noticed, with the "involuntary", or better put "survivalist" take on degrowth, which argues that growth is coming to an end, whether we like it or not, and "we" better be preparing to adapt and become "resilient to" in order to survive. This framing of the issue hides the fact that we are not all equally responsible or equally vulnerable; it opens the potential for authoritarian responses to save "us" from disaster; and it is politically disempowering and demobilizing, as it suggests that we can do nothing to change the system and its trajectory, only prepare and "survive with our peers".

The discourse of the "always forthcoming", never yet here, climate change disaster has done very little to mobilize people to take action against it. As you acutely analyze in your piece, responding to climate change will require a dramatic reorganization of life projects and social structures, which most people are reluctant to undertake. Your response is that "they will undertake them", when there is no other option and the disaster will already be there. We doubt that this will be automatically the case. The socioenvironmental disaster is already here (I am writing from Greece), and rather than adaptation, what we see is oppression and conflict. In the absence of a positive vision, in the face of a disaster many people will simply recoil, close borders, accept "leaders" that promise to save them, and try to shift costs to others, if need be by violence. A social change, if it is to take place, requires desire, materialized into an alternative political vision, a vision driven by a quest for the enjoyment of life, not by fear of a looming disaster, or a pure survivalist spirit. If by being Southern Europeans, we bring a much needed "enjoyment of life" perspective in the "limits to growth" debate, this is good, and I don't understand Brian why you frame it as a weakness of the book. And our optimism is commendable, given the far from "enjoyable" and fully involuntary disaster that we do experience in our countries currently.

Note also your own contradiction. If climate disaster, degrowth and whatever else the future holds for us is "involuntary" and the best we can do is to become "resilient" in "transition towns", then what is the point of an international "cap and share", like the one your propose, or any other mitigation action for that matter? Cap-and-share is a voluntary, and deeply political action, for which people would have to be seriously mobilized and organized to get it institutionalized. How would this ever be done without a positive, political vision about the future? And why do it, if the future is pre-determined? According to your logic, we can only let climate change take its path, while preparing for adapting and surviving. Why act now, if not in order to create a better and more enjoyable world tomorrow? Why act now if we don't believe that it is in principle possible to change the future, i. e. that we are not slaves to external "involuntary" forces, but that we can make our own history?

Our distaste of the a-political involuntary/survivalist perspective, does not mean that we underplay that there are real "limits to growth". Our ambition was to integrate the "limits" literature of Georgescu-Roegen, Odum and Herman Daly, in which the three of us are trained in our ecological economics school in Barcelona, with the "vocabulary" and concepts of a Franco-phone and "Southern" literature, which we have more recently come across, and the likes of Castoriadis, Gorz, Illich, Bataille or Escobar. It is in that sense that we claim that this is the first book about "degrowth" in English. Degrowth is much more than the Anglophone "limits to growth" literature.

Your comments about the use of French words in our book are a little bit off the mark and contradictory with your own argument. Take dépense, your example. If we had called it "expenditure", its meaning would be completely confusing to the reader. Expenditure has a precise meaning in English, which does not capture all that Bataille wants to talk about. We called it dépense, and this made you think you don't understand it, and you had to read carefully our chapters as well as the originals of Bataille to understand what it is (and you did understand it very well!). That was precisely the point of using the original in French.

Concerning our thesis with dépense, you got it right: we wanted to question the assumption of an eternal scarcity (and of external limits), which we see as a central idea of modernity, capitalism and neoclassical economics, and instead argue that the problem has always been the management of excess, i.e. the decision of what we do with the surplus. This, and only this, was our main point. A Nazi celebration, a Soviet parade, Tibetan monks and cannibalistic Aztec ceremonies, are all in a sense dépense, but some are desirable, others not. Exactly: we were not elevating dépense to be a normative principle; unproductive expenditure is a central feature of all societies, and the way they give sense and meaning to themselves; that's an observation, not a proposal. A degrowth society should develop its particular forms of dépense, that will be different from those of capitalistic society (as well as reduce part of its accumulation and increase its dépense).

You raise a lot of valid questions about "which dépense", "where", "how," "how do you define surplus"? These are the types of questions and debates we hoped our epilogue would prompt. This is not the conclusion and closure of the book, but the introduction of a new (and let us admit, not fully developed) idea, that will hopefully spur new debates and new research. And your excellent review and debate makes me think that we succeeded.

"Intellectuals and indigenous groups in Latin America ... don't want growth, but "buen vivir" (the good life), a term that for us Greeks is familiar since Aristotle wrote about it. Unfortunately we might have to endure the same level of suffering that the Latin Americans did the last 30 years to reach their degree of wisdom."

Image: "Under the asphalt, lies the sand". Grafitti in Paris, 1968

Part VII: A view from the South (of Europe)

25. The growth curse. How the tigers became PIIGS

Author's note: This is an article written in Greek and for the Greek audience of the website Greeklish. *It seems to me like yesterday, when in 2008 and upon my arrival in Barcelona, I was reading a* Financial Times *cover in front of a kiosk at Las Ramblas. The* FT *was preoccupied with the economy of Germany, "the great patient", as it was then called. Two years later Germany was an "engine of growth". As the patient was transforming to an engine, so did the tigers become pigs. My argument is that the crisis in Greece and other European countries was not because of the lack of growth, but because of growth. If I had time to write an academic article on this, I would call it "the growth curse".*

A few years can seem like centuries. In 2004 *The Economist* was applauding the miracle of Ireland, the "Celtic Tiger", and wanted to see its example replicated elsewhere. In 2008, the year that I arrived in Barcelona, Zapatero's Spain was celebrating because the country's GDP had surpassed Italy's for the first time. That same year the IMF informed us that the Greek economy was blossoming and that it would remain strong for the coming years.

The subsequent developments are more or less known to everybody. A few years later the tigers had transformed into the PIIGS.[1] Prophets after the fact, the analysts now suddenly remembered the small reservations that they had included as footnotes to their triumphant projections: Greece was hiding its increasing fiscal deficit, Spain and Ireland had real-estate bubbles. According to the dominant narrative, together with the glorious growth there were also faults. But are we certain that these problems were independent of growth and not results, or prerequisites, of growth itself?

Examining why some economies were hit much harder by the crisis than others, Karl Aiginger, the Director of the Austrian Institute of Economic Research (WIFO) found a statistical correlation between how hard a country was hit by the crisis and the extent of its borrowing (public and private) as well as its trade deficit prior to the crisis.[2] No surprise here. In contrast, much more interesting and unexpected is the finding

1 An acronym that came to be used to refer to the five Eurozone nations that were much weaker after the financial crisis: Portugal, Italy, Ireland, Greece, and Spain.

2 Aiginger, K. "Why growth performance differed across countries in the recent crisis: the impact of pre-crisis conditions." *Review of Economics and Finance* 1(4): 35-52.

that the higher the growth rates of a country before the crisis, the more intense the recession afterwards.

Let us focus on the example of Greece. In the mid-1990's the country went through an extended period of stagnation in average per capita income.[1] The stagnation had begun in 1974 with the oil crisis, but the policies of wealth redistribution of the Andreas Papandreou government and its investments in public goods, in parallel of course with an increase in debt, allowed the living standards of the average Greek to rise despite there being no growth in national income. Greece was not fundamentally different from other developed OECD economies, which during and after the 70s also saw a drop in the rate of GDP growth following the end of the "golden" post-war period. Growth rates, according to economic theory, are higher when an economy is recovering from a catastrophe, or when a relatively poor economy, like China today, converges with richer ones. But following the completion of the basic process of growth, the tendency is to stabilize at a lower growth rate. It is easier for a country which has only one car to add another than it is for a country which has 1 million cars to turn them into 2 million cars, then 4, then 8, and so on.

How each country responded to the conditions of the structural economic stagnation explains how it was affected by the crisis. For Greece, as for the other comparatively poorer countries of the EU, the issue at the beginning of the 90s wasn't only its emergence from stagnation, but its "convergence" with the larger economies in light of the coming monetary union. For the Simitis government the goal of convergence was the aim of all of its policies. Indeed from 1995 until 2007 the rates of growth in Greece were exceptionally high for a developed economy—on the order of 3-4% per annum peaking at the positively "Chinese" rate of 6% in 2004, the year of the Olympic Games.

How did this "miracle" happen? Very simply. Through an increase in public borrowing that funded state spending. Entry into the monetary union and the Euro increased Greece's creditworthiness and reduced the cost of borrowing. We should not be fooled here by the fact that state expenditures did not appear to increase as a percentage of GDP following Greece's entry into the monetary union until the crisis. They were increasing at the same rate as GDP (that is why the ratio remained stable), something which is not necessarily the case unless the increase in GDP is a direct result of state spending.

1 Gogos, S. G., Mylonidis, N., Papageorgiou, D., & Vassilatos, V. (2012). "Greece 1979-2001: A (first) Great Depression seen from the basic RBC model perspective." *AUEB–Department of Economics, Working Paper Series*, 01-2012.

We didn't do anything worse than Ireland or Spain or even the United States or Great Britain—countries which relied on private instead of public borrowing and property bubbles to maintain their growth rates. The only difference is that, given the peculiarities of the Greek economy which passes largely through the state, here it was the state which was borrowing whereas in other countries it was employers and households. Throwing money into the market, the state ended the period of stagnation. Speaking back in 2002, then-President Simitis was insisting on the need to sustain the already high growth rates in order to converge to the rest of the EU[1]. National investment programs, EU support funds, and the Olympic Games, he argued, will propel the economy, and will facilitate the expansion of Greek businesses and banks to the rest of the Balkans, making Greece the geo-economic core of Southeastern Europe.

On the surface, at least until the crisis arrived, nobody saw anything wrong given that public debt, even without creative accounting, remained stable as a percentage of GDP. And so the praise from the IMF in 2008. The entire economy, however, was built on a cycle of lending and growth: we borrow to grow and we grew to maintain the debt at a stable proportion of GDP. The cycle was broken when the global crisis brought growth to an end, causing the cost of borrowing to skyrocket.

I don't think the Greek state had the degree of control over the economy needed to determine how much growth it wanted and when. I am referring primarily to a dynamic, and a confluence of circumstances, which the pre-crisis governments promoted to a certain degree through state spending and which it certainly didn't do anything to prevent as it could have done. The growth allowed increases in wages and their convergence with those in the rest of Europe which was a pressing need following the dramatic increase in the cost of living which the euro brought. Why would a government put the brakes on the economy that was "growing" and "converging"—which was the goal and which everyone was praising?

It wasn't growth itself, some might say, but the fact that growth in Greece had rotten foundations. We need "healthy growth" according to some or "smart growth" according to others. Unfortunately I am not aware of a developed economy, smart or stupid, which can grow at rates of 2-3% per year with healthy foundations. With the collapse of the financial bubble, so too collapsed the myths of the supposed increased

1 2002, 20 August. "Εμμονή Σημίτη στη σύγκλιση." *Kathimerini*. Accessed on 14 August 2016. http://www.kathimerini.gr/127129/article/epikairothta/politikh/emmonh-shmith-sth-sygklish

economic productivity in the USA during the 1990s or the "technological miracle" of Ireland. Despite the revolution in the information technology sector and even with the huge bubbles which gave misleading figures for GDP, the rates of growth of the USA over the last decades pale in comparison to those of the 50's or the 60s. If economists like Robert Gordon are right, the age of growth has come to an end for developed economies.[1] Even politically conservative economists such as Robert Lucas, who consider themselves optimists in comparison to Gordon, looking forward to never-ending technological progress, speak of growth rates on the order of 1.5 to 2% per year.[2]

For Greece to begin to reduce its debt, it requires growth rates higher than the interest rate—that is the rate at which the debt increases. In the best case scenario we hope for a low interest rate on the order of 5%, that is, to begin to pay off our debt we need growth rates roughly greater than 5%. Such an unnatural growth rate may be achieved for a short period in an economy recovering from a catastrophe. However, to be maintained, it requires new bubbles and new loans. And as Aiginger's research shows, the greater the bubble, the greater the subsequent destruction.

When I heard from the 2008 Greek governments' grandiose programs of growth, convergence, and modernization I felt like I entered a time machine. History repeats itself. Unfortunately not as a farce but as a continuation of the tragedy.

1 Gordon, R. J. (2012). *Is US economic growth over? Faltering innovation confronts the six headwinds* (No. w18315). National Bureau of Economic Research.

2 Lucas, R. E. (2014). "The Wealth of Nations in the 21st Century." Retrieved from https://www.youtube.com/watch?v=5oOgx_JF9ww

26. Extractivism, the Greek way

Author's note: our group in Barcelona, under the lead of Joan Martinez-Alier, is known for its work on ecological distribution conflicts and the study of environmental injustices around the world. Joan's famous book The environmentalism of the poor *traces the "metabolism" of capitalist economies (that is the materials that fuel production and consumption) and the conflicts between local communities, corporations and states at the territories where materials are extracted from and wastes disposed to. In Joan's book, written in 2003, most of these conflicts—over mining, oil, tree plantations, or industrial waste—take place in the exploited periphery and the ex-colonies of the Global North: Latin America, South-East Asia or Africa. In this essay I tried to make sense of the reappearance of the "commodity frontier" back in places that thought they were at the centre, like my home country Greece. At the time of writing, in the village of Skouries, in the peninsula of Chalkidiki at Northern Greece, battles were raging on the streets between protesters and police forces protecting the opening of a new gold mine. In newspapers, conservatives and "progressives" were reveling about the unexplored oil wealth of the country in the Aegean Sea, and how it could pull the country out of the crisis. Back then (2012), the price of gold and oil were at record highs. But as I predicted in the text, this boom of extractivist expectations could soon be over, which it sure was. One core insight of this essay remains relevant: crisis and indebtedness renders natural resources exploitable that would otherwise be out of reach. In a market economy "the poor sell cheap": not only their bodies but also their environments.*

In the popular imaginary, oil and gold are hidden under the ground. A lucky guy (it is always a "he") stumbles upon them one day and gets rich.

Reality is more banal. Minerals may lie under our feet and may still not be really "available". Extraction in a capitalist economy makes sense only if the profits outweigh the costs. Profits depend on the money the mineral can fetch on the market. Cost includes wages, operating machines. The deeper the mineral the costlier it is to get it out. The dirtier it is, the more expensive it is to process it. And the more damaging the extraction is, the more difficult and costly it is to get the legal permission for it.

With oil and gold prices at historical highs, there is suddenly "more" oil and gold to be extracted. Where was all this "wealth" hiding? Nowhere, it was always there. But now it pays more to extract more. And it pays more to find more, hence companies invest in exploration and reserves keep growing.

No matter how high mineral prices get however, we have already eaten the low-hanging fruit. The new reserves are in remote places and are dirtier. Think of the oil in the Amazon forest or the tar sands in Alberta, Canada. New technologies are developed to drill deeper for oil or capture less concentrated gold ores, but their costs are high.

Economic crises then come as good news for investors. "The poor sell cheap" as the saying goes. Royalties and taxes are a main cost for multi-national investors. Indebted countries, such as Greece or Cyprus, are willing to give their rights away as if in a "fire sale". Environmental and health regulations are seen as costs and circumvented with "fast-track" and other extra-legal processes[1]. The natural environment or peoples' health are no longer values to be protected, but costs and obstacles to the speed of investment. Low wages are an added bonus for investors (though probably not the most important since extractive industries are mostly capital-intensive).

As Jeremy Wrathall, chairman of Perth-based Glory Resources told *Bloomberg* about gold investments, "it is bizarre that Greece is virtually unexplored because of the political situation that prevailed before the crisis".[2] It is hard to see which "political situation", he was referring to. The "bizarre political situation" was probably what we used to call democracy and rule of law—the features of any dignified developed nation that is not willing to sell itself at a discounted price. Greece, as any EU country had environmental laws, and these laws mean that you cannot extract gold wherever and whenever you fancy. Probably Manhattan is also unexplored but it wouldn't occur to Mr Wrathall to look for gold there.

What Greece experiences today is a regression from a developed to an extractivist state, similar to the process many Latin American countries underwent in the 1980s. An extractivist state is one whose sole function is to provide the global economy with cheap raw materials, often at the cost of its own people and its own development.

It's a small consolation that there might be little oil actually in the Aegean or that low oil prices may render such oil again "unexploitable".

---

1 "Fast-track" refers to a concept introduced as law in Greece, whereby for investments of "national importance", the requirements of legal processes that slow down the investment may be temporally suspended. For example, environmental impact assessments necessary for prior authorization often take a long time to be completed or battled in higher courts. If an investment is on a "fast track" it means that the project can start before the impact assessment is completed.

2 Biesheuvel, T. (2012, 10 October). "Greece Welcomes Gold Miners to Rank First in Europe: Commodities." *Bloomberg*. Retrieved from http://www.bloomberg.com/news/articles/2012-10-09/greece-welcomes-gold-miners-to-rank-first-in-europe-commodities

Gold prices also may soon bust and citizen resistance in Chalkidiki make it too expensive to dig gold out of the soil. Yet the saddening fact remains the ease with which the Greek political elite and a substantial part of the population run to the extractivist dream. Ready to risk everything of value for the sake of waking up back to the blissful and meaningless prosperity of the 1990s.

Lesson learnt from the crisis? None. It's all about easy money, stupid. It was the stocks before, now it is gold and oil. It is easier to imagine turning the Aegean Sea black with a huge oil spill than to think that perhaps we could work hard in common and suffice with the simple beauty that this country offers in plenty.

Intellectuals and indigenous groups in Latin America, experiencing firsthand the "benefits" of extraction have gone beyond extractivism, beyond even alternative development and talk today of "alternatives to development". They don't want growth, but "buen vivir" (the good life), a term that for us Greeks is familiar since Aristotle wrote about it. Unfortunately we might have to endure the same level of suffering that the Latin Americans did the last 30 years to reach their degree of wisdom.

Giorgos Kallis

27. Islandizing the city

Author's note: This is the only written piece from a research project I hold dear at heart but hasn't yet materialized despite years of interviews and ethnographic notes. My interest is in the Greek Archipelago; the alternatives to growth-based development that it produces and signifies, and the ways it encounters and is transformed by such development. I first encountered "degrowth"—in the very broad sense of the term as the imaginary of a simple, dignified, and playful living in contact with nature—in the shores and cobbled streets of the Aegean islands, as a kid spending my summers happily in the company of my family and friends. I am aware by now that this romantic encounter with "the other" of my urbanized life was part and parcel of the transformation of this "other". Me, my family, and our friends were caught, active and passive subjects, in the historical process that was gentrifying and suburbanizing the very paradises that we were escaping to. Our romantic gaze valorized the deserted islands and turned them into prime locations for capital accumulation. With my research I seek to better understand the processes through which capitalism sucks difference out of difference, and the role of those of us who long for other worlds, in making these worlds valuable for capital. In turn, I am interested in how this encounter with difference and with the existence of other worlds changes us in the process, making us active agents of producing different worlds "back home".

In the 1930s, Nobel laureate's Odysseas Elytis' poetry helped place the islands of the Aegean at the centre of the Greek national imaginary. Since then, the development of tourism and of vacation housing, especially during the last two decades, has brought dramatic changes in most of the Greek islands. There is a huge gap between the islands of an imaginary past and the islands of today. Santorini alone, an island of 170 square kilometers, saw 2 million people in the summer of 2013. My summer visits to favorite islands are nowadays accompanied by a ritual exchange of nostalgic memories with other regulars. "Do you remember when…." "This old coffee-house closed, too..". "The visitors these days do not appreciate the island for what it really is..". Our Athenian narrative about the islands is one of "paradises in peril", paradises lost since we ourselves discovered them.

This narrative of paradises "before development", is far from the dominant narrative among most locals who time and time again have been asking for more "development": roads paved with asphalt, better ports and faster connections to Athens, airports, hospitals, electricity. While islanders want their islands to become more like a city, that is they desire to eliminate both differences and distances from Athens, some of us urbanites want exactly the opposite, namely to keep the islands as different as possible from the city. If it were possible, we would like the small islands of the Aegean to remain remote and hard to reach, keep their dirt roads, have no electric lights so that we can see the stars. Islanders, we dream, would continue living off the land, offering genuine hospitality free of charge.

Of course the above juxtaposition of locals and Athenians is a caricature, more so since the boundaries of islanders and outsiders are increasingly blurred. Island natives spend more and more of their free time, especially during winter, in Athens (if they are not on holidays in Thailand or the Caribbean). On the other side, many foreigners and Athenians, especially pensioners, but also more and more young people led out of the city by the crisis, spend most time of the year in islands. In the hybrid island societies that are taking shape, opinions vary about what genuine development is. I have met many young people in the islands desperately fighting against the forces of globalization in order to maintain and improve what they love most about their territories, from traditional music instruments and popular feasts to food orchards and the Aegean architecture. Even those that benefit the most from tourism lament the changes in the social fabric of the islands and the loss of the "old ways", though they may be unable to express or even imagine what could go differently, and how.

I won't deal here with what could change in the islands. I have some ideas on this, but I am only an occasional visitor. Changes in the islands are to be imagined and enacted by the people who live and produce there. What concerns me instead is what the islands may mean for "the city", meaning the city or cities where I live in and produce. My idea is this: if some islanders dream of their islands becoming more like a city, why don't we, island-loving urbanites, dare to think that our cities could become more like the islands of our fantasy? In a world that is increasingly urban, it may be that only by "islandizing" the cities, the islands may not totally urbanize.

Many fellow island-lovers will find all this too theoretical and maybe unnecessary. They will argue that the beauty of a summer experience in the islands lies in its temporal character: they never wished to live the whole year as if it were summer. They want a temporary escape, not to change their everyday life in the city. They want holidays, not politics.

Unfortunately, this escapist desire is self-defeating. Many young people experience a summer in an island as a temporary revolution, a taste of non-alienated life: walking naked on the beach, sleeping under the stars, forgetting what time it is, not using money, fishing their food in the sea. This however ends as soon as they come back to the city in September, put on their suits, set the alarm, charge their credit cards and go to the supermarket. Capitalism has found a grand opportunity for profit in this intense desire to escape from capitalism itself. As the numbers of temporary escapists increase, so do profits. Free camping inevitably becomes rooms to let, hospitality turns into tourism, and the barren land of the islands offers prime locations for real estate speculation. Not only is revolution commodified, but any latent desire for social change in the city is diffused into a temporary, elusive escape that acts to reinforce the status quo.

If escapism leads nowhere, how could then one bring the islands to the city? It is worth asking this question. What is it that animates our fantasies in the islands and how could everyone have it in the city? Is it the different biorhythm? Is it our right to be lazy? Is it the fact that in the islands we could once eat natural, organic products from the earth and the sea? Or is it maybe that in an island everyone knows and says good morning to one another? Is it the convivial town squares and the cobblestone alleys? Is it that we can live simply without luxuries? If so, why not imagine systemic transformations that would make all this possible in our cities and not only "out there" in the countryside?

Let me conclude in a more optimistic way. Maybe we do not even have to imagine, only to look around and see what is already happening in the cities. Islands already shape the city because, we Athenians, bring something from the islands back with us every autumn. For many friends it was a summer in an island that made them realize the superfluous in their urban lives and the value of simplicity. It was after a summer in an island that many decided to throw away their TV. I have seen friends leaving their corporate jobs, downscaling to a simpler life, with all the sacrifices this takes. True, a few became permanent escapists, getting by in the winter, and waiting for the summer, each summer traveling farther and farther away, to discover a new paradise whose destruction they themselves will set in motion. Others, though, no longer wait for the summer for their personal revolution. They bring the islands to their art. They bring the values and rhythm of the islands to their work. They work with others to turn parking lots into public squares, to cultivate unused land into food orchards in the center of the city. They initiate networks of gifts and barter, set up food or housing cooperatives, provide for the health or the care of their kids and the elders in common. They occupy squares and claim their right to the city.

As the Paris '68 saying goes, "under the asphalt, lies the sand".

Further reading

Alcott, B. (2005). Jevons' paradox. *Ecological Economics*, 54(1), 9-21.

Ariès, P. (2005). *Décroissance ou barbarie*. Golias.

Bataille, G. (1933). *La notion de dépense*. La Critique Sociale, 1(7).

Baykan, B. G. (2007). "From limits to growth to degrowth within French green politics." *Environmental Politics*, 16(3), 513-517.

Carlsson, C. (2008). *Nowtopia: how pirate programmers, outlaw bicyclists, and vacant-lot gardeners are inventing the future today*. AK Press.

Cattaneo, C., & Gavaldà, M. (2010). "The experience of rurban squats in Collserola, Barcelona: what kind of degrowth?" *Journal of Cleaner Production*, 18(6), 581-589.

Coote, A., Franklin, J., & Simms, A. (2010). *21 hours: Why a shorter working week can help us all to flourish in the 21st century*. London: New Economics Foundation.

D'Alisa, G., Demaria, F., & Kallis, G. (2014). *Degrowth: a vocabulary for a new era*. Routledge.

Dale, G. (2012). "The growth paradigm: a critique." *International Socialism*, 134.

Daly, H. (1996). *Beyond growth: the economics of sustainable development*. Beacon Press.

Daly, H. (2011). "What should we tax?" Retrieved from http://steadystate.org/what-should-we-tax/

Daly, H. (2013). "A further critique of growth economics." *Ecological Economics*, 88, 20-24.

Dean, B. (2014). "The economic "growth" frame – and its opposition." Retrieved from https://newsframes.wordpress.com/2014/08/27/economic-growth/

Ellul, J. (1967). *The technological society*. Vintage books.

Foster, J. B. (1992). "The absolute general law of environmental degradation under capitalism." *Capitalism Nature Socialism*, 3(3), 77-81.

Foster, J. B., Clark, B., & York, R. (2010). "Capitalism and the Curse of Energy Efficiency: The Return of the Jevons Paradox." *Monthly Review*, 62(06).

Fournier, V. (2008). "Escaping from the economy: the politics of degrowth." *International Journal of Sociology and Social Policy*, 28(11/12), 528-545.

Georgescu-Roegen, N. (1971). *The Entropy Law and the Economic Process*. Cambridge.

Georgescu-Roegen, N., Rens, I., & Grinevald, J. (1979). *Demain la décroissance: Entropie-écologie-économie*. P.-M. Favre.

Gibson-Graham, J. K. (2006). *A postcapitalist politics*. University of Minnesota Press.

Gibson-Graham, J.-K. (2008). "Diverse economies: performative practices forother worlds". *Progress in Human Geography*, 32(5), 613-632.

Harvey, D. (2000). *Spaces of hope*. University of California Press.

Harvey, D. (2014). *Seventeen contradictions and the end of capitalism*. UK: Oxford University Press.

Jackson, T. (2009). *Prosperity without growth: Economics for a finite planet*. Routledge.

Jackson, T. (2012). "Let's be less productive." *The New York Times*. Retrieved from http://www.nytimes.com/2012/05/27/opinion/sunday/lets-be-less-productive.html?_r=0

Kallis, G. (2011). "In defence of degrowth." *Ecological Economics*, 70(5), 873-880.

Kallis, G. (2015). "Yes, We Can Prosper Without Growth: 10 Policy Proposals for the New Left." *Common Dreams*. Retrieved from http://www.commondreams.org/views/2015/01/28/yes-we-can-prosper-without-growth-10-policy-proposals-new-left

Kallis, G., & March, H. (2015). "Imaginaries of hope: The utopianism of degrowth." *Annals of the Association of American geographers*, 105(2), 360-368.

Kallis, G., Kalush, M., O'Flynn, H., Rossiter, J., & Ashford, N. (2013). "'Friday off': reducing working hours in Europe." *Sustainability*, 5(4), 1545-1567.

Kallis, G., Kerschner, C., & Martinez-Alier, J. (2012). "The economics of degrowth." *Ecological Economics*, 84, 172-180.

Klein, N. (2015). *This changes everything: Capitalism vs. the climate*. Simon and Schuster.

Kothari, A. (2014). "Radical Ecological Democracy: A Path Forward for India and Beyond". *The Great Transition*. Retrieved from http://www.greattransition.org/publication/radical-ecological-democracy-a-path-forward-for-india-and-beyond

Lafargue, P. (1969). *The right to be lazy*. Solidarity Publications.

Lakoff, G. (2014). *The All New Don't Think of an Elephant!: Know Your Values and Frame the Debate*. Chelsea Green Publishing.

Latouche, S. (2009). *Farewell to growth*. Polity.

Le Guin, U. (1974). *The Dispossessed*. New York: Harper & Row.

Martinez-Alier, J., Kallis, G., Veuthey, S., Walter, M., & Temper, L. (2010). "Social metabolism, ecological distribution conflicts, and valuation languages." *Ecological Economics*, 70(2), 153-158.

Mitchell, T. (2011). *Carbon democracy: Political power in the age of oil*.

New York: Verso.

Mitchell, T. (2014). "Economentality: how the future entered government." Critical Inquiry, 40(4), 479-507.

Norgaard, R. B. (2006). *Development betrayed: The end of progress and a co-evolutionary revisioning of the future*. Routledge.

Odum, H. T., & Odum, E. C. (2008). *A prosperous way down: principles and policies*. University Press of Colorado.

Rowan, M. (2014, 27 February). "We need to talk about growth. (And we need to do the sums as well.)." Retrieved from http://persuademe.com.au/need-talk-growth-need-sums-well/

Sahlins, M. (1995). "The original affluent society." *Sociological Worlds: Comparative and Historical Readings on Society*, 2.

Schneider, F., Kallis, G., & Martinez-Alier, J. (2010). "Crisis or opportunity? Economic degrowth for social equity and ecological sustainability. Introduction to this special issue." *Journal of Cleaner Production*, 18(6), 511-518.

Schor, J., & White, K. E. (2010). *Plenitude: The new economics of true wealth*. New York: Penguin Press.

Skidelsky, E., & Skidelsky, R. (2012). *How much is enough?: money and the good life*. Penguin UK.

Turner, G. M. (2012). "On the cusp of global collapse? Updated comparison of The Limits to Growth with historical data." *GAIA-Ecological Perspectives for Science and Society*, 21(2), 116-124.

Žižek, S. (2011). "Nature does not exist." [Video] Retrieved from https://www.youtube.com/watch?v=DIGeDAZ6-q4

Žižek, S. (2011). *Living in the end times*. Verso.

Useful websites

French website on degrowth: http://www.ladecroissance.net
French degrowth party: http://www.partipourladecroissance.net
Research & Degrowth network: www.degrowth.org
List of prominent degrowth publications: http://www.degrowth.org/publications
Degrowth media library: http://www.degrowth.de/en/media-library/
Florent Marcellesi's writings on degrowth: http://florentmarcellesi.eu/category/decrecimiento/
Degrowth: A vocabulary for a new era (book): http://vocabulary.degrowth.org/

Academic publications by the author

Please email *giorgoskallis@gmail.com* if you do not have access and wish to have a copy of a paper.

Asara, V., Profumi, E. and G. Kallis, 2013. "Degrowth, democracy and autonomy." *Environmental Values*, 22: 217-239.

Ashford, N. and Kallis, G., 2013. "A four-day workweek: A policy for improving employment and environmental conditions in Europe." *European Financial Review*, April- May 2013: 53-58.

Calvario, R. and Kallis, G., 2016. "Alternative food economies and transformative politics in times of crisis: Insights from the Basque Country and Greece." *Antipode*. 10.1111/anti.12298

Cattaneo, C., D'Alisa, G., Kallis., G and C. Zografos, 2012. "Degrowth futures and democracy." *Futures*, 44: 515-523.

D'Alisa, G. Demaria, F. and G. Kallis (eds), 2014. *Degrowth. A vocabulary for a new era*. Routledge-Earthscan. (translated to French, German, Spanish, Catalan, Brazilian Portuguese, Greek, Dutch, Croatian).

Kallis, G., 2011. "In defense of degrowth." *Ecological Economics*, 70: 873-880.

Kallis, G. 2013. "Societal metabolism, working hours and degrowth. A comment on Sorman and Giampietro." *Journal of Cleaner Production*, 38: 94-99.

Kallis, G., Gomez, E. and C. Zografos, 2013. "To value or not to value? That is not the question." *Ecological Economics*, 94: 97-105.

Kallis, G., Kalush, M. O' Flynn, H. Rossiter, J. and N. Ashford, 2013. "'Friday-off': reducing working hours in Europe." *Sustainability*, 5: 1545-1567.

Kallis, G. Kerschner, C. and J. Martinez-Alier, 2012. "The economics of degrowth." *Ecological Economics*, 84: 172-180.

Kallis, G., Martinez-Alier, J. and R. Norgaard, 2009. "Paper assets, real debts. An ecological economic exploration of the global economic crisis." *Critical Perspectives on International Business*, 5 (1/2): 14-25

Kallis, G. and H. March, 2015. "Imaginaries of Hope: the dialectical utopianism of degrowth." *Annals of the Association of the American Geographers*. 105 (2): 360-368

Kallis, G. and Sager, J., 2016. "Oil and the economy: A systematic review of the literature for ecological economists." *Ecological Economics*, 131: 561-571.

Martinez-Alier, J., Kallis, G., Veuthey, S., Walter, M. and L. Temper, 2010. "Social metabolism, ecological distribution conflicts and valuation languages." *Ecological Economics*, 70 (2): 153-158.

Otero, I., Kallis, G., Aguilar, R. and V. Ruiz, 2011. "Water scarcity, social power and the production of an elite suburb. The political ecology of water in Matadepera, Catalonia." *Ecological Economics*, 70 (7): 1297-1308.

Schneider, F., Kallis, G. and J. Martinez-Alier, 2010. "Crisis or opportunity? Economic degrowth for social equity and ecological sustainability." *Journal of Cleaner Production*, 18: 511-518.

Sekulova, F., Kallis, G., Rodriguez-Labajos, B. and F. Schneider, 2013. Degrowth: from theory to practice. *Journal of Cleaner Production*, 38: 1-6.

Videira, N., Schneider, F., Sekulova, F., and G. Kallis, 2014. "Improving understanding on degrowth pathways: an exploratory study using collaborative causal models." *Futures*. 55: 58-77.

van den Bergh J.C.M and Kallis, G., 2013. "Growth, agrowth or degrowth to stay within planetary boundaries?" *Journal of Economic Issues*, XLVI (4): 909-919.

Degrowth: A vocabulary for a new era

Edited by Giacomo D'Alisa, Federico Demaria, and Giorgos Kallis

Degrowth is a rejection of the illusion of growth and a call to repoliticize the public debate colonized by the idiom of economism. It is a project advocating the democratically-led shrinking of production and consumption with the aim of achieving social justice and ecological sustainability.

This overview of degrowth offers a comprehensive coverage of the main topics and major challenges of degrowth in a succinct, simple and accessible manner. In addition, it offers a set of keywords useful forintervening in current political debates and for bringing about concrete degrowth-inspired proposals at different levels - local, national and global.

The result is the most comprehensive coverage of the topic of degrowth in English and serves as the definitive international reference.

"... 'Degrowth' for many signifies a variety of initiatives proposing an alternative to capitalist accumulation and the reconstruction of our reproduction on more cooperative terms. This then is a volume that those committed to building non exploitative relations will need to consult as it offers a map to the world of alternatives to capitalisms.

— Silvia Federici

"At a time in history when political, economic and intellectual leaders assure us that nothing fundamental can any longer be questioned, nothing could be more important than the movement – of thought, and of action – that this volume on Degrowth represents..."

— David Graeber

"This book is one of the most thorough and insightful presentations and discussion of economic theory and practice in the field of de-growth economics, a revolutionary attempt to understand the economy as if humans and Nature matter."

— Manuel Castells

"A thought-provoking, wide-ranging, spirited, and deeply original analysis; this book is a must-read on degrowth debates."

— Karen Bakker

Visit http://vocabulary.degrowth.org/ for more information and to purchase the book.

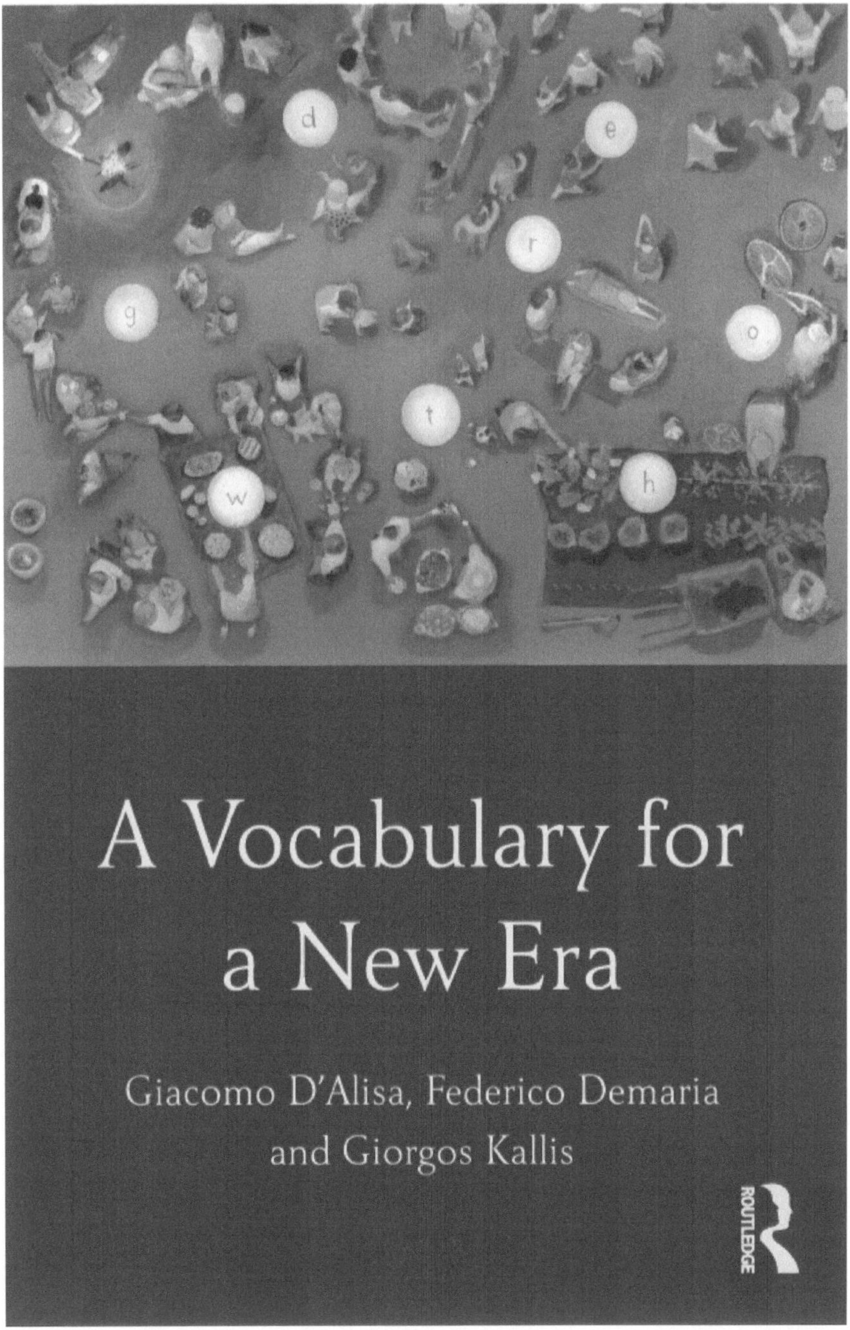

A Vocabulary for a New Era

Giacomo D'Alisa, Federico Demaria and Giorgos Kallis

www.ingramcontent.com/pod-product-compliance
Ingram Content Group UK Ltd.
Pitfield, Milton Keynes, MK11 3LW, UK
UKHW041845200726
13854UKWH00005BA/2172